MW00905729

To Experience *Wonder*

Edna Staebler
A Life

Veronica Ross

THE DUNDURN GROUP
TORONTO · OXFORD

Copy-Editor: Jennifer Bergeron
Design: Jennifer Scott
Printer: Transcontinental

National Library of Canada Cataloguing in Publication Data

Ross, Veronica
To experience wonder : Edna Staebler : a life / Veronica Ross.

Includes bibliographical references and index.
ISBN 1-55002-462-0

1. Staebler, Edna, 1906- 2. Food writers — Canada — Biography. I. Title.

TX649.S73R68 2003 641'.092 C2003-903527-1

1 2 3 4 5 07 06 05 04 03

We acknowledge the support of the **Canada Council for the Arts** and the **Ontario Arts Council** for our publishing program. We also acknowledge the financial support of the **Government of Canada** through the **Book Publishing Industry Development Program** and **The Association for the Export of Canadian Books**, and the **Government of Ontario** through the **Ontario Book Publishers Tax Credit** program, and the **Ontario Media Development Corporation's Ontario Book Initiative.**

Care has been taken to trace the ownership of copyright material used in this book. The author and the publisher welcome any information enabling them to rectify any references or credit in subsequent editions.

J. Kirk Howard, President

Printed and bound in Canada.
Printed on recycled paper.
www.dundurn.com

Excerpts froom Edna Staebler's writings used by permission.

Dundurn Press
8 Market Street
Suite 200
Toronto, Ontario, Canada
M5E 1M6

Dundurn Press
2250 Military Road
Tonawanda NY
U.S.A. 14150

for Irene

Praise to God for this goodness
That in woodland I write well.

— Anonymous, ninth century,
found in the monastery of the Irish St. Gall,
translated by Maire MacNeill

Contents

Introduction

Then, after minutes of moving silence, one prisoner said to another, "How beautiful life could be."
— Viktor Frankl, *Man's Search for Meaning*

Somehow there is excitement in its monotony. Though nothing happens, each day brings wonder and a new delight. There are so many simple things to be aware of: a chicken to laugh at, a dog to pat, a kitten to fondle; there are always birds and boats to watch.
— Edna Staebler, *Cape Breton Harbour*[1]

It is fall, the air is crisp and the leaves are changing in the twin cities of Kitchener and Waterloo. At the corner of King and Erb in Waterloo is the old hotel where years ago my husband, Rick, took a photo of Old Order Mennonite girls spooning yogurt while they waited to catch a bus.

Kitchener-Waterloo is in the middle of Mennonite country, an area settled by the Erbs and Schneiders who came up from Pennsylvania in their Conestoga wagons. Immigrants from all over the world have since joined the original families, and the Twin Cities have the usual urban problems, but it seems apt to be thinking of Mennonites on this fall day because my friend Joyce Spring and I are on our way to visit Edna Staebler, author of the *Schmecks* cookbooks. The first, *Food That Really Schmecks*, popularized the Old Order in the sixties when many local people thought of them as backward and simple-minded.

You can still see the Old Order in K-W, the women in long dresses and shawls, the men in black suits and shirts without collars. Conestoga Mall even has hitching posts for the horses that pull their buggies.

In the countryside, Mennonite farms with their big barns seem like illustrations out of a children's book. You might see women hanging out the wash, or girls hoeing neat rows of peas and beans. Windows gleam. There are no curtains, but geraniums bloom on windowsills, and in the summer the flowerbeds are magnificent. Roadside stands offer bouquets and canning jars for your loonies. Signs read: "Quilts," "Summer Sausage," "Fresh Eggs," "Apple Butter," and, always, "No Sunday Sales."

It is all so pretty, the stuff of cute folks on paper napkins, but beneath the charm lies the strong faith that has sustained the Anabaptist followers of Menno Simons since the sixteenth century, when they were hounded out of the canons of Switzerland and Southern Germany. They are pacifists who will not go to war, and many died for their beliefs. They believe in practising frugality, working hard, and helping their neighbours. They do not carry insurance. Instead, everyone gets together to rebuild a barn that has burned. The strictest of them do not allow photographs, electricity, or telephones. They are wary of *Hochmut* — pride.

Their way of life is a billion times removed from war and terror, worlds away from the modern life of fashion, getting ahead, and looking out for number one.

"I have learned so much from my Mennonite friends," Edna says. "They find such joy in simple things."

Edna is in her late nineties and lives alone in her winterized cottage on Sunfish Lake. Her place is obviously a writer's house, filled with books and art and comfortable old furniture. And cat stuff: pillows and pictures and one real feline, Mally (Mally with an *a* because she came from a mall), draped over the IBM Selectric by the big window overlooking the lake. Your eyes are drawn to the red cardinals and chickadees at the feeder. Edna points out squirrels and chipmunks and Copper, the neighbour's dog, who comes to visit.

I have known Edna for years, casually at first, a bit better when we drove to Kingston together by limo when Edna gave the Margaret Laurence Memorial Address at the annual general meeting of The Writers' Union of Canada, and much better now that I have started working on her biography.

There is no one like Edna, Joyce and I agree as we drive through Waterloo. We're going to stop for lunch. We used to arrive at Edna's at one until we found out she usually naps after lunch. But Edna didn't want to say anything.

She has done a lot of other writing beside the cookbooks — journalism for *Maclean's* and *Chatelaine* in the fifties and sixties; *Cape Breton Harbour*, a literary book, and her favourite, about a fishing village in Cape Breton; *Whatever Happened to Maggie and Other People I've Known* about folks she met while writing articles; and a book about the Kitchener area called *Sauerkraut and Enterprise*. And then there was *Ruby's Letters*, a collection of her sister's letters about ordinary life in the fifties, which Edna edited, and a series of small, thematic cookbooks.

She's kept a journal since she was sixteen. There are thousands of letters, spanning sixty years. She wrote quietly for years; her husband said you weren't a writer unless you were published. Her mother said Edna had no talent.

She has lived on a Hutterite colony, on a Mennonite farm, in a fishing village, on a Mohawk reservation, in St. Pierre and Miquelon, and in a mining town. And during the time she spent in all these places, she always wrote about her friendships with the people.

She thought her life was over when she divorced at age fifty-six after twenty-eight years of marriage. Her husband, Keith, was an alcoholic who left her for her best friend. Edna and Keith hadn't had sex for more than twenty years, but divorce was still a scandal for middle-class people in Kitchener in 1962.

She was sixty when her first book was published, sixty-two when her first cookbook, *Food That Really Schmecks*, came out, and seventy-three when the second one, *More Food That Really Schmecks*, appeared and her publisher sent her across Canada on a publicity tour. *Schmecks Appeal* was published eight years later in 1987.

Edna always wanted to write fiction, and unpublished poems and stories, including a hilarious novella about a gadfly manhunter, Molly, who goes to Europe, are in her archives.

Edna never intended to write cookbooks. A magazine article about Mennonite food led to a query from Ryerson Press, tentatively suggesting a cookbook.

But it was the cookbooks that sold and sold and made Edna financially secure. When Margaret Laurence stayed with Edna overnight in 1983, she told Edna that the *Schmecks* books to date had earned more in royalties than her total oeuvre.

The cookbooks are as much stories as cookbooks. Fans say: "They changed my life," "I keep your book by the bed for bedtime reading," and "When I'm sad I read your books about the Old Order Mennonites and having sticky buns and tea with Eva Martin." Never mind nouvelle cuisine or fifty-dollar bottles of wine. Her recipes are about feeding hungry people, using local ingredients.

"The steaming soup bowl is passed around Bevy Martin's table at suppertime and we ladle into our plates its clear, fragrant broth, thickened by tiny dumplings. Bevy says, 'Grossmommy Brubacher always told me drepsley [dripped batter] soup is especially nourishing for the sick.'"[2]

Edna has received the Order of Canada and an honorary doctorate from Wilfrid Laurier University. She has given money away in endowments.

I was the first writer-in-residence at Kitchener Public Library under Edna's endowment. She funds the Edna Staebler Award for Creative Non-Fiction, which is administered by Wilfrid Laurier University. Edna has also given money to the Joseph Schneider Haus, where you can watch costumed employees and volunteers quilt and bake Eppe cookies, as well as the Gerald Noonan Bursary in Canadian Literature and the George G. Blackburn Scholarship in Canadian History.

I haven't seen Joyce for a while. We've been friends for about ten years, ever since her book *Daring Lady Flyers* came out and Tricia Siemens of Words Worth Books suggested Joyce call me because we shared a publisher.

Joyce had triple bypass heart surgery in the summer of 2001. A grandchild had died the previous year, and another from the same mysterious blood disorder nine years ago.

My problems are tiny compared to Joyce's: I have a huge book project that has gone on and on, occasional gloominess and worry, and a tendency to complain.

Yes, there is no tea, how can this be in a Scottish restaurant? I sigh as I pour orange juice into a glass. I catch myself: what does it matter? I am with a good friend, the day is fine, and after lunch we go upstairs to the arty shop selling Celtic stuff. I want a witch's ball to hang in the dining room window, or maybe a clay goblet I've had my eye on.

Happiness can be simple, I think as we get back in the car. I've learned this from Edna, who, it seems to me, has made a conscious decision to be happy; or, as Lawrence McNaught, a filmmaker who's been working on a film about Edna for a long time, told me, "She's a lady with attitude. And that attitude is to be happy."

Edna learned this way of thinking during the bad years, when Keith was out all hours, drinking and running around and becoming severely depressed when one of his lady friends dumped him.

I thought a lot about this as I began working on her biography. No one writes about happiness unless it's in a gooey, self-help, greeting-card sentimental kind of way. People are happy, of course, sometimes fleetingly, often as a result of events like falling in love or attaining success, but happiness as a conscious decision, as a work of the mind and coupled with intelligence, is rare.

"He has shown me I am privileged to experience wonder," Edna wrote about Dr. John Robins, her mentor, in the forties.[3] She met Robins when he addressed the Canadian Club in Kitchener. Edna was into this and that, a committee person who longed to write books while she anguished about her husband's drinking and affairs.

Edna wrote in her journal, but it wasn't until 1943 when she visited Neil's Harbour in Cape Breton that she was drawn out of her introspection. In 1948 she wrote a story about swordfishing and sold it to *Maclean's*. She took it to Toronto herself, wearing a new hat. The editors loved it and commissioned other stories.

"Pierre Berton always said no one could edit my work because my style was so different," Edna says. But perhaps it wasn't just style. Her writing about ordinary people reveals the extraordinary.

And I think it is her hard-won positive attitude that has made her writing luminous. Her words almost cast a spell.

Privileged to experience wonder: acknowledging the wonder is also why Edna draws people to her. The president of Wilfrid Laurier University visits her regularly to eat blueberry muffins. A lawyer involved in the "Cookie Wars," the brouhaha involving Nabisco and Procter and Gamble about Edna's recipe for Mennonite rigglevake cookies, flew from B.C. to attend her ninety-fifth birthday party. An Old Order friend also came, calling it a gathering because parties were taboo for her. Edna's cleaning woman, Becky, was there, as well as librarians, neighbours, artists, writers, and politicians.

Young men invite her for lunch. For years, Pierre Berton and his family stopped at Sunfish Lake on their way to the Stratford Festival.

"I'd rather be out at Sunfish with Edna than anywhere in the world," a woman from California told me. Kevin, thirty-two, Edna's next-door neighbour, checks on her every day and often accompanies her to social events. Kathryn of the Wilfrid Laurier University bookstore brings dinner. Wendy fetches her for alfresco dining at her peacock farm. Edna's calendar is filled with engagements.

Happiness — who said this? — may not be the purpose of life, but as a hard-won achievement, as a refinement of mind, it is a power that draws, not as an inappropriate response to suffering, but rather as a possibility, a choice where possible, and never as a denial of the dark times.

Edna isn't a saint and certainly not, as she stresses, "a sweet dumpling of a cookbook author." Her publisher says Edna keeps them on their toes; she's never afraid of writing to them if she feels her books aren't available or has any other problem with them. You forget her age. She is a modern woman with an interesting past.

I'm enthralled by the letters I've read in her archive at the University of Guelph: letters about relationships, worries, philosophy, and thought. I've just seen letters she wrote to Keith during a three-month jaunt to Europe: ten-page letters detailing her adventures. Venice one day, Florence the next, Lausanne and the Rhine and back to Lausanne to visit the interesting Alphonse: "I dread the adjustment period of my coming home," she wrote Keith on her second trip two years later, "but I thank God I do have my writing."[4]

She's a complicated woman. I feel as if I am only beginning to understand her. I want to find out more about how she arrived at her positive attitude. And how is it possible to enjoy the world when you are suffering? She is anxious for me to write her biography and she's told me a lot about her adventures and relationships in her long life, but she's still a bit of a puzzle.

After lunch, Joyce and I drive along Erb Street, past the yellow brick and blue-shuttered condo that was once Seagram's Distillery and then a restaurant where writers, and I, too, have read, past the big New Order Mennonite church, past strip malls and the big plaza, then right at the Kitchener-Waterloo Bilingual School. Soon we're in the country, nearing Erbsville.

Last winter Joyce drove and made a wrong turn coming home, landing us almost in Petersburg. Go further and you're in St. Jacobs, Jakobstetl, where the main street is lined with shops selling quilts, pine furniture, handcrafted jewelry and pottery. And beyond, you will find Elmira, New Dundee, and Mount Forest, where the Mennonites are buying farms as land around Kitchener is gobbled up by developers.

This is Edna's country. Her great-great-grandfather was the first permanent settler in Wilmot Township. He was a Mennonite, but his son married an Irish woman, Susan MacMahon, from County Clare. Edna's mother was born on a farm just down the road from Sunfish.

We go by farms and an old school and turn left at Conservation Road. A field stretches beside modern houses but soon we're in the bush, on a road between high firs. We are only minutes from town, but we could be in Muskoka.

"I've been so looking forward to seeing Edna," Joyce says as I navigate the car down the narrow road. "Isn't it miraculous that she still lives alone out here?"

"I can't imagine her in an apartment."

Edna considered moving to a high-rise for the winter months a few years ago, but she said Mally wouldn't like an apartment and there'd be no birds for a cat to watch, and she just couldn't be parted from Sunfish Lake. She still goes out in ice and snow to fill the bird feeders. She used to walk out half a mile to fetch the mail, but Kevin picks it up for her now.

Around the corner, over the narrow patch of road, and we are at Edna's green cottage set back from the road, nestled among trees. Sunfish Lake is right behind the house. Until recently Edna swam there in the summer. She could afford a mansion in town, but after her divorce she sold her big brick house on Simeon Street and winterized the cottage. She has been there since 1962.

It's so still out here. Autumn trees and the quiet lake. A stone path leads to the door. There's a pumpkin on the step and a cat picture taped to the mailbox.

"Your own bit of Eden," a friend wrote Edna about Sunfish Lake.

The door is unlocked. I tap the knocker and we enter.

Edna rises from her chair by the window overlooking the lake. Birds are at the feeder; Mally stretches on the sofa. There are books on both sides of the fireplace and on shelves over the windows. Hooked mats, two big Linda Johns paintings, books on the coffee table, and her current reading, *A Fine Balance*, on the windowsill.

"Here you are." Her voice is glad, and there's a big smile. She's wearing sweats and a Mexican vest and one red sock, one blue. Round cheeks, jaunty white hair, and bright, intelligent eyes.

I feel the familiar contentment of Sunfish. And, for a moment, a bit of guilt. Or perhaps incomprehension. How to square contentment with what is happening in the world, with the fear that anything awful and terrible could happen at any time? I worry about things — car accidents, for instance; I dream about my purse being stolen on foreign journeys.

But not Edna, who decided not to worry about robbery after someone broke in and stole jewelry and other things when she was away. No security alarms here, and cats would trip them off anyway.

Car accidents? "Just put your car in low gear," she said last winter when I worried about her narrow, icy lane. (My mother wanted my husband to drive me on these dangerous journeys.)

"All these 'what-ifs'," Edna sighed when she decided to stay out at Sunfish and family and friends worried about her breaking a leg/having a stroke/not being able to get to the phone and call for help.

All this sounds — I know, I know — so Polyanna-ish. But you need toughness to live so long and so successfully. And so intelligently. I think of one of the fan letters. "I have before me five golden leaves of Neil's Harbour bread and six gleaming jars of relish ... The sun is shining and I imagine I am in Clara May's kitchen in Neil's Harbour..."

Bread and relish: not big accomplishments, surely, but here is something you can do at this minute, this time. Happiness and contentment can be in front of you.

You can have this moment.

A year later. Fall again, and summer weather has lingered far into October. I visited Ireland in the summer, and I signed a contract for Edna's biography after a year of visiting her every week to learn more about her life. I've talked to her friends and gone with Edna to visit the farm of a Mennonite friend. But I'm still not quite through the archives at Guelph — boxes and boxes of letters and papers — and what is this? Who is this? And what about the long letters in 1943 and 1944 to Earl Bailey, the Lunenburg artist who painted with his mouth? And all those painfully confiding letters to Helen, the woman who would run off with Keith? Oh Edna, so much material, I've sighed, so many surprises. I can see everything, she says, and I can quote from it. I have about thirteen hundred pages of photocopies.

"You know more about me than I do," Edna says, laughing. "I've had such a long and wonderful life. How're you going to do it all? Maybe you should write a series. So many things would make a book. Fred, for instance. I wanted to write a book about Fred but no one was interested in another book about a convict."

"And the letters. All your letters. Dr. Robins's letters. Your travel letters from Europe. Love letters to Keith."

"I haven't read those in years. Did you find letters from Harold Horwood yet?"

"Yes, sure. I had some copies made."

"And all those crazy, searching letters I wrote to men in the forties. Many of them unsent."

We are writers, plotting together. The plot is Edna's life. Full of surprises and dramas and ponderings, making sense of things.

"I should have just gone to bed with them, instead of writing all those letters," Edna says, chuckling. "Say, by the way, someone from Neil's Harbour called me the other night. I knew right away it was a Cape Breton voice. Travis Budge, I knew him long ago at the Harbour. Now he's a retired RCMP officer. He read about Jay Leno."

Jay Leno is the latest thing in Edna's life. A local writer, Nancy Silcox, wrote a piece about wonderful Edna and all the company she has at Sunfish for the Kitchener-Waterloo *Record*, and the Jay Leno people apparently read the article on the Internet and invited Edna to appear on the *Tonight Show* in California.[5]

Edna had never seen the show and watched it with Mally. Not a big fan of stand-up comics, she wasn't impressed by the crazy clapping of the audience, and Mally wasn't impressed either, and anyway, Leno's chin reminded her of Brian Mulroney. And a trip to California all expenses paid wasn't a big deal to Edna, who's been to Europe eight times. Edna told her friend, journalist Judy Creighton, about the incident; Creighton wrote a story for CP. Edna was on the front page of the *Record* and reporters from everywhere and nowhere have been calling.

"Just because of an American talk show," Edna said. "There wasn't as much fuss when I got the Order of Canada. Can you imagine? But maybe I should write Jay Leno a note — it wasn't personal."

Nancy Silcox has been back this week, with oil of oregano for Mally, who has a sore, the size of a quarter, that won't go away. Earlier in the week, Ted and Janni Schafer, who live in California part of the year, brought Mally chicken-flavoured ointment, but that didn't work. Lawrence McNaught has been out with a cameraman to film for his ongoing film about Edna. And, oh yes, on the weekend someone from London came and brought lunch. And Edna's nephew drove her to the denturist in Galt — she's had trouble with a bottom denture — and guess what? His friend's dog escaped from the car and landed in the pound. It cost forty dollars to spring him.

"Oh, and I had call from the Roger's Cable. They want to interview me next week. And did you see this?"

She pulls a big photo out of an envelope. It's a copy of another picture that appeared in the *Record*, in an article about hormonal replacements, which Edna has taken for fifty years.

It's a striking shot, Edna pictured against a backdrop of red maple leaves.

"Sometimes photographers say they'll send you a copy but they don't. He did though — such a nice man. But you can see my rolled up sweatpants. Oh well, that's the style these days, Wendy said."

"It's a wonderful picture," I assure her. Edna's vain about photos.

"Oh, by the way, did you get invited to that meeting?"

"Barb Naylor phoned me." Some of Edna's friends are getting together to make sure she'll be okay for winter, that she has food, the bird feeders are kept filled, and so on. "It's Monday night. I'll be there."

"Who knows what they'll talk about. What are we going to talk about today? How about Paris?"

I've read a lot of travel letters, some written on toilet paper. Edna wrote all the time in Europe and sent the letters home, in lieu of her notebook. She wrote on trains and in cafés, describing the people around her. She used a lot of the details in her sassy, unfinished novella, "Molly."

"Oh but I didn't put everything in the letters. I couldn't write everyone at home everything that happened. We haven't talked enough about Europe, I think. Europe really changed me, made me more sophisticated. I've been thinking about it. And Portugal — it was all so wonderful. I learned so much. I just went. I was afraid until a friend said, 'One day at a time.' Our husbands were at AA together. And that's what I did, one day at a time. Something and someone always came along. I wasn't naive, just trusting."

So many stories.

I pull out the notebook and think of Edna, in her forties, wearing her grey tweed travel suit, sitting in a train compartment and describing the big, ugly, brown suede shoes of the German man sitting across from her. She wore the suit most of the time and had it dry-cleaned in Switzerland. A woman with reddish hair cut short who looked much younger than her age. Later she bought a big plaid suitcase to hold her purchases. And how many hats did she buy on that first European trip? Fifteen? I must check my notes; the number is there somewhere. Mostly straw hats, I believe. Edna, hats! Why hats? I think of a photo of a Canadian Authors' Association convention circa 1950 and the silly dumpy hats some of the women wore. And Edna, identified as Mrs. Olive Staebler, with a big purse dangling from her hand. And a really matronly belted dress with a little collar. All those nicely groomed authoresses and poetesses. Their propriety bleeds the heart.

"And the gondola ride in Venice. I haven't told you about that," Edna says.

Am I going to write about the gondola ride?

Where will I ever begin to tell the long, involved story of Edna's life? How can I tell all the stories? The stories that keep coming and coming?

And how will I ever be able to stop telling the stories?

Spring 2003. I have almost finished the book, after a long, hard winter — hard because my mother died in December of liver cancer, diagnosed in September, right after I signed the book contract.

Driving out to Sunfish in late fall was always a reprieve from sadness and worry. Going to the country and turning down the narrow road to Edna's cottage was, as I heard from one of Edna's friends about another friend, like passing through a hole in the trees. And to me it was, too, almost like moving into another time, not in a nostalgic way or goofy time travel way, but into a standing still time of peace.

Sitting in Edna's cottage, watching the lake and the birds at the feeder, looking at her books and art and petting Mally, a normally reserved cat who always comes out of the bedroom to greet me, talking to Edna, listening to her life's stories as dusk fell over the lake, I felt tension disappear.

I hated to leave but bad weather had started, and I didn't want to chance the narrow lane with ditches on both sides in the dark.

And then I did not come for a while, and although I tried to move my mind into Edna's way of looking at the world, grief dispelled all effort. Later, it was time to write again, to return to the archives. Edna, the professional writer who knew what it was to sit at your desk day after day, understood.

The war was just about to start in Iraq on a shiny spring-like day — snow finally melting, the ice disappearing seemingly overnight — when I reluctantly took a day off writing to speak to a class at the University of Waterloo. The undergrads were using my collection, *Order in the Universe*, and I couldn't disappoint them, but it was with great reluctance that I pulled myself away from my desk.

I thought of Edna, and mentioned her as someone whose life has been writing, while the students asked me, "What did you mean by…?" I knew Edna hadn't been well. In 1996, just before receiving the Order of Canada, she suffered from a virus that affected her balance and she started using a cane. She has diabetes and sometimes her blood pressure goes up. She hasn't driven in a year. Her teeth bother her and there's occasional facial pain from an annoying tic douloureux. Not that she discusses her ailments. She usually seems spry.

But this time there was redness and such big, painful swelling that she couldn't even wear her glasses.

And her sister, Norma, died shortly after her ninety-fourth birthday on December 23, 2002, after being ill a long time. Long ago, the baby sister had been Edna's Christmas gift. I think of those girls in middy blouses, in their big yellow house on Spetz Street. Years later, Norm and Edna bought the land at Sunfish together. Norm and her family used to come to the lake for dinner and Parcheesi, the family game. The sisters had sisterly spats, but as Edna's niece, Barbie Wurtele (who lives only a few miles away from Sunfish), said, "If you could have heard the three sisters reminiscing about their childhood…"

Now only one sister remained, Ruby in Peterborough (with whom Edna knits catnip mice; Edna has made more than thirty thousand of them), and Norm's death has surely made Edna think of her own mortality. I know she thinks about her death: what will it feel like, what will happen, when will it occur, but, Edna-like, she always makes herself think of something else.

I had an overwhelming urge to see Edna after my talk, so when it was over I drove out to the Zehrs grocery store in Waterloo and phoned her. Her place was only ten minutes away.

Could I come? Sure. Peter Etril Snyder, the artist famous for his paintings of Mennonites (and other subjects too), and his wife, Marilyn, were there. So was Nancy Martin, an Old Order friend of Edna's. I knew all of them, had visited Nancy with Edna in the summer near Heidelberg, where Nancy lived with her over-ninety father. Nancy liked to read good books, literature: Tolstoy and Dostoevsky, and modern things too. I'd wanted to talk to her about Edna, and she told me how impressed she was that Edna treated everyone the same way, and how much Edna had added to her life. Nancy helps scholars with Pennsylvania-Dutch dialect and folklore; I liked her at once.

On the way back, Edna and I stopped at the Heidelberg Inn and ate veal schnitzel and sauerkraut at the corner table where Edna always sits. The waiter/owner rushed over to say hello, and I remembered Edna's story about going there with Harold Horwood, her friend Gerald Noonan, and others, including a strange, pessimistic young man, George Dawes, who lived in his truck, admired Hemingway, and felt everyone wanted to do him wrong.

(Gerald Noonan, writer and professor, almost forty years younger than Edna, was dead too. Cancer. He referred to Edna as "my best friend.")

I'd seen Nancy again in — what, early January? — when she was visiting Eva; two New Order Mennonites had driven them to Edna's. We'd all had tea together and talked about what we were cooking for the men for dinner (and other things). Eva and Nancy each had gifts bags of books Edna hadn't been able to get to them by Christmas; once she would have hopped into her car and driven the few miles to their farms.

I knew from Edna that Nancy's father had died; I wanted to see her, and the Snyders too.

Edna's lane still has ice on it, and I see her front yard — really the backyard, as she reminds me, because the front yard faces the lake — is squishy. I'm glad I have boots in the backseat.

Tea is almost ready when I arrive. Marilyn and Nancy have both brought some home baking; I stuff my raspberry squares from Zehrs into Edna's fridge. Edna is thrilled with the daffodils I picked up and shows me the azaleas I gave her in the fall: still blooming, aren't they lovely? Did I give her the azaleas? Really? Oh, to be so observant about small things.

Especially when she is in pain. Edna's face is red and swollen, but she says it is "much better." She called her cousin, Marcia Smith, a retired doctor, on the weekend because she didn't want to sit in the emergency room for hours. Marcia came right over and said Edna should call her doctor for antibiotics. Edna's face was so swollen she could hardly see, and another visitor remarked that she looked like the elephant man. Someone else brought soup she could sip with a straw.

The swelling has gone down — some — but the skin is red. She still can't get her glasses to stay on, so she can't read or watch television comfortably.

"I just have to sit here," she says, with a small laugh.

It's a pleasant visit, and if the sign of the infection weren't visible, you'd never know Edna was not feeling the best. She takes part in the conversation, wants to know how my cat, Thomas, is — he's had kidney trouble — and Edna talks about a wonderful new dog she's met, Sherlock, a German pointer, who saw the newspaper in its plastic wrapper and carried it over to her.

Peter and Marilyn share news: they've returned from a cross-Canada trip. Peter took photos everywhere for painting later, and Marilyn wrote in her journal. They'll combine her words with his art: a book to look forward to.

We talk about Nancy's father. Might someone write about him for "Lives Lived" in the *Globe and Mail*?

Edna says she's almost finished the anthology of Maritime poetry I gave her for Christmas, but sometimes she doesn't think modern poetry is really poetry.

The Snyders and Nancy leave after the tea things are washed and put away. Edna and I sit as the room grows dimmer, as we have so often over the past two years.

Edna says everyone is waiting for the biography to come out, is anxious for it. I know. One person, eyes wide, asked me: Is it true the biography won't be published until Edna is dead?

I am anxious, too, but for different reasons: will I meet the deadline? I still need a few more days in Guelph for some items I've missed.

And: what will Edna think of it?

Not seeing her for over a month has made me realize how much I missed her. We have, I think, grown close. We have shared books. I lent her the first memoir and the novel by Nuala O'Faolain, my latest favourite writer. Edna loved them. I gave her a quirky vest with animals on it (she said it was the Christmas present of the year) and she gave me her little red travelling typewriter, which I plan to use for poetry.

Edna agrees I must write what I deem right, but what if she is upset by the biography? What will her friends think? All the *Schmecks* fans?

In the weeks ahead Edna will ask me to change certain names. And I will agree.

Whenever I am with her, I forget her great age: ninety-seven now, this past January. And she is not this dear old lady, but an adventuresome free spirit, still the way she was when she was thirty-nine and found herself alone in a Cape Breton fishing village where she knew no one; still the same as the spiffy forty-two year old in her hat with the flowers and the "new look" outfit when she boldly marched into *Maclean's* and presented the editor with a manuscript; still the same as the woman who spent three months alone in Europe in 1954.

Always the same, for years and years: drawing people to her with her writing and with her being.

She seems Irish somehow, I think as dusk falls, as if something has filtered down from her Irish ancestor, Susan MacMahon. Edna used that name as an alias in an unpublished short story way back when. And like a mythic old woman in Irish lore, while not growing younger, she is timeless and seems to create life anew.

"I've had a wonderful life," she says. "I'm so lucky and so grateful."

Part *One*

Chapter One
A Berlin Childhood

Monday, January 15, 1906, a cold and damp early evening. The lights and celebration of Christmas have passed in the town of Berlin, but electric streetlights glow on the main street.

Berlin is known as "the German town of Canada,"[6] a prosperous place of factories, solid houses, and churches. The rich have their villas and mansions on Queen Street, but even workers live in brick houses; frame construction is forbidden in this town settled by Mennonites, and by German artisans who arrived with their tools and ambition. Railway tracks of the Preston-Berlin line run down the centre of King Street. In rainy weather, the street is muddy, but tonight the snow is packed down and the occasional horse-drawn sleigh or buggy passes by.

Mrs. Markham tugs her long coat close as she hurries by the stores — Langs (which ran a Christmas story contest with the prize of a big doll, which lucky Nellie Brubacher won), Weber's Hardware, Weserloh's clothing, August Boehmer's Jewellers. Lights gleam in the Walper House Hotel, but the city hall and the market are dark.

A mother is always nervous with a first child, but perhaps young Louise Cress is overly anxious, Mrs. Markham thinks, because Louise's poor mother, Rosine Sattler, died six days after Louise's birth. A sad story, one that is known in this town where everyone seems to know everyone else.

Louise was born in January, too, and six days later, Rosine's parents, the Shiefles, fetched the baby and took her to their big home in Waterloo. John Sattler did not see his daughter for eleven years. And now Louise's grandparents are dead, and there is no close female relative to rejoice at the birth of a daughter.

The midwife turns left on Scott Street and continues up a block to the house on the corner of Spetz Street, a house bought with Louise's inheritance, Mrs. Markham has heard, and it is surely a finer house than John Cress could have afforded on his own. Louise Cress likes her finery, her hats, and now she has her big house in Berlin. He's a boy from St. Jacobs, really, a descendant of Mennonites.

Dr. Noecker's buggy is still tied up outside the Cress house. Gaslights burn and candles flicker upstairs in the bay window; the Cresses do not have electricity yet.

John is waiting by the door, holding a lantern, and ready to relieve her of her satchel. He's a quiet-looking man with a dark mustache, usually reserved, but tonight his face is creased with a smile as he takes Mrs. Markham's coat.

Dr. Noecker is coming down the stairs. Doctor and midwife shake hands.

"A healthy daughter," he says. "Mother and child are both well. You will have an easy time of it, Mrs. Markham."

You can hear his German accent. Mrs. Markham speaks a bit of German, too, and understands when the doctor says, "*Der lieber Gott war gut.*"

God was good.

After the doctor has gone (more handshakes, congratulations again to the father), John leads her upstairs to the big bedroom where Louise, decorously covered with a quilt, smiles up at her. The young mother's face is soft in the candlelight as she lowers her eyes to the infant resting in the crook of her elbow.

They have waited for this child. John has loved Louise ever since he saw her at her aunt and uncle's house next to his repair shop in Waterloo. Now the shop has expanded to the Waterloo Spring Company, and here they are, man and wife with their firstborn in this big, solid house that smells of polish and candles. The cradle is ready for the child; baby nighties and nappies are neatly folded on the bureau. John Cress smiles down at the tableau.

This child will be blessed, the midwife thinks.

Every child should have such an enchanted beginning. Edna Louise Cress, born on that wintry afternoon, had a happy, privileged, and secure childhood, youth, and early adulthood. Her ancestors had lived in the area for almost one hundred years. She knew who she was and where she belonged and that family cared about her.

The happy memories of those early days brought self-confidence and reinforced her positive attitude. “When we were young children we were never allowed to hate anything. My parents used to say it was wicked. I remember once saying I hated watermelon and got the very devil for it because — they explained — God made watermelon. I must not hate anything that God made and God made everything so I must not hate anything,” she wrote a friend years later.[7]

Childhood was also the source of many of the stories she wove into the cookbooks that would bring her fame and fortune.

Today the Cress home houses a law firm. It’s a big, yellow brick house in downtown Kitchener. Office furniture has replaced tables and chairs and sofas, but there is a sense of permanence and prosperity in the big rooms. Beams and stucco cover the ceilings; original dark wood panelling gleams. The lawyer’s office is in what was once the children’s playroom with its cupboard full of toys, the piano, and a singing canary in front of the bay window. The solid staircase curves at an angle.

Before electricity was installed, Edna and her sisters climbed these stairs in the dark before they hopped into bed. Upstairs is the master bedroom, now an office, where Edna was born and where, as a teenager, she recuperated after a sledding accident to receive her friends in style.

Higher up, accessible by a narrow staircase, is the attic where the girls roller-skated until their mother couldn’t stand the noise any longer.

It’s easy to imagine the three Cress girls, Edna, Norma, born four years later on December 23 (a Christmas present for Edna), and Ruby, born a year after that, laughing and playing in this house, girls dressed in old-fashioned dresses, in middy blouses. Or at Christmas, with a German Christmas tree with real candles set in the window.

John Cress’s strong arms have rolled out Lep cookies and Springerle and now the cookies sit on glass plates, awaiting Santa Claus to come calling at the door on Christmas Eve.

And later, the girls squabbling about whose turn it is to do the dishes, about a borrowed pair of stockings. The whole family eating Edna's favourite noodle soup (made with beef and lots of parsley) on her birthday or Louise's candy pie, made with maple syrup and crumbs. Or the mocha cake that was her specialty.

And on the porch steps — is this where they showed Edna Haley's Comet when she was ten?

There's a parking lot across the street now, but once a widow — they called her the neighbourhood witch — lived there. Her garden covered the whole block and was filled with cherry trees. Next door (the house is gone) lived the Georges,* who had daughters the same ages as the Cress girls. The two families did not speak. Mr. George drank, and the Cresses could hear the fights. "They didn't use nice words," Edna remembers. Louise Cress wouldn't let her girls have anything to do with the Georges, and they never did, even to say hello, when as adults the Georges and Cresses passed one another on the street. The Cress girls always obeyed their mother. Edna used to worry that Mr. George would burn their house down when he was drunk. Edna feared fire after seeing sparks from a blaze at a neighbour's house on Frederick Street.

To the south is Pearl Place, Mascott Lane in Edna's childhood, where Catholic workers lived. A Foreman boy would chant: Catholics, Catholics, ring the bell, Protestants, Protestants, go to hell. But a few streets over lived Dentist Roberts* and his wife, who golfed, with their five children. Fay Roberts* was Edna's age, and the two were best friends from kindergarten on. They played hide and seek and run sheep run in Fay's backyard; in the winter they built snow forts. Edna's friends came from her parents' tight social circle and they were usually friends for life, girls like Margaret Snyder and Jean MacMillan.

Just up the street and around the corner on Frederick is Suddaby School, which Edna attended. You can imagine Edna traipsing down the porch steps of the house on Spetz Street and skipping to school. A thin girl, a bit of a tomboy, with reddish hair, brown eyes, freckles, and, alas, two prominent front teeth.

---

* An asterisk following a name indicates the name has been changed.

Perhaps Edna resembles her Irish great-great-grandmother, Susan MacMahon. As a teenager Edna liked to talk about this ancestor, but for the rest, she is of Mennonite and German descent.

Her birth announcement appeared two days after she entered the world, on Wednesday, January 17, in the German language *Berliner Journal*: 15 Jan. in Berlin, John C. Cress, *Tochter*.[8]

John must have walked to the newspaper office on the sixteenth to arrange for the announcement in the newspaper. The *Berliner Journal* was written in old script and was German in theme and sentiment, reporting on the doings of the beloved Kaiser and his family and carrying articles about travels in the Fatherland, Reisen Durch Deutschland, in case anyone had a hankering for castles along the Rhine or hiking trails through the Harz Mountains.

The big news in December 1905 was the revolution in Russia and the rumour that the Kaiser was sending troops to the Baltic.

Both John and Louise understood some German, or Pennsylvania Dutch as it was called, and would if necessary speak a few words, but English was their main language. Still, John obviously felt an allegiance to things German.

John's ancestor Simon Cress was a Mennonite from Pennsylvania, and the first permanent settler in St. Jacobs, a few miles north of what is now Kitchener-Waterloo, in 1806. His son, Ephraim, married Susan MacMahon, an Irish woman (actually a girl; she was only sixteen), most probably from County Clare, whose family emigrated before the Great Famine. Like the Cresses, the MacMahons became a well-established and respected family, Ida MacMahon working as the first librarian at the Mechanical Institute, and her brother, Fred, heading the County Home on Frederick Street.

Louise's roots were also deep in Waterloo County. The first Shiefle, sometimes spelled Shiefly, arrived in St. Jacobs around the time the Cresses did. They had all come over from Pennsylvania, and both families were Mennonite, originally from the area of Alsace Lorraine, Switzerland, or the German Palatinate. Mennonites liked to stress that they were Swiss, and some said they were descended from the Celts, but they spoke German and ate German food.

After suffering discrimination, harassment, and martyrdom for their Anabaptist faith, they immigrated to the Commonwealth of Pennsylvania, where land was plentiful and they were assured they would not have to fight in a war, as they were pacifists. But would the new American government honour the pledges given to them by the English king? Perhaps not, and there lay Canada across the border. And land. The Mennonites of Pennsylvania were prosperous, thrifty farmers, and liked to pass on farms to their sons. Scouts came up and reported that what was to become Waterloo County was rich and fertile. The German Land Company was formed, and by 1807 over five hundred people lived in the Waterloo area.

Simon Cress was born in 1764 in Path Valley, Franklin County, Pennsylvania. In 1806 he and his wife, Catherine, and their five children, Mary, Elizabeth, Rachel, Jacob, and Ephraim, along with about forty other Mennonites, made the thirty-two-day trek from Pennsylvania to Upper Canada. They followed north along the Susquehanna River and forded it before crossing the Allegheny Mountains. It took nine hours to climb the three miles; six horses pulled one Conestoga wagon. Sometimes oxen were used.

They forded the Tonawanda River in New York by cutting trees and erecting a bridge. And then they had to cross the Niagara River. By 1806 a rude ferry existed, but the Beverley Swamp remained, a boggy area that was treacherous for the horses and the heavy wagons.

Simon and his family stayed a few months at the farm of John Erb in Preston before heading to their new land in what is now the village of St. Jacobs. Simon Cress, Jr., was born there in 1806. By 1813 the First Mennonite Church had seventy-three charter members. Simon's land, purchased from John Erb, cost 196 pounds, 17 shillings, and 6 pence. His lot ran from the Conestoga River to St. Jacobs. He soon built a log house.[9]

Louise Cress was not curious about her ancestry and vaguely said her family was Swiss, although her father, John Sattler, was descended from Konrad Sattler, born in 1819 in Grossherzog, Sinsheim, Baden in Germany. In 1885 Louis Sattler purchased a harness shop, which his son, Rufe, turned into a prosperous leather goods store.

Louise felt uncomfortable around Mennonites, although she bought *Schmierkase* and *Kochkase* from the Old Order farmwives in their dark clothes at the Saturday market. She definitely wasn't thrilled when she overheard a Mennonite woman at the market whisper that she, Louise, a city woman, didn't know anything.

Descendants of Mennonites, who had come up in the world, considered their distant Old Order relatives with their plain dress, simple ways, and odd speech to be country cousins. Edna's articles, and later her cookbooks, contributed to the change in people's perceptions of the Mennonites, and Waterloo County became known as Mennonite country. But an aunt chastised Edna for writing about the family's Mennonite ancestry: "Did you have to say it?"

Joseph Schneider, Abraham Weber, and Benjamin Eby, Mennonites from Lancaster County, Pennsylvania, were the first settlers of the town. Joseph Schneider erected a log cabin on what is now Queen Street; the frame farmhouse he soon built is now the Joseph Schneider Haus, a national historical site. More Mennonites quickly followed to clear the land.

The hard-working Mennonites quickly had the rudiments of a small settlement, more a crossroads than a village, which they called Sand Hills, and later, Ebytown. They had their sawmill and gristmill, a tavern/inn, a church, and a school.

German artisans began to arrive, and in 1824 Ebytown became Berlin. A furniture shop was started, and there were shoemakers, a weaver, a potter, a wagon maker, and so on. The newcomers were mostly from Hesse and the surrounding states and they carried with them not only their tools but also their language and belief in hard work. Church services were in German. A printing press hauled by ox team from Pennsylvania ensured the printing of a German newspaper and books. Berlin was incorporated as a village in 1853, with one thousand residents.

Berlin became a town in 1870. By the time Edna was born, it was a solid, prosperous town of fifteen thousand. The elite were people like the Breithaupts, Langs, and Seagrams; Louis Breithaupt came to Berlin to buy hides and stayed to found a tannery. Hartman Krug and others started furniture factories. There were also four button factories for a while.

It was a very German town. You had to speak German as well as English to work in a store there. Owning your own house was important, and often an entire family worked in the same factory to meet the mortgage payments. Even girls worked in factories. People kept pigs and perhaps a cow in the backyard, where they also grew vegetables.

For entertainment, there was music: music festivals and groups, *Vereins*, were popular. An opera house, attached to the Walper Hotel, was built in 1896. Beer gardens were popular. Of course there was always churchgoing on Sundays.

Ties to Germany remained strong. The Berlin anthem was "Wacht am Rhein" — "Watch Along the Rhine" — and people remained closer in sentiment to the Kaiser than to Queen Victoria, whose robust statue looked grim in Victoria Park.

"At home amongst ourselves we speak this language [German] but we are thoroughly Canadian," wrote a Berlin teacher transplanted to the West.[10]

While the factory owners lived in fancy villas and rode in fancy broughams, ordinary folks were heartened that J.M. Schneider started out making sausages on his kitchen table and another businessman used to lace his shoes with string. Thrift and hard work were celebrated; the businessman was king.

There were no slums.

Edna described Kitchener and neighbouring Waterloo in an essay in her first book, *Sauerkraut and Enterprise*, published in 1966 as a Centennial Project, as clean, prosperous, and hospitable places. It's a laudatory piece of writing, but sometimes this praise reveals the other side:

> Both cities have a passion for cleanliness and order. Upkeep is a sacred duty to all. Anyone driving around on a summer evening will see people painting their houses and manicuring their green velvet lawns: on

> Brubacher Street the family of Fritz Herschenbaum, rubber worker, may be decorating a porch; on John Boulevard, Tom Seagram, whose millionaire grandfather started distilling V.O., may be seen mowing his grass; on fashionable Stanley Drive, Brigadier Walter Bean, O.B.E., Honorary Colonel of the Highland Fusiliers of Canada, and President of the Waterloo Trust and Savings Company, might be snipping sprigs off his hedges.[11]

One is reminded of W.V. Uttley, an earlier historian who lauded Mr. Reinhart Boehmer, who, at age eighty-four, went to bed at eight, rose at five, and took lots of cold baths, followed by rigorous exercises, including ones for the eyes.

It's all a bit rigid and not exactly conducive to creativity. Kitchener was known for its music, but few writers have written about the place in novels or poetry. The old town of Berlin may seem cozy in retrospect, the way women wearing hats in sepia photos appear to be quaint and mysterious, but it hardly provided the colour or drama needed for creative literature. Other towns had social cliques, of course, but probably they were seen more seriously in Berlin than elsewhere.

Certainly, another writer who lived in Berlin as a child in the years following Edna's birth, Ross MacDonald, did not share any version of Edna's cozy childhood. He found his mother's Mennonite relatives rigid and unloving, and he and his mother were so poor that he was almost placed in an orphanage.

By the time she wrote her words of praise about Berlin/Kitchener, Edna had found inspiration for writing not in her prosperous native city, but in a poor Cape Breton fishing village; the *Schmecks* cookbooks came along much later.

John and Louise had wanted a son, and planned to call him Edward. Instead, here was this big, eight-pound girl with reddish hair and alert eyes.

They decided to call her Edna Louise, Edna for Edward and Louise because that was her mother's name and the second name of her deceased grandmother.

Edna was slow to walk, but talked early. "A slow walker and fast talker," she jokes today. She was a shy and skinny girl, a bit of a tomboy who did not like dolls too much, although she was upset when Norma broke her doll. John called Edna "Buster," after one of the Katzenjammer kids.

John provided a good living for his small family, but the Cresses weren't up there with the Breithaupts, Seagrams, and Langs. The Seagrams kept horses, which they raced at Woodbine; cosmopolitan Mrs. Lang was from New York and "entertained 200 guests at home in honour of her sister-in-law of Berlin, Germany. … Present was her debutante daughter."[12] But the Cresses were respectable enough.

Until he bought his first car, a Briscoe, John took the trolley to Waterloo every day to run his company, the Waterloo Spring Company. He had perfected a technique of tempering steel for springs for upholstered furniture, which he sold to factories in Berlin and Kincardine.

John was quieter and less ambitious socially than Louise, who loved fashion and had her hats made by a milliner. She always wore white gloves when she read the paper. She dressed her daughters beautifully, hiring a dressmaker for a week, spring and fall, to make their outfits. She bought hats for them too, including a straw poke bonnet for Edna, which prevented her from fully seeing the elephants in a parade. Sometimes they all went to Toronto to shop for clothes, and for shoes for Edna's very narrow 7 1/2 AAA feet.

They had lunch at Child's Restaurant, where butter cakes were made in the window. The trip took four hours on the unpaved roads, and John was always looking for a shortcut. Once they got lost and ended up back on Dundas Street in Toronto.

The girls called John "Daddy," and Louise "Mother."

Family opinion is that Louise was the boss in the family. She even bought a building lot in Waterloo against John's objections because she'd always wanted to live there; she would move to

Waterloo after John's death. John enjoyed country drives and going fishing; Louise preferred to see the sights of the town.

They had a close social circle. The Cresses played bridge but did not golf, which was all the rage then. The family attended nearby St. Andrew's Presbyterian Church, not out of religious belief, but because respectable families went to church on Sunday; they always occupied the second pew from the back, in front of Mr. Kerr, whose body emitted cat noises. The wall clock, donated by Sheriff Davidson, caused Edna to imagine the sheriff riding like a sheriff in the movies.

Unlike her working-class sisters, Louise did not go out to work. No wife of her class worked; it was unthinkable. She wanted to learn to sew when she was eighteen, but her grandmother didn't let her. Like other women of her class, Louise hired a maid, Aggie Brubacher. The girls loved Aggie, who looked after them while Mother, a very good cook, prepared the meals.

Once Aggie kept them in the kitchen while Louise entertained. Unnoticed, Edna ate a mass of cream puffs and summer sausage and became ill enough for her mother to call the doctor. (Edna's first memory is of pulling down the tablecloth and eating cake batter while her mother dashed to a neighbour, Mrs. Hassenauer, to borrow an egg. She can still see the blue bowl and taste the batter.)

Louise was a kind-hearted mother; punishment for an infraction was making a child sit on a little chair in the pantry — "never a strapping," according to Ruby — but she was not overly demonstrative with hugs and kisses.

Each girl had her own room. The kids were seldom allowed in the parlour, where Greek tiles adorned the fireplace, but they did have a playroom. Edna, who took piano lessons from Mr. Tibbett, recalls playing the piano when she was nine or ten and a visitor remarking, "That child has such beautiful hair. An artist from New York would pay thousands of dollars to paint that hair." It was fine praise for Edna, who wanted to pay two dollars for a solution to get rid of her freckles.

There was a beloved cat, which accompanied them once on a train trip to Lake Huron. Sometimes they visited Grandpa and Grandma Cress in nearby St. Jacobs, where Grandma, a tiny woman, made pancakes for Edna. There were also cousins, Ethel and Katherine, with whom Edna and her sisters often went to the general store, today the site of Stone Crock, a restaurant serving Mennonite food, where Edna has often eaten. Later, Edna told *Maclean's* that she had "to learn some Pennsylvania Dutch in St. Jacobs or be deprived of the adventure of catching pollywogs in the Conestoga River with children who spoke English only in school."[13] On Saturdays, as soon as she was old enough, Edna accompanied her mother to the market, just a few blocks away, pulling a little wagon.

Yes, it was a wonderful childhood, but one thing set Edna apart: reading. The Cresses were not bookish. They took the daily paper and Louise purchased a set of the Books of Knowledge (and Edna did not mind putting her hand up in school to show what she knew), but books and book-reading were not part of daily life on Spetz Street.

As soon as she could read, Edna began going to the Carnegie Library two blocks away. She would visit several times a week because patrons could take out only two books at a time. Mabel Dunham, author of folksy books about the area, including *Kristli's Tree*, was the local librarian. She was strict, chastising Edna for putting a book face down and bending the spine. "I was afraid of her — a real disciplinarian. She could be quite mean," Edna recalls.

But never mind. Edna discovered beloved books there, not the classics like *Treasure Island*, but children's favourites like the Cousin's series, Jimmy Skunkin's tales about animals, the *Cornerhouse Girls*, and *St. Nicholas Magazine*, in which Augusta Hewell Seaman wrote mystery stories.

It was the beginning of her lifelong passion for literature, and also of an inner dreaminess that set her apart from her sisters. Sometimes the dreaminess led to feelings of being different, and occasionally there were feelings of inferiority. She minded her two buck teeth, thought she was skinny and that Norm was the pretty one who resembled John Cress, but these whispers of sadness were the feelings most children experience.

Edna was an average, and sometimes indifferent, student who would later have trouble with math; she wasn't angelic and once got a strapping for putting her slate cloth into Loren Holtz's mouth.

Reading at night was easier once the family had electricity. Niagara Power arrived in Berlin in 1910; it was the first city in the world to receive electric power at 110,000 volts. It was a big improvement over getting undressed (Edna was adept at removing bloomers, garter belt, underpants, and stockings in one swoop and setting the arrangement on a chair so she could put everything back on at once in the morning) and going to bed in the dark. Now Edna could read in bed. And hide books under the mattress.

She didn't dream about being a writer. Not yet.

Edna was eight years old when the First World War broke out. She was visiting Aunt Nelly (a lousy cook who made ham and boiled potatoes and rice puddings without raisins) and Uncle Henry at Seaforth for three weeks — she wasn't homesick; she would never be homesick. As soon as war broke out Aunt Nelly bundled Edna up and sent her home.

Nice quiet Berlin changed at the outbreak of war. Suddenly these German Canadians were at war with their cousins in the Fatherland. Were they loyal citizens or not? Would the young men of Berlin enlist or were they traitors? The year 1914 saw the beginning of dissent and even riots. German had been taught in the schools but was soon dropped. Edna's German teacher, Mr. Wiegland, a nice man who wore a cape, disappeared. Soon German was no longer spoken in the streets.

But Berlin men were not eager to enlist, and strong-armed and devious tactics were used by army recruiters, who cornered men of eligible age on the street and urged mothers and wives to taunt and shame men into signing up. It was terrible for Berliners, who did not feel a real affinity for the British king while they remained loyal Canadians.

And what about the unfortunate name, Berlin?

It was an uncomfortable time for Edna's parents. She recalls, still, her parents being against the actions of the infamous Captain Blood, an Englishman who was the ringleader of the get-them-in-the-army-or-else faction.

"My family was so mad at Captain Blood, a Cockney — so anti-German and anti-Mennonite," Edna recalls. The Cresses were also against the town's name change to Kitchener in 1916. There were riots by then. The German Concordia Club was ransacked and the Kaiser's bust was torn from its pedestal and thrown into Victoria Lake. The Cresses do not seem to have taken an active stance in the matter. John was not a civic leader, and certainly no proper wife was going to get involved, but their opinions and their privately expressed anti-Anglo sentiments embarrassed Edna, although the war troubles do not seem to have affected the flow of her childhood.

Despite her feelings, sometimes, that she was homely, she was a self-confident young girl, with a witty sense of humour and a love of adventure, who already had the sharp eye of a writer.

When she was fifteen, she travelled alone by train to Toledo, Ohio, to visit her mother's friends, the Gilberts. Wearing a new dress with a Bertha collar, she noticed everything about the journey (a man wearing "the strangest platinum ring set with a large emerald … remarked about the heat occasionally and I heartily responded. … He asked me if his face was dirty; it was. Then at Chatham … a boy smiled at me 3 times and winked. Snubbed him."), the way she would do all her life. She loved everything about the trip, although her new dress wasn't in style in Toledo. Mrs. Gilbert took her shopping and bought her a tangerine sweater for $2.98, "cute and all the rage."[14]

Edna's letter to her mother shows her already distinctive voice. And her spunk:

> Yes, I promise to write a letter every day & here it's the 4th day and the first letter. I've been SO busy I have had only a few minutes to spare. Listen, Mother old girl, in order to save time, money and expenses, I'll send you my diary (I'll have to write it first, see?).
>
> How are the goaters? Jason, one of Marion's friends, thought that goaters were little goats and you know that goaters are beards. Consequently, I mean how are Norm & Ruby? I'm expecting a letter from you all. Really, Mother, I'm not a bit homesick. Gee, I don't even have time to think of home. Jean has spent tons of money & I still have 90 cts left out of the first $10. Things are so different here. We're so polite &

> I'm sure they think I'm a Society Belle (I'm so polite, tee hee). Here they say wha (meaning what) and they say yeah (meaning yes). Golly but it's queer, Golly, Gosh, Darn. Damn is a very common expression.[15]

No wonder this bright girl had many friends, including boys. As she grew into a teenager, there were wiener and corn roasts in Martin's Grove and sledding parties on Lancaster Street. Sometimes they snowshoed all the way to Preston; there seemed to be so much snow in those days. Parents allowed house parties; the kids rolled up the rugs and danced to a hired pianist.

As they got older, Edna and her friends went to elegant dances in the Crystal Ball Room of the Walper Hotel. There were dance programs. Edna's page was always filled two weeks in advance.

It was all innocent. No one discussed sex or drank, or if someone did, it was a big scandal (at least in their crowd; a few years later, Ross MacDonald did plenty of drinking in Kitchener, and gambling, too). Dr. Lackner's son was tipsy at a Walper dance and everyone talked about it — a doctor's son!

Edna's crowd went around in gangs, although they did date in a very proper fashion, with the sons and daughters of people your parents knew.

Edna had her share of dates. Mother finally allowed Edna to cut her hair fashionably short (after insisting on doing it up in rags, even when Edna was in Grade 8, to make it curly) and photos of the period show an intelligent face, not chocolate box pretty, but interesting and alert.

Walter Bean, mentioned as the good gardener in *Sauerkraut and Enterprise*, took Edna to a corn roast. "You always went with the first person who asked you in case no one else asked you. He was so homely," she says.

And there was Stanley Weber. "Oh, instead of phoning a girl he'd send a card. 'Your presence is requested by Stanley Weber.' You'd send the card back. He was a weirdo — short and stocky. [At the dance] I was twirling and he said, 'We must dance properly.'"

Edna was with Stanley when she had her sledding accident. A group of kids went with him; he attached the toboggan to the car. Edna was on the toboggan when it swerved into a car. Her thigh hurt but she didn't tell anyone and went along to a restaurant. At home, her thigh was purple. "Daddy woke Mother up and they called the doctor the next day. I was in bed for weeks. The doctor used Epsom Salts, then lanced my thigh. Stanley came to see me — I was in the best bedroom. Stanley sat down and the leg broke on the wicker chair. Stanley took the chair to his father's furniture factory … [Later] at Varsity he asked me out to Massey Hall. We walked up Yonge Street. I would do an extra step and he'd have to keep up."

Franklyn Keeler, a window dresser at Goudie's Department Store, also had a crush on Edna. He was "nice-looking but once he crossed his knees and I could see white skin between sock and trousers."

The writer's sharp eye for the telling detail was developing.

By the time she was sixteen, she was writing in the journal she would keep for the rest of her life. She was also a counsellor at CGIT Camp, a nature officer — the Books of Knowledge came in handy again — and a young camper had a crush on Edna and slept with her sneaker.

School was less of a success. Her report card for spring 1920 gives her an average of 50.7 percent, with 23 in Arithmetic, 19 in Algebra, and 23 in Latin. In 1923 she failed Algebra (36 percent) and Chemistry (37 percent). She had to spend two extra years at the Kitchener-Waterloo Collegiate Institute to bring her math marks up so she could get her senior matriculation; in those days students repeated an entire year if they failed a single subject.[16]

She finally graduated in 1926, when she was twenty.

She was determined to attend the University of Toronto, to experience something other than Kitchener. She was idealistic, too, and wanted to "save the world" in some way, although she is not sure today what she meant by that. As a younger child, she thought about becoming a missionary and going to India to see the Taj Mahal. There was another idea of going to work in a Chicago factory.

But mostly she wanted to be a writer, the natural dream of a bookworm. It was a vague dream; she was not sure, exactly, what being a writer entailed, but the idea was there. It was a dream that would be less vague in the years ahead. She was obviously ambitious: not for wealth, but for some undefined adventure, for a different life. She could have easily gotten a job — matriculation meant something then — but she was determined to do something different.

Although it was unusual for women to attend university then, several of Edna's friends were also going. Kay Tracey, whose father owned a big store, enrolled at U of T and would room with Edna. Also, Fay Roberts had enrolled at the Ontario College of Art.

Edna's parents agreed to pay her tuition and board at the University of Toronto, where she enrolled the following autumn. They provided her with a big, cumbersome trunk — "that damn trunk. I unpacked it and never saw it again," she remembers. They also gave her some advice: "Work hard, study hard and pass or you won't go back. If you get in trouble, stay away."

"Getting in trouble" meant getting pregnant, which would bring shame and scandal to one's family in those years of social convention and no knowledge of birth control.

The Cresses didn't have to worry. Edna had already met the man she would marry seven years later. She'd had "lots of kisses but no one got my clothes off," and she would be a virgin when she married.

Chapter Two
University and Beyond

Edna enrolled in the general arts program at University College in 1926. She took full advantage of Toronto's cultural and entertainment offerings, attending concerts, films, performances at the Royal Alex and Massey Hall, and dances at Hart House with a myriad of dates. Murray's Restaurant had just opened on Bloor Street. Toronto was still largely Anglo and Protestant; the Orangemen's Parade was a big thing and Society mattered. *Saturday Night* was filled with the doings of Lord and Lady So-and-So.

Hemingway had come and gone, Faulkner was publishing in the States; Edna Ferber, Willa Cather, and Colette all published novels that year, and Dorothy Parker ("Men seldom make passes/ at girls who wear glasses") went on being smart in *Enough Rope*.

It was the flapper age, and Edna and her friends danced the Charleston, but Edna's world remained staid in comparison to the goings-on elsewhere.

Classes were held in the morning, leaving afternoons free for cultural events and window-shopping along Yonge Street where Edna looked at dresses in Simpson's and Eaton's windows and took note of fashions she could sew for herself. She made a lot of her own clothes, sewing by hand, with French seams. Sometimes she took a sleeve from one dress she'd seen, a collar from another. She was proud of a velvet evening wrap she made, with an inner lining, and of a watered silk, apple green evening dress.

She also liked Junor's, which sold lovely china.

She would say later that her University of Toronto days were the happiest of all because she found soul mates with whom she could discuss serious subjects, but getting married was the most important thing. You wanted your diamond; you hoped to plan a perfect wedding. You wanted to be Mrs. Somebody. Many of her friends would get engaged while at university.

But Edna also dreamed of travel, of seeing the ocean. And there were still the stirrings about writing, the ideas for stories that came and went, and sometimes she saw something — a sparrow in the park, wet leaves against the pavement — but these were only glimmers, vague memories. Not real life, which was exciting, but what to say about it? Anyway, life was busy with studies and socializing. And with sewing.

She joined the *Varsity* staff and eventually wrote a short piece about drinking buttermilk. Sigma Phi, the writers' sorority, invited Edna to join. She was supposed to write something to get in, but she joined without submitting anything.

She had her own room in Queen's Hall. Today the rules read like quaint regulations for a girls' boarding school: "Students must be in residence by 10:30 p.m. ... Students may not go to dinner at a hotel without the permission of the Dean ... No student is to go to public restaurants after the theatre at night ... Tin boxes must be used for all food supplies ..." and so on.[17]

Getting around the rules was fun and took ingenuity. You were supposed to have a letter from your hostess if you wanted to stay out overnight. Girls regularly wrote hostess letters for one another. Sometimes they were caught and punished, which meant they couldn't go out for so many days or weeks. "I had the longest gating ever," Edna says.

Edna's first-year classes were: English, French, Psychology, Zoology, and Religious Knowledge. She earned a *B* in English and *C*s for the rest. She was technically a second-year student, having received credit for her senior matric subjects.[18]

Her friend from home, Kay Tracey, took Home Economics. Naturally there were no males in Home Ec, and no women in Engineering, only five in Medicine, but many in arts.

Edna listened to English lectures by Dr. Wallace and wrote the odd essay for Professor MacDonald, brother of J.E.H. MacDonald. She dissected a frog in Zoology and paid careful attention to Dr. Taylor, who taught Religious Knowledge. It was a revelation to find out about other religions. *This Believing World* made her think about what she had been taught at St. Andrew's Presbyterian Church. She had always believed what the minister said, and now she began to question his opinions. It was the beginning of a long quest.

Morley Callaghan's first novel, *Strange Fugitive*, had just been published and Edna went to hear him read, the first Canadian writer, except for strict Mabel Dunham, she had ever seen. It would be years before she read *Barometer Rising* by Hugh MacLennan and became passionate about Canadian writing.

In 1929 she weighed 106 pounds. Her long, thin figure suited the flapper look of dropped waist and knee-length skirt. Her personality attracted people. She liked to laugh, to "lighten things up."

Bob Boehmer, a fellow Kitchenerite, bet her five dollars that she'd start smoking at university, but she never did. Ken Cunningham from home took her out. And sometimes she went down to the Art College to see her friend, Fay Roberts, who was part of the Students' Arts Council League. Fay had been athletic, but a bout with polio left her with a slightly withered leg. While she recuperated, she started painting as a hobby and discovered a lifelong passion. From 1926–27 she studied with G.A. Reid, J.E.H. MacDonald, and Arthur Lismer.

It was through Fay that Edna met Mac MacLean, a promising artist also studying with Arthur Lismer. It was a platonic relationship with much earnest discussion of art and life; Mac introduced her to *The Prophet* by Kahlil Gibran, and although they were never intimate — never even kissed — Mac asked her to marry him.

But there was someone else. F. Keith Staebler (*F.* for Frederick but he was known as Keith) of Kitchener was working at an insurance company in Toronto and staying at the Central Y. He and Edna had met in Kitchener. His sister, Elizabeth, was Edna's friend, and a gang of them shared a car one day. Edna and Keith both had other dates, but Edna was immediately attracted to him with his beautiful curly brown hair and lovely eyes. There was chemistry there, a connection.

The Staeblers were musical, and Keith was a talented pianist; he had a chance to play piano on the lakeboats, but Keith's father, Leslie, insisted he learn the insurance business and enter the family firm. Keith loved jazz and had, at some point, visited Harlem and noted how many musicians more talented than he did not make much money, and apparently, as his step-grandson recalled years later, decided he did not want to be poor.

The Staeblers were prominent in Kitchener; Keith's grandfather had been mayor. Keith's brother, Nort, was also a talented musician and played the violin.

Keith would become a successful businessman and civic leader in Kitchener, head of Rotary and Gyro and so on, but music always remained his first love.

Later he would say he chose insurance instead of music and made a decision to learn the business "by the seat of my pants,"[19] and probably the spectre of having little money really was a factor. The Staeblers kept up appearances. Mrs. Staebler, a Christian Scientist practitioner, always had a maid, but the three kids were clothed by taking insurance premiums out in trade, a difficult thing for Keith, who liked snappy clothes.

He was the life of every party and in demand as a pianist. He was two years younger than Edna, and she soon fell in love with him. It was too early for a commitment, and neither had any money, but they went out frequently to Massey Hall or just to walk in the park. Sometimes they read aloud to each other.

Edna also made lifelong friends in residence: "Wicky," who married Dr. Ross Carruthers; Glad Arthur; and Helen MacDonald, from St. Thomas, who would steal Keith away almost forty years later, ending a long marriage and breaking Edna's heart.

But that was all in the future. For now, days were innocent, demure.

It was boiled onions in cream sauce and boiled potatoes and ham on Saturdays, on Fridays, fish, and glue tapioca one night a week. Sometimes she took the train home to Kitchener on the weekend.

Edna worked for the Kitchener-Waterloo *Record* in the summer of 1927, rewriting items for the women's page. It was writing of sorts, but it had nothing to do with those vague inner stirrings. What did it mean to be a writer, anyway? She had no idea, and she never mentioned writing to Keith — then.

The next fall she moved into Kaufmann Mansions on College Street. She shared a two-bedroom apartment with Helen MacDonald, Glad Arthur, and Helen Wickwire. "Wicky," a few years older, engaged and working at Simpson's, was the official chaperon. The apartment meant more freedom. Boyfriends or fiancés could visit (but not stay overnight).

In her second year at university Edna took English, Ethics, Psychology, and Zoology, in which she dissected a rabbit and received an *A*.

Keith was back in Kitchener, working for his father. And Fay Roberts had gone home, too. Her mother had died and her father needed her to look after her younger brothers and sisters.

Edna wrote to Keith all the time and would continue to do so until she returned permanently to Kitchener. Her letters are gushy and bright, full of longings and avowals of love, and addressed to "My darlingest." There's a slap-dash quality to the letters; they are written in haste — Edna is always ready to go to bed or has to study.[20]

Keith calls her "ducky."

Sometimes Edna teased Keith. She had met Rance on the train. He carried her bag and sat with her and wanted to come to her apartment. "Isn't he dreadful, darling?"

They had an understanding, but did not officially become engaged until 1931. Edna graduated with a pass BA in 1929 and returned to Kitchener to look for a job.

She was a flop at business.

Simpson's in Kitchener needed a manager; Edna applied for the position, proudly saying she had a BA; the interviewer suggested she start as a salesclerk.

Instead, the *Record* hired her to tally the money paperboys brought in. She didn't last long. Her figures never added up.

"What's the good of university? She can't even count," someone at the paper said.

Her next job was at the Waterloo Trust Company, where she sat in a teller's cage and filled out customers' passbooks. No one could read her writing; the boss made her practise figures on foolscap. She earned thirteen dollars a week.

She decided to return to school in the fall, to earn her OCE teaching certificate. It meant a year away from Keith. They were engaged, although there was no formal announcement or ring. Edna could hardly wait to be married. Glad Arthur was married; Fay Roberts had married a young professional, Howard Adams* (who had been fond of Edna, but Edna was in love with Keith, and arranged an introduction to Fay); the Carruthers were married; and Helen MacDonald was engaged to a young doctor, Bill Kergin.

The Depression had started, and for Edna and Keith money was a problem. Some furniture factories closed in Kitchener, but the city was not as hard hit as other places were. One thinks "Depression" and pictures the Prairies and men riding the rails, but for much of the country life went on. *Saturday Night* still devoted itself largely to society news. History hadn't happened yet; the focus hadn't been defined. Louise Cress sometimes gave food to people who came to the door, and there were people so poor they collected coal along the railway tracks, but Edna's family didn't suffer and the Waterloo Spring Company survived.

By 1933, there would be forty-five hundred people on relief in Kitchener, but the people in Edna and Keith's circle do not seem to have been greatly affected.

Still, there was not enough money to get married on. You needed things: tables and beds and linen and dishes. A place to live. You had to have a real wedding with attendants and fancy wedding clothes and a reception and honeymoon. Eloping was scandalous; what was there to hide? Was the girl pregnant? Did they have to get married? L.M. Montgomery almost had a nervous breakdown when her son eloped; she didn't write in her journal for two years.

Edna complained about the time they had to wait. "[I want] to be near you — and feel your strength and be thankful for such a dear god man to look after me. … Oh Darling, we couldn't make it sixty-eight weeks, could we? — but — I must be patient — only I love you so much and I want you so much that I can hardly wait to try all the things that I am always thinking about…"[21]

They necked and "almost went all the way" but there was no intercourse until they married. Today Edna says she mistook sexual arousal for love; no one else had aroused her sexually and she thought the powerful feelings meant you were supposed to marry the man.

Keith's letters are also to "Darlingest," but they are less gushy and more direct. He has been playing badminton; he wonders what to get Edna for Christmas; he has been to a concert; and so on. He plays bridge with Howard and Fay Adams, the young married pair, and was amazed that Howard was "a little more assertive." Perhaps he and Edna had better not play bridge when they were married to avoid marital strife.

He's close to Edna's family and relays messages: Louise Cress can't go to Toronto shopping, but suggests that Edna buy things and send them COD. Perhaps Edna can buy a diamond ring and her mother can pay for it COD, Keith suggests tartly, adding that her mother will get over her pique at the idea of Edna marrying, and probably she'll be like other mothers and get a big bang out of the wedding (Louise Cress fussed when each of her daughters married and said she wished they could remain with her and be like sisters).

Edna seems to have speculated about a more bohemian existence. But, no, Keith did not want to live in a garret, artist-like; they needed the basic necessities at least.

Unlike Keith, Edna had never had to think about money.

Perhaps Edna was influenced by Mac MacLean. Unlike Keith's practical letters, Mac's surviving letter is about art and the meaning of life, subjects that would consume Edna in the years ahead.

Mac is enchanted with the beauty of the world: "The aim in this universe, or God's aim is a greater unity or a greater completeness … Each thing in the universe being complete is adding to the whole … therefore if we are complete, we are adding our bit." And: "One thing in life's great problem is trying to fuse the spiritual with the physical; it is a religious problem, the painter's problem, the poet's problem. Thus the great trouble with the materialistic business world."[22]

Edna's letters to Mac have not survived, but the philosophical tone of his letter suggests Edna wrote in a more questing way to Mac than she did to Keith. Despite her focus on marriage, Edna was enchanted by the outer world, by the beauty in things she saw around her, by startling images of nature or a wet autumn street. She also thought a lot about the meaning of life and creativity.

Perhaps if she and Mac had been intimate, and she had been aroused by him as well, she might have considered marrying him, but platonic romance did not stir her the same way as personal intimacy did, and she decided to marry Keith, who made a more fervent plea for her, in person if not in letters.

And, really, she did not want to live in a garret either. Keith had bought her a hope chest (his mother was jealous) and she wanted to fill it. She'd spend the next year "hemming a million things," she wrote Keith.

Soon, instead of buying a ring, they spent one hundred dollars on bedroom furniture. Fred Boronsky, a Kitchener artisan, made them a solid mahogany (with French polish) set of twin beds, two bed tables, dressing table, bureau, mirror and stool, which they stored in the attic on Spetz Street.

Edna felt better, really engaged, when the furniture was stored in the attic on Spetz Street. There was no ring, but "to hell with that." She started a scrapbook, filling it with clippings of furniture and houses.

Furniture, not art.

She wanted to teach, too, but studying for her certificate was hard. And she had other things on her mind. "Oh darling, I am so desperately discouraged that I don't know what to do. I've worked harder this year than I ever have before but I seem to be getting less for it. I know I won't pass in French and later on, any of my commercial subjects [she was taking typing, bookkeeping, and shorthand for a teaching certificate in those subjects] and my marks are apparently so low in French that none of the teachers here will recommend me for a position. I might as well pack up and come home," she wrote Keith.

She did pass French, and not only obtained her teaching certificate, but was offered a job in Ingersoll for $1,700 a year.

"I got my job and I'm just so pleased I don't know what to do. He phoned me sharp at 9 o'clock and asked my religion and I told him, he said that was fine and they had appointed me & congratulations … and they'd send me the contract immediately.

"But Keith I have to go to Summer School — July 6 to August 7 — and exams … and I am still having to write 3 commercial ones…" She had to take classes in Physical Education: "Swimming and softball and basketball and calisthenics and swinging from things — Holy Cats!"

The best thing was that she didn't have to take "commercial work" in the summer.

In the fall, she taught Phys Ed, Geography, Composition, French, Latin, English Literature, and Spelling in the Lower School of the Ingersoll Collegiate Institute. Ingersoll was about eighty kilometres from Kitchener, and she came home every weekend, taking the train. Keith, who still did not have his own car, borrowed the Cress car to drive her back.

She boarded with a Yorkshire family, the Swallows, who would remain close friends. Sometimes Keith stayed for roast beef and Yorkshire pudding Sunday nights and played the piano. The Swallows had three sons. Every Sunday evening was like a party.

Letters to "Darlingest" and "Dearest" flew back and forth several times a week. Keith addressed his letters to "Miss Edna Cress, BA." He was "Keith Staebler, Esquire." The letters are warm, hopeful of the future, but often too practical to be deeply passionate.

Keith hopes for a son who is musical and wants to hold musicals after they are married and teases Edna about being a gadabout. He hopes Edna will not go out as much after they're married, leaving him to look after the children. But he reassures her about her weight; Edna had gained a few pounds during her physical education training. She's not the tiniest bit hefty but he wouldn't care if she weighed 180 pounds.

Edna constantly assured him of her love and admiration.

"I wish I could curl up close to you and feel your dear warm hands," she wrote. "I love them darling — they're so strong and understanding — like you…"

She was sewing and doing cross-stitch embroidery on linen. Her chest was in the Swallows's attic. She was also taking woodcarving and made a footstool, which she still has today, and other items. "I have carved another candlestick. I just have the bottoms to do now — two more lessons."

Edna wanted to carve all their furniture and even bought a lathe, which she never used.

She thought the last pre-wedding year would go quickly. "Every weekend will be scurrying around buying stuff and looking for houses, tiny wee ones we can fix up cheaply."

Keith suggested they could use tapestry for blankets. They can go to sales, argue with secondhand merchants.

Edna was too busy getting married to think about writing at all.

Where is Edna Staebler, the writer, in this pre-wedding year?

One does not sense her, or feel her, as she rushes off to her carving class, or draws diagrams for Keith of a dress she is making. Anyone who knows her long writer's — and writerly — life, will find her out of focus here. She could be any happy, busy bride-to-be, yet her voice is as distinctive and forward-reaching as the voice in the letter she wrote her mother from Toledo.

"Maybe if I'd had a happy marriage I wouldn't have become a writer," she speculates today.

It is a thought. And would the idea of being a writer have seemed to be a consolation, if she could have looked ahead? One suspects not. Certainly, the prospects of being a writer were not in her mind as she hemmed and carved to make pretty things for her home. She was too busy, and making things made her feel creative.

Her life was going the way it should: education, marriage, a proper home. Hopefully, too, children. She wanted to be perfect for Keith and their children.

To Edna's dismay, her teaching contract was not renewed for the following year. She seemed too young to be a teacher, she was told; the principal didn't like her doing somersaults in front of the students.

She applied for another job in St. Mary's, and had a good letter of reference from Ingersoll, but she wasn't hired and returned to Kitchener in the summer of 1932 and helped as an assistant at the library. Her father became ill that autumn with Hodgkin's disease. Mother, who had never been openly affectionate to her husband, didn't like caring for invalids, and so Edna carried meals to him and generally looked after him. He died October 23, 1932, only fifty-seven years old. More than fifty years later, Edna wrote in her journal about holding his hand as he lay dying.

"He was shy, dominated by my mother. … He made a good living … I was never aware of money as such. We always had what we wanted."

While John Cress was sick, the trust company appointed Edna to look after the business until it was sold. For two years, even for a few months after her marriage, Edna "called on customers." She loved the work and was good at it. Keith said she could sell refrigerators to Eskimos. October 14, 1933, was the big day, the culmination of Edna's hopes and dreams. Autumn leaves, marigolds, and chrysanthemums decorated St. Andrew's Presbyterian church. Uncle Rufe Sattler gave Edna away, and Keith's brother Nort played selections from Saint-Saëns. Norma and Ruby were bridesmaids.

Edna made a startling picture. She was beautiful in a gown of suede thread lace in an ivy leaf pattern. A round neckline, leg of mutton sleeves fitting tightly at the wrists, and long, fitted princess lines widening into a full train characterized the medieval design. The veil hung in a point to the bride's waist over her face and extended several feet beyond the train. The cap, appliquéd with a wreath of the leaf design of the dress, had a twisted roll of the veiling coming to a peak in front. An arm bouquet of lilies completed the effect.

Louise held the reception at the house, which was decorated with chrysanthemums. She wasn't overjoyed at losing her eldest daughter to marriage and wore black velvet. Mrs. Staebler also wore black, "a black sheer gown of the Edwardian period."

All this black was ominous, but never mind. Edna recorded the ninety-nine gifts in "Gifts and their Senders" ("Attach numbered stickers to each gift as received and enter under the proper number") in her wedding record: carpets, a Sheffield plate, pewter dishes, vases, sterling teaspoons. Kay Tracey gave walnut end tables. Dottie Shoemaker, her good friend from the library, gave a set of Shakespeare. There'd been showers, too. Elizabeth Staebler held a treasure hunt at hers. Edna's university friend, Helen Wickwire, now "Mrs. Ross Carruthers," attended another one. A bridge and tea took place at the Westmount Golf and Country Club.[23]

Blessed with this cornucopia, surely excited by the festivities, Edna and Keith went on a honeymoon to the United States and Ottawa. Edna wore a grey corduroy velvet frock and a felt hat and carried a Harris tweed coat, which came in handy when it snowed as they passed through Quebec.

They were together at last as the verse said in their gift register:[24]

Now the rite is done
Now the word is spoken.
And the spell has made us one.
Which may ne'er be broken.

Who would have thought in those happy days of getting married that all hell would break loose in a few years?

Chapter Three
Early Marriage

Who knows what goes on inside a marriage? The marriage that started with such piquant tastefulness and so much hope and the chest filled with embroidered treasures would change Edna's life in a way she could never have imagined when they returned from their honeymoon. The failure of that marriage would contribute to her fulfillment as a writer in the years ahead, and to a whole new life, but she had no idea of any of this in the fall of 1933.

All those wedding gifts, all the things she had collected to make a pretty home: one can sense her pleasure in the attainment, and sixty years later she still speaks fondly of her dining room set, now in her niece Barbie's house; she says she visits her dining room furniture at Christmas.

The footstool, carved in Ingersoll, is in Edna's living room, as is the hooked mat of a snow scene, draped over a sofa, and the braided rug is on the floor.

Finally, she was Mrs. Keith Staebler, a bride like all her friends, and if she felt a letdown in the physical act of consummation — what was the big deal in that quick act, she wondered, comparing it to the years of slow and passionate arousal — she kept these thoughts to herself. No one talked about sex then, not even the closest of friends or sisters.

Marriage meant having a home, and the happy couple installed their new belongings in a house they rented for thirty dollars a month on Simeon Street. It was only a few blocks from Spetz, and while Louise Cress would be miffed as each daughter married (Edna could have done better, she said, although the Staeblers were probably more prominent than the Cresses), she and Edna remained close, talking on the telephone daily if they did not see each other in person. Norm and Ruby were still at home, too.

Edna was not as outgoing as Keith, but they were soon a popular couple in the business and professional circle in which they moved. Music was a big part of their lives. Nort and Leslie Staebler were both involved with the Philharmonic, and Keith played piano wherever they went. *Saturday Night* had even mentioned Leslie Staebler in the fall of 1933 for his contribution to the local music scene, and his sons carried on the family tradition.[25] Musical evenings at Edna and Keith's home were common, and they often hosted out-of-town musicians. Edna was a gracious hostess, serving home baking (cinnamon buns, recalls Hannah Schlenker, a Waterloo piano teacher).

Keith's sister, Elizabeth, a schoolteacher, soon married Ed Devitt, also a teacher. Both became prominent in Kitchener society. Nort would marry Helen Waimel, a talented sculptor who'd received a Governor General's medal and a scholarship to the Ontario College of Art when she was only in her teens. Helen, born in Estonia, was European and glamorous, and the City of Kitchener bought pieces of her work to display in parks. The Staeblers were proud of her.

"So Norton married an Estonian lady of artistic culture," Ephraim Weber, a Kitchener native who lived out west, wrote to Leslie Staebler, "modelling with plastics with a preference for sculpture! And what honours she took at the College of Arts! We wish she had some way of disposing the sculpture she'd like to fashion — or has fashioned perhaps. But art of any kind is a cruel thing to pin one's hopes to in this philistine era of industry."[26]

None of them was interested in writing, but you could say Edna was the unaccomplished one among the young Staeblers in those days. "They are very clever and really talented," Edna wrote a friend a few years later. "I am the only one who has little to offer to the group. I am the inferior one."[27]

She was also the more open among the bunch, dispensing with the little snobberies. Helen's sister, Endla, recalls Helen suggesting that her sister and friends, kids from the farm, use the senior Staeblers' back door. Not Edna. "Hi girls," she'd say, welcoming them to the front door with a wave.

There were labour problems in Kitchener, and strikes, but the young Staeblers did not know any working-class people personally other than the cleaning woman and the people Keith sold insurance to. Money was tight, but a bit of liver and bacon cost ten cents at the butcher's. They did not own a car.

Edna finished her work for her father's company, but there was no question of her holding a job. Kitchener women had always worked in factories, providing cheap labour and contributing to family income, but for the white-collar and professional class, a woman being employed was an insult to her husband, implying he could not look after her. Middle- and upper-class married women kept the home going, entertained, played bridge and golf, and maybe sat on committees. They did church work.

For a while, Edna and Keith attended the Presbyterian Church one Sunday, the Christian Science one the next. Edna would soon stop going to any church, having decided she could think for herself and that the "rigidity and paganism" of institutional Christianity had ruined Christ's message. But for now attending church was a way to keep parents happy. Keith was only twenty-five when they married, but he soon joined Gyros and Rotary and a sales club. Today it all seems like dull stuff for a musician, but Keith took civic duty seriously.

Children, the musical boy, the offspring Edna would be perfect for, would wait until they had more money. Dr. Cliff Wilson fitted Edna with a pessary.

In 1934, the Staeblers purchased a building lot at 51 Simeon Street for $650 and the construction of the house began the next year. Edna took out books of house plans from the library, and they picked out a plan created by American architect Royal Barry Wills and hired the Stroh Company to build the house. John Cress had made provisions in his will to lend money to Edna for a house; the house was put in her name.

To save money, Edna and Keith moved in with his parents on Ellen Street while the house was being built. Mrs. Staebler, who was from Guelph, "the Royal city," turned her nose up at the industrial Kitchener. She spent hours reading Mary Baker Eddy.

There was always jealousy on Mrs. Staebler's part; she'd been jealous of Edna's hope chest, saying, "Don't tell Dad about it, he'll worry he couldn't buy me one." Later she would blame Edna for problems in the marriage, and for stealing her boy away from Christian Science, and Edna would come to resent her mother-in-law, but in these early days of marriage, the two women got along.

Edna visited the building site every day right after breakfast to watch the workers. She had designed the house herself. Built of red brick, with straight lines and white shutters, it was a classic house with little fuss about it. She had the living and dining rooms painted soft apple green; the trim was knotty pine. The kitchen was pale blue and the front hall had a flagstone floor. There were three bedrooms upstairs, and a smaller room, meant for the nursery, would be used as a sewing room for the time being. They planted four cherry trees and two apple trees in the backyard.

Edna loved that house, and remembered it with "the greatest nostalgia as the most beautiful, comfortable and satisfying [place] with its sturdy red brick and white paint pseudo-colonial ivy spreading over the chimney, spruce trees brushing its walls…" And inside: her heart warmed to the "living room with its mellowed pine woodwork, its furniture upholstered in crimson and forest green plaid, the thick braided rug covering the floor, and lamps that give good light for reading, a cat purring on the hearth and my husband playing his reconditioned grand piano," she remembered. Away from home, she "yearned for the French Provincial mahogany of my dining-room, the high dresser with the old pewter and precious Chelsea candlesticks, the polished refectory table, the Sheffield service on the cabinet and the pine cupboard displaying ceramics…"[28]

She made frilly curtains for all the windows, hooked mats, and braided the big living room rug.

She didn't know how to cook, but she clipped recipes from Mary Lowry Ross's column in *Saturday Night* — Louise said if you could read, you could cook, and she grew to love cooking for Keith and for friends. The Staeblers and their friends, the Nashes, Wilsons, and Whaleys, got together for international meals — Edna recalls cooking Swedish food — followed by bridge. They also saw the Breithaupts, the Beans, and Fay and Howard Adams. Everyone wanted Keith to play the piano.

Edna still loved sewing clothes: "a candy-striped white satin dress with a green frill and puffed sleeves, buttons down the front ... I felt so smart in that dress ... [and] I made this beautiful winter brocade grey boucle Princess line [coat] with frogs down the front ... a little collar of grey lamb ... I had a coat once before with quite deep Persian lamb cuffs and I used a cuff for a Cossack hat." She also knitted sweaters and dresses.

As Keith made more money, she bought her clothes at the smart places on Bloor Street in Toronto.

She was "really busy." She had a cleaning woman, Mrs. Dietrich, for fifty cents an hour, but cleaned the hardwood floor with a hairpin herself. She read English literature — J.M. Barry, Edward Burke, Katherine Mansfield, the Bloomsbury group — when Keith was out in the evening, collecting insurance premiums. Edna joined the University Women's Club soon after returning to Kitchener, and the club also founded a reading/study group, which Edna still attends today.

Sometimes she and Keith read aloud together, or Keith played the piano or put on records while Edna did her knitting. Sex was no better, nothing fantastic, but she remained in love and often watched him while he napped after lunch — he would come home at noon and she'd have a meal waiting for him and think how handsome he was, how wonderful, and he was all hers. And then, dishes done and kitchen tidied, she'd change her clothes like the proper wife she was.

Add a dog, Buddy, and the kitten, and you have a charmed and easy, happy life.

It was true she often found social life boring — they went to so many parties — and she hated playing bridge and gossiping. Sometimes her university education made her feel superior, and yes, she missed Toronto and the intellectual talk of university friends. But Fay Adams, still painting and a member of the Kitchener Society of Artists, was there to talk to, and Edna's friend Dorothy ("Dottie") Shoemaker, from another old Kitchener family — her father was a well-known pharmacist, intelligent and wise and always trying to understand people — was the librarian at the Kitchener library. Edna soon involved herself with library affairs, lobbying to have women on the board.

Still, glimmers of artistic creation, of something else, those shots of joy she experienced seeing a sparrow or a leaf on wet pavement, remained.

The Staeblers subscribed to *Atlantic Monthly* and *Saturday Night* and Edna copied out favourite passages from articles and books for her commonplace book. She called it her bible and often read from it over the years. Thomas Burke's quote about artists painting and writing is from the thirties:

> Why does he do it? They ask. What has he got to show for it? Well God knows and a few people on earth know why the artist starves himself for the joy of painting, why the poet writes poetry that doesn't pay, why the composer continues to compose though he is never performed… The spiritual face behind each of them is the same face — a face which common sense will never know, or if it did know, would profane.[29]

And from 2 Timothy: God has not given us the spirit of fear but of power and of love and of a sound mind.

She didn't write. She didn't write in her journal much, either. There wasn't time, and really, she did not have the inclination, the discipline, or the compulsion in these early days of marriage, of cooking and entertaining and being happy. Making pretty things was satisfying. Here were the curtains; here was the dress she had designed, she could put it on and wear it and receive compliments, unlike the poet with his unread poems or the composer whose music was never performed.

There was an exception, however. One of the activities Edna and Keith enjoyed was participating in K-W Little Theatre, an amateur troupe staging plays locally. It was an active group made up of prominent people who held regular meetings at Kitchener City Hall. There were competitions and studio meetings and gala presentations at high school auditoriums.

"Local Folk to See Brilliant Play," wrote the *Record* about Somerset Maugham's *The Circle*.[30]

Some of the Staeblers' friends and relatives were also members. Nort, Keith's sister Elizabeth and her husband, and Edna's sister Ruby, all sometimes acted or directed.

It was all great fun, but seen seriously, with warnings that memberships had to be paid by a certain date ("Positively no renewals or new memberships will be accepted after that date"); meetings were at "8:00 p.m. sharp."[31]

Keith was soon president. Edna, on the selection committee, read hundreds of plays. She acted, too, playing Anderson in *The Devil's Disciple*.

In June 1937 Little Theatre announced a play-writing competition. Edna submitted a play, *The White Waistcoat*, and won (not nepotism; Keith received the sealed entries but forwarded them to the judges, B.K. Sandwell, editor of *Saturday Night*; Professor H.W. Auden of the University of Western Ontario; and Graham Llewelleyn of Huron College).[32]

This was Edna's first real piece of writing. She was thirty-one years old and chose as her subject the music lovers among Kitchener society.

The story involves a famous violinist, Frantz Neumann, who plays in Kitchener. After his performance he visits the home of one Mrs. Aikin, age "60 or thereabouts." People fawn and gush over Neumann and are generally gauche. It's coffee and sandwich time and Neumann will not have a Canadian beer because he has had German beer. Some awestruck teenage girls crash the party and in short order managerial Mrs. Aikin has them helping in the kitchen.

Alas, one guest is Margaret Craig, age thirty. She is a young widow with a son, and what a coincidence it is but she knew Neumann years ago in Leipzig, and hey, her little boy is really Neumann's son. Big secret. She hadn't wanted to hold back Neumann's career. All he'd cared about was wearing a white waistcoat, like the one he wears tonight. He's been pretty anxious to get off on the train, but Margaret reveals the secret and he announces his plans to marry her. He's pleased to miss the train and never mind about his engagement in Los Angeles. "My days of slavery are over."

The romance is trite and not quite believable, but the observations about society and the characterizations are astute. Edna based Neumann on the violinist Nathan Millstein, who had performed in Kitchener, and recalls today Mrs. Motz saying of Paul Robeson, "Isn't he cute?"

The local characters, all prominent citizens, are well meaning, earnest, bumbling, and somewhat pretentious. Not attractive folk; the president of the musical society is bald, his wife is "dumpy." A Mrs. Prindle says artists must be bored by receptions: "I make a point never to speak to them at all." Miss Allbright ("not young"): "Oh, I love to talk to them. Some of them are so queer." Flashily dressed Mrs. Welden, "our treasurer," makes Frantz autograph a picture with "Love to Ethel from Frantz." She spells out her name. Loudly. Poor Mr. Watson sounds Frantz out about how much it would cost to engage Marion Anderson and Paul Robeson.

It's all credible and witty and Edna obviously knows her characters, having listened with a writer's ear to similar conversations at receptions. Both Sandwell and Auden praised Edna's characterizations and her "dexterity." There's an ease with which she quickly captures someone's essence; she finds the telling gesture, the physical trait that sums someone up. Years later, Pierre Berton would say she was most graceful writer *Maclean's* ever published. Edna has always described people well and has a good ear for dialogue, but none of her later published writing shows the sharp satire found in *The White Waistcoat*. Her characters here are not the loving Bevvy Martin or hopeful Maggie of *Cape Breton Harbour*, but social climbers who do not realize how crude they are.

Satire was mentioned by the adjudicator, Professor Carl Klinik, when *The White Waistcoat* was staged the following January at Waterloo Town Hall (Nort Staebler played Neumann and Ruby was one of the gate-crashing teenagers), but he said the "love-interest" balanced the play.

It was a big occasion. Three to four hundred attended the performance (and the runner-up, a play by a Dr. Johns, was also staged). But — what did people think? Did anyone wonder if Edna looked down on the friends she met at social dos?[33] We have no way of knowing.

Her photo in the paper shows a serious but fey face that gives little away. This is not the smiling, expansive Edna of later photos, the Edna with the glad face of someone who enjoys the world the way a child does. She's not yet that woman. There's an astuteness in *The White Waistcoat* that speaks of a certain distance, of a coolness in looking at the world. The author knows what's what and doesn't mind saying it. You could see this author writing a witty English-type comedy of manners.

It's interesting to compare *The White Waistcoat* to another play Edna wrote around this time. *The Departure* received a mention in another Little Theatre competition, but it was never staged.[34] Here her characters are Old Order Mennonites, people she knew at this time only from seeing them at the market. The women's clothing is a bit wrong, and she chuckles today because she has a young Mennonite girl knitting socks with a red pattern. But she shows more warmth in this play, if less smart wit, than in *The White Waistcoat.*

The story is simple. Peter Brubacher, age twenty-two, is moving to live with his uncle in the city. Peter is looking forward to the bright lights, the stores and cars, and Mrs. Brubacher worries Peter will lose the Mennonite way of life.

Mary, who hopes to marry him, arrives with the inappropriate gift of socks, and Peter tries to persuade her to move to the city with him.

But Mary says she can't bear to leave her home.

"Here I can stay with my own people and hoe in the garden and milk the cows and make the butter and even if I get myself a man our children could hunt bees and run in the fields."

Peter and Mary love each other, but how can they be together?

"I guess I'll be an old maid — like Salome," Mary says before she rushes out of the door.

But — warmth or wit? Edna would never write in such a telling way about proper Kitchener again. Other humorous pieces, including, later, a hilarious novella about Europe, would never be published, but the possibility that Edna could have become another kind of writer altogether lingers. She would try to publish fiction for years — it was what real writers wrote; the first cookbook happened almost by accident.

She received a plaque and twenty-five dollars for *The White Waistcoat*; there was hoopla in the local press and many congratulations came her way, but she did not write again for years. She had shown she could do it, though.

One omission in *The White Waistcoat* is politics. If Neumann is based on Millstein, he is Jewish, and when Edna wrote the play, restrictions against Jews in Germany and the possibility of war were realities. Bringing this into the play would have made it an entirely different play with another focus: would Frantz risk taking Margaret to Europe? He did live in Switzerland, but what about performing in Europe? He has studied and worked in Germany.

But still. History as we know it hadn't yet happened and it certainly did not intrude on the musical evenings at 51 Simeon. Politics and the larger goings-on have never played a big part in any of Edna's work. Anyway, war was still only a remote possibility for the average Canadian when the King and Queen visited Canada the following year (they passed through Kitchener in their special train but Edna didn't go to see them).

She and Keith were pacifists, big fans of Beverley Nichols, and the war would have a great effect on both their lives.

Part *Two*

Chapter Four
All Hell Broke Loose

Edna and Keith stopped having sex in late 1939. They did not separate for another twenty-two years, but they were never intimate again. It still seems incredible and difficult to understand. Today couples would discuss the problem with a doctor or therapist and perhaps with friends, or even separate, but in 1939 Edna and Keith's lack of a sex life remained their secret.

Sex had never been a big deal — quick acts, a couple of times a week. Was this normal? Edna had no way of knowing; she had never had sex with anyone but Keith. One didn't discuss intimate matters, and perhaps she had always been naive about sex. She had no knowledge of homosexuality, for instance, until Keith gave her a copy of *The Well of Loneliness* by Radclyffe Hall. When a stranger exposed himself to her while she was in university, she came home in tears to Keith on the weekend.

Was Keith as naive? What did he really think? It's impossible to say. Who knows? Something must have been wrong, because in 1939 Keith, the loving husband, went to an insurance convention, had sex with another woman, and never had intercourse with Edna again.

"He said he was afraid of giving me a disease," Edna says. "He said he was impotent ... Later, his psychiatrist told me Keith saw me more as a mother."

But what of it? They had the nice house and the friendly dog and the cat and the frilly curtains and the musical evenings and the cozy hours, but at the end of each day was this dark secret. What had all the anticipation and hopes for the wedding and for consummation been for?

What about all those embroidered things?

Edna was terrified someone would discover their secret.

She was thirty-three, Keith thirty-one, and they should have had years of intimacy ahead of them. Edna hadn't gotten pregnant, although doctors didn't find anything wrong with her or Keith. Now there was no chance of having a child.

Nothing in Edna's life had prepared her for this. Had happiness been a delusion?

Why, anyway, did he confess his dalliance?

Edna does not seem to have been furious. She always tried to understand, she says, the other person's point of view, but Keith's little fling was surely a shock, a disappointment. And there was no warning.

In the spring, Edna had driven to Florida with her mother and sister, Norma, who had married Ralph Hodgson, an employee at the Mutual Insurance Company. She wrote to Keith regularly and he replied almost daily, saying he missed her, that it felt so strange coming in the house alone, that the house felt clammy. He loves her letters but would rather have her; he's busy, which is good because he'd be so lonely otherwise.

When the war broke out in September, she and Keith were in Gananoque, visiting Eldon and Walter Staebler, sons of Keith's grandfather, who had been married twice. Except for the news about the war, it was a normal weekend for a couple visiting relatives.

Did the war have anything to do with the change? Unlike his many friends, Keith did not enlist because his father needed him in the business. Keith would later join the Scott Fusiliers Reserve, but he felt guilty about not actually being in the war; he felt like he was not quite a man, haunted because he'd never been shot at.

Edna and Keith had been confirmed pacifists, but the war changed that, at least for Keith. Unlike in the First World War, when Berlin men did not rush to the enlistment office, Kitchener supported the war and the rubber and auto industries particularly helped the war effort. There had been some marginal support for Hitler early in the thirties, but people of German descent were quick to prove their allegiance to Great Britain. For instance, Keith belonged to the Sales and Advertising Club, which raised money to buy a tank.

Kitchener became an army training centre; barracks were hastily erected on East Avenue. People were only too glad to invite servicemen to their homes and to organize dances and card parties.

Keith had made his patriotic feelings known the year before. Charles Lindbergh had questioned the right of Canadians to draw the hemisphere into a European war because of Canada's loyalty to the British Crown.

Kitchenerites were furious and "openly dared Lindbergh to set foot in Kitchener. Veteran Ben Warren said, 'I'd favor rounding up all the old eggs available several days in advance.'" Someone else suggested the Little German Band could serenade him and "He'll get decorated again if he comes here, but it won't be the same kind of decoration he got from Hitler."[35]

Keith, "prominent in Little Theatre," sounded pompous when he voiced his opinions in the *Record:*

> We cannot deny a person the right to think and a person may think and say what he likes but it was certainly bad taste for Col. Lindbergh to give expression to his line of thought regarding Canada, even in the United States. It would certainly be ill-advised for his part were he to enter Canada to give further utterance to this same line of thought. I believe such a move on his part would do harm to the friendly relations existing between Canada the United States. There would certainly be incidents at any public gatherings he might address that would not contribute to friendly relations. People in the United States are much annoyed at what he said and that also applies in greater degree to the people of Canada. His coming to Canada would create intense resentment and there is no predicting what would happen. He would certainly not be welcome in Kitchener.[36]

Was this really Keith? He was only thirty when he made these comments; the language suits a much older man, and there's a rehearsed air to it, as if he's saying what would sound weighty, what people expect him to say. This is the community leader speaking, the fellow who in the future will want to buy a bigger house so he can get elected to the executives of important committees. He wasn't a snob, Edna says, and he helped many people over the years, but being prominent in the community mattered to him. There must have been a dichotomy between the outer reality of the big businessman and the artistic musician. Private demons, perhaps. We do not know.

"He always struck me as not quite real. He was too friendly," an old acquaintance said.

At the end of March in 1940, K-W Little Theatre hosted the Western Ontario Drama League. It was a big occasion, with theatre groups from all over eastern Ontario congregating in Kitchener to put on nineteen plays. London won with *Nellie McNab*, by Lois Reynolds Kerr, a member of the Playwrights Studio Group of Toronto; Galt Little Theatre earned the Hanna Shield. Brantford and St. Catharines also received praise.

Despite, or perhaps because of, the war, the festival was "free from gloomy and gory pieces."[37] It was a respite from the war, and tentative plans were made for a larger festival in Sarnia the following year. Keith was appointed to the board as an executive member.

It was all forward-looking and hopeful, but sometime that spring Keith had a nervous breakdown.

Why? What happened? Again, we do not know. Coupled with impotency with his wife, Keith's breakdown suggests a dark despair, a change of life, a new direction that would be permanent.

Edna is vague on the date, remembering only that it was in the spring and that Keith stopped to visit his mother on the way home from the office and fell apart at her house. His mother put him to bed and kept him there for two weeks "as if he did not have a wife at home."

Edna did not visit him. Like the woman in the Simone de Beauvoir story who cleans the apartment because she isn't sure whether her husband will come home or not, Edna painted all the bedrooms.

She must have been stunned. Sex over — but was it for good? And now this. These things, this darkness, weren't supposed to have anything to do with the happiness she had created at 51 Simeon Street in the wonderful house; they weren't supposed to have evolved after the perfect fall wedding. This new, private torment remained hidden, secretive. There was the outward life of being Mrs. Keith Staebler, and this other new, parallel existence she had never expected.

These dual roles would go on for many years. She would come to feel she was more housekeeper than wife as she accompanied Keith to parties, entertained their friends, and became more involved in the community: prominent member of the library board, working for higher staff salaries and establishing the film, record, and picture library; president of the Canadian Club, an organization that brought in stimulating speakers. She was an executive member of the Women's Voluntary Service during the war ("What did we do? I have no idea").

Also in the forties, she did surveys for the Gallup Poll, a project no one else in the University Women's Club wanted to take on. For the first time in her life, Edna met working-class people in their homes; she'd always listened wistfully to Keith when he talked about the insurance clients he visited, and she found these people more vibrant than the middle-class crowd she hung around with.

She had never before, for instance, seen a man in an undershirt drinking beer. Keith might drink but he was dapper and never sat around in his undershirt. It was a telling statement about the tight social circle she and Keith moved in, but then her own friends had always come from the same circle, even in childhood when the Cress girls avoided the girls next door because their father drank. Now, conducting the Gallup Poll was another startling change in these upside-down war years.

Privately she looked for answers and a new way to live. Feeling lonely, she began to think again about writing. She had this feeling that she had to write, she must write; sometimes she even felt guilty about not writing. Dottie Shoemaker, who knew nothing about Edna's sexual problems with Keith — Dottie never married and only ever had non-romantic dates with a musician when he returned home to Kitchener — encouraged her: "Ed, you have to write. You must write." Dottie, who always tried to understand people and who never said anything nasty about anyone, obviously recognized a growing hunger in Edna.

"So many things have happened to me in the past few years — I'm a different person really," she wrote to Helen Kergin in 1944.

Keith's lack of attention, the loss of intimacy with him, would lead Edna to flirtations and platonic friendships involving long, searching letters. Men sensed her loneliness and made advances.

She wondered what was wrong with her. "Am I like a bitch in heat? I read butterflies can tell for miles." Keith stayed out late at night and wasn't jealous. "He welcomed it." He kissed other girls at parties; Edna kissed other men. "We are in a sophisticated crowd — where lovemaking is light and meaningless and tossed off like a cocktail and forgotten as quickly," Edna blithely wrote a few years later, exaggerating and meaning kisses and flirting, not sex. At least that was how she understood it then.[38]

She became introspective as she tried to make sense of this new life. Others might have become bitter, casting blame, but Edna found strength in her thoughts. It was the beginning of a liberating transformation that would lead to the conclusion that all humanity was spiritually connected, the realization that just as the eye cannot see an atom, so it was with the spiritual life. Every action or thought that a person has influences other people.

> So every single person is responsible for the rest of the world. That thought might be frightening but if we have faith to let ourselves be used as an instrument through which positive spiritual power can work, we need have no fear. Jesus was completely receptive to it. As a result his personality radiated such power that he wrought miracles. I believe this power could be as available as the other forces which have been discovered.[39]

She still believes in this philosophy, saying, "Everyone has an effect on the world, even an aborted baby, but it's not something I talk about very much."

And she knew that she could not count on another person for her own happiness. This inner strength led to joy in the world around her. She would teach herself to focus on a child in a red snowsuit, a blooming tree, or a kitten despite personal sadness, to lose herself in concentrating on others.

Sometimes on long walks, she would feel enchanted by people who passed by, seeing them much like Thomas Merton described: people walking around, shining like the sun. Merton found knowledge and realization in the solitude of a monastery; Edna had her own kind of monastery, that of the mind; it was "a private Algonquin," as Dr. John Robins, who would become her mentor, called it.

It was a remarkable transformation, one that enabled her in the years ahead to think deeply about the people she wrote about and to come to a way of writing about them honestly but with love and understanding. The transformation deepened over the years, creating the powerful charisma that continues to draw people to her and the ability to banish dark thoughts, to think of something else.

"It's not hard to be happy, you know," she says today.

In the meantime, she tried to understand Keith. What had happened? She was determined to love him no matter what, but he drank more than before and he was out until the early hours most nights. Where was he? she asked her friend, Fay Adams. Like Edna, Fay was lonely; her husband, Howard, was overseas.

They talked daily; Edna was glad to have someone to talk to, but she knew self-pity was her enemy and she was determined to remain happy despite the changes in her life.

And gradually, fumblingly, desperately lonely, she began to write.

The war changed Edna's life. The city was soon filled with soldiers taking basic training and living in the barracks on Stirling and East Avenues; the Canadian Women's Army Corps trained at Knollwood Park. There were dances at the barracks on Saturday night with big-name bands, and swimming and cards at the YMCA. On Sunday, people came and passed out invitations for meals. Who knew what would happen to these young people going overseas to war? There was a sense that tomorrow might never come. The young men might die soon, and some women whose husbands were overseas were lonely, looking, as Edna wrote to a British airman, "like hungry pathetic little birds with their mouths open ... I have felt so darn sorry for them and I'd rather die than look like that."[40]

Well, Edna's husband was around, but she was a hungry bird all the same. And no wonder. She was a normal young woman who should have had a husband who made love to her all the time.

She and Keith went dancing at the officers' mess, where officers wanted to kiss her; they invited young recruits to 51 Simeon. They picked up hitchhiking servicemen and several became friends. A Cockney English soldier, Bill Reeves, was a frequent visitor whose company they really enjoyed and his whose wife, Kath, came over from England to visit. The Reeves would be Edna's friends for life.

There was another Bill, who soon went overseas. She met a British airman, Geoff Henson, whom she and Mrs. Swallows from Ingersoll picked up hitchhiking. Geoff was handsome and young and visited 51 Simeon Street. Edna spent many hours writing him long letters, most of them unsent: witty letters poking fun at the campaign against venereal disease that was worrying school kids; about the old couple she met doing the Gallup Poll — "So sweet but so smelly" — who had magazine cut-outs of royalty on the wall; about Thomas Wolfe's new novel.

She sent Henson cookies, and created a fictional character, "that damn gal R," who fantasized about yanking the covers off Geoff's bed. Sometimes she referred to herself as "poor lovesick Ednie," although Henson had a girlfriend.[41]

It was fun; it was sad. She was terrified of being unfaithful and being found out. Despite the supposed sophistication of their crowd, real infidelity, especially for women, was considered immoral. There was a big scandal when a woman had a child by another man while her husband was overseas. People gossiped about the Staeblers, who often had Fay Adams with them.

At least the letters, with a presumed if imagined audience, different from her private diary, provided a writing outlet. And a safe one, too.

She still wanted to change the world. How? She did not know.

In November 1941, Edna and Keith invited a young soldier, Fred Kruger, to 51 Simeon Street. He looked, Edna thought, like an Indian. He had spent most of his youth in jail for theft and other offences; he'd started his criminal career by stealing turkeys. His father was an alcoholic, his mother just thirteen when he was born.

"I am a thief. I live by stealing," he answered when Edna asked what his work had been. Fred's statement "did not even throw her off her stride, but rather was the source of more and more questions about myself," he said.

Secretly, she wondered if he'd steal her silver tea service.

Fred became an important person in Edna's life, she said, "because he extended my horizons. It was a fabulous experience, good for Fred, but better for me. I'd never met anyone like him before."

They remained in contact until shortly before his mysterious death in 1981. Edna always wanted to write a book about Fred and over the years approached various publishers with the idea, but they weren't interested at all in another story about a convict.

In 1941, Fred was often at 51 Simeon Street to talk to Edna and to play checkers with Keith.

Fred was soon back in jail after going AWOL and breaking into a service station. He wanted Edna to pretend to be his sister so she could write to him, but Edna wasn't going to be devious. The prison authorities didn't give her permission to write to him, but she appealed to the new chaplain, who permitted the correspondence.

Edna wrote to Fred for the four years he spent in prison. Perhaps it was Edna's encouragement that made him upgrade his school education to Grade 9; he was put in charge of the library and read books by Joseph Addison and others.

Released, he came straight to the Staeblers, who had agreed to take him in. He would help with the spring housecleaning, always a big production, by washing windows and floors ("Don't be preachy," Fred wrote to Edna when she rhapsodized about the joy of making things sparkling clean).

He arrived wearing "an awful blue suit, made in the prison. Keith gave him a suit."

That first night, Keith was out and Edna awoke to find Fred standing over her. "Get out of here!" she cried. He ran away, sobbing. Edna gave him a sedative.

"I had this compulsion to help," she explains.

Keith found him a job at Goodrich.

"Fred's clothes were smelly; awful. I washed them; I had a wringer washer. He was with us for three months, then he got a place to stay and a job in a shoe factory where there was an order to make shoes for the police department in Cambridge."

Edna's family was kind to Fred. Her mother invited him for Christmas dinner; it was the first time anyone had ever done that for him.

But he was psychotic when he was with them. Once he ranted and raved that he'd planned to build this tank thing in prison to rob banks; he'd found maps in the library.

"I thought, This is a really dangerous man."

She wouldn't dance with him when he wanted to learn from Arthur Murray records. She didn't want him touching her; he spoke about the many rapes for which he'd never been convicted.

He was soon in trouble with the police again. The police blamed him for a break-in at a flourmill in Preston, but he wasn't guilty. Keith hired a lawyer and Fred was released from jail.

Edna is right: Fred's story would make a book. His life was a tale of hopeful new beginnings leading to new failures. He worked as a waiter in Kitchener, Windsor, Detroit, and Toronto. He was often fired for his temper. He lived with a woman, had an affair with someone else. He returned to prison for the statutory rape of a young teenager; he said he pleaded guilty so the girl wouldn't have to testify. He took a course as a maître d' and opened a shoe repair business. When he didn't know how to repair the new hollow high heels and the business failed, he walked away from it because he didn't know what else to do and thought he might get in trouble with the police.

Edna advised him to write things down. He began in a scribbler and wrote for years — an autobiography, a thriller — but he was never published. Edna suggested they write a book together: he'd write his version of their friendship, she'd write hers.

In "Decriminalization" Fred described Edna's ease with strangers.

> I met Mrs. Staebler on November 22, 1941, at the Y.W.C.A. in Kitchener, Ontario, County of Waterloo. I encountered directly in moments; long enough for me to know that I had come from the West for my Basic Training ... and catching then a fleeting glimpse and another soldier who was there also, she turned quickly to me and said, "There is a Western outfit: The Lone Scouts." I turned just as quickly to look what their emblem might be like, and seeing that she had made a mistake in the name of the regiment, that it was not the Lone Scouts at all but rather the Lorne Scots, She just laughed over it. Although I was unable at that time to speak anything like good English we did manage to strike up a means of communication between us. We sat talking the remainder of the evening.[42]

Kruger relates the story of their friendship and how he learned about music from Keith and books from Edna. But he was plagued by feelings of nausea, which overcame him when he had the urge to steal; talking with Edna, who made him think logically, always helped.

People flocked to her door, and would do so for years, especially after Keith became involved with the John Howard Society and later with Alcoholics Anonymous. Pierre Berton, who got to know Edna a few years later, recalls the people Edna took under her wing.

"I had a lot of lame ducks — some people were always teasing me," Edna says.

One man stole all of Keith's clothes; Keith did not press charges. Johnny, a safe cracker, stayed with them, and Keith got him a job at Smiles & Chuckles. He held Edna captive on the couch all morning while he raved about plans to rob the Bank of Montreal. Another fellow swallowed suppositories, calling them pigeons.

Fred was the longest lasting of these unusual friends.

Through it all, he stayed in touch with Edna — sometimes he called her "Auntie Ed" — and would visit sporadically over the years, even taking a taxi out to Sunfish Lake.

Harold Horwood, a well-known author, was writer-in-residence at the University of Waterloo in the early eighties and met Fred. Horwood thought Fred was a terrible person, totally amoral, "with no guilt for sexually attacking little girls, for instance. But Edna entertained him at Sunfish without a qualm. Her ability to befriend a dangerous convict, alone in the woods, always astonished me."[43]

Despite her kindness, Edna had no illusions about Fred and recognized that he was amoral. "He wanted to pay a Jamaican girl for her nine-year-old sister."

In 1943 Edna took the train to Halifax, where Ruby's husband, Bob, worked for the Mutual Insurance Company. Ruby and Bob had two children, John and Mary Lou, and their babysitter, Marj Corkum, was from Lunenburg, which Edna wanted to visit because it had been founded by Germans in the late 1700s, Protestants recruited to settle Nova Scotia. The Germans were from the Palatinate and had been farmers, but they soon learned to fish and to build boats. The famous *Bluenose* was built in Lunenburg dockyards, and trawlers regularly went to the Grand Banks and traded in New England.

Keith said Edna's letters about Lunenburg were better than a good book. Why didn't she try writing travel books? The proceeds could pay for more travel and she'd have lots of fun. Edna loved the harbour town and found the houses with their widow's walks on top charming, and she loved the sight of the town rising on a steep hill above the harbour. She "wasn't into food then" but enjoyed Dutch Mess, a dish made with potatoes and dried cod.

Later, she thought about "the hills and the harbour —the vessels tied up at Zwicker's, the view from Corkum's back porch. Felsensouth across the water, when the light hit the houses and the church from the side just before sunset. I thought about the oxen drawing the carts and the funny towers that aren't towers in front of the houses. … I thought of Blue Rocks and the people there — the lobster traps and the dories."

She wrote these words to Earl Bailey, a well-known artist she had met there. Bailey was a cripple, with an adult's head and a child's body, as the result of polio. He painted with his mouth and was looked after by his brother, Don. His creativity and sensitivity inspired Edna and she spent hours talking with him as he sat in his wheelchair. He liked to read, and she knew "art talk" from her artist friend, Fay Adams. Bailey and Edna agreed to correspond.

Letters soon flew back and forth between Kitchener and Lunenburg. Edna was used to writing prosaic letters about everyday things to her family — "On Mon. I did such and such." "Mrs. Somebody or other has had another baby." "I bought a new striped dress. [description following]" — and smart letters to Geoff, but here was someone she could write real letters to, someone far away; a talented, intelligent man, one she could never see as a lover, but one who inspired her to think — and to write.

There was a parallel between them, too: neither had a real sex life, Bailey because of his disability and Edna because of Keith's impotency. Edna felt sorry for Bailey. And, possibly, Edna saw Bailey as someone to save.

It was after she met Bailey, and maybe because of Keith's suggestion about travel writing, that Edna enrolled in a correspondence course for writing with the Newspaper Institute of America for which she wrote small pieces that were critiqued. Edna wrote the institute in March 1944:

> I am interested in developing a personal literary style, not straight newspaper reporting or to sob stuff sort of thing. I hope I have developed a fair critical sense because of my wide reading. I have started writing a wide variety of things — stories, articles, sketches, poetry, plays — but I have seldom finished them because they always fall short of what I consider good writing. I despise the obvious and sentimental but probably haven't the ability to write anything good.[44]

She lists her community work and adds: "it is easy to find out that I don't have time to write, though I have wanted to do that more than anything else all my life."

Only a few assignments have survived, and the writing is awkward, not at all like the fluency of her two plays:

> Earlier in the evening Herbie had told us he'd rather listen to classical music but he'd rather play in a jazz band. While playing in a symphony orchestra he could play only what was written whereas in a jazz band he is free and can let his musical imagination soar.
>
> His variations on a theme are not unlike these of the great composers. This thing happened last night — this conversation between Herbie and Buck is exactly the thing you hear…

And:

> And the men themselves… they are all so lovable. Being with them warms your heart… It is a wonderful privilege to know them — to be fond of them. They are so alive. This creative thing that's in them is so terribly vital.[45]

Edna was writing about what she knew, Keith's musically inclined friends, but it was wooden, clichéd.

"HES" of the institute commented that Edna had stated her facts "flatly," although earlier the organization reported that her aptitude test showed she had it in her to become a successful writer.

She didn't stay with the institute for long, and didn't complete many assignments, but it was a beginning, a tentative move towards her goal, although she felt she had "nothing to write about." She wanted to write fiction, for that was what great writers wrote, and she was reading Thomas Wolfe and Katherine Mansfield; she loved Mansfield's story, "Bliss." But what could she write about?

She explored these ideas, as well as others, in her letters to Bailey, in flowing prose that was nothing like the dead attempts sent to the institute.

Bailey's letters have not survived, but he seems to have written her about desiring a woman, a partner, as well as discussing Life and Art. Sometimes Edna wrote a batch of letters to him and sent them all at once. Her letters are warm, effusive, and confessional. She does not spell out her real troubles with Keith, but tells Bailey that there are different ways of loving someone; one person cannot fulfill all your desires. She hints that sexual frustration can have its advantages:

> But that intense longing that almost burns us up sometimes and for which there is no satisfactory physical outlet must be the energy that can be used for creative art. I do believe there must be someone to provide us with that motivating spark, someone we can feel does understand — someone who calls forth our best thoughts and gives us faith in ourselves — or is this wishful thinking too? Is a friend enough? you ask — much better than a relationship based on a purely sexual urge that engenders fear of loss — a friend is constant — but does a friend give you the spark? Can people of the opposite sex ever be just friends — isn't there something more involved somehow? For me there is — it may be latent or subdued but if I am honest with myself I know that it is a very different feeling — more compelling than that I have for girl friends. Oh dear — how do I know the answer? I'm never satisfied, physically or mentally, I'm always searching.[46]

He was the perfect person for Edna to unburden herself to. "You, Earl, I find one of the most stimulating people I have ever known. I would like to feel free to tell you anything and everything that might be in my mind about you or me or things in general."

She does just that and he seems to be the first person with whom she really discussed her writing dreams and the growing guilt that she does not write. She sometimes calls him "darling"; she says that their friendship will endure.

> I have that awful feeling of power inside me that is being wasted and not used but how to counteract it is the worse feeling of having nothing inside but a helluva lot of nerve to even think that I might be able to do something worthwhile. Do you know what I mean? And so I flounder around in my mind and analyze and grope and get absolutely nowhere. I suppose because I can't write a gem of literature in one sitting I do nothing. I have written a lot of stuff but it is lousy. I never finish anything. I know good writing when I read it and mine isn't good — so I argue with myself — why try to clutter up people's minds with more stuff that isn't any good — it would be better for me to sop trying but then that damn something or other inside keeps niggling away saying I have got something. I'm not like 50 thousand other people.

She couldn't get away from those powerful urges to write:

> I want when I am terribly thrilled to express that intense emotion that I feel — but how can one write anything about those fleeting moments one has at times that are pure magic. Those are the things that make me want to write, to make other people know those moments too. You must know what I mean — they're like the gate of heaven opening up and giving you a glimpse — you couldn't take more than a glimpse — you couldn't bear it— a glimpse is enough... There is no accounting for those magic moments — they come often so unexpectantly from

> the simplest things — as Wordsworth said — Sometimes while looking at a star — the ships and the sea gave it to me … a young girl's face on a streetcar in Toronto — five years ago — but I have not forgotten.[47]

These glimpses, she writes Bailey later, are connected to something larger. Suddenly she has found the key:

> All the petty troubling things will have no meaning. Only this great wonderful thing that carries us will. You've felt the power of this thing — but … you've been tied by your body, the fear of friends and relations — so many things … it's all coming to me clearly now — I've had glimpses off and on for years — it will no doubt be a long time before it's worked out in my mind, but I think now it's like this Creative spirit, Power, cosmic energy, God, Karma, Spirit. Our self — call it what you will — is in everything and everyone — and it is alive — eternal — it flows like a fast moving stream … I'd been struggling, working towards it — discovering bits of the pattern but I couldn't fit it all together because I hadn't found the key — and now I've got it. Oh darling, isn't it wonderful? Of course all I have to do now is lose my fear — cut loose entirely from the shore — and be myself be carried along — learn all I can — be aware of everything that fits into my pattern and forget my self. That's simple, isn't it? But it is, because I have faith now to do it. Are you still with me, lover? I think you are, you know. That's why I know I love you — because we are so close — in this thing together — wanting the same things — in much the same way — both loving not only each other but other people — other things — ideas — we want the spirit in us to be loving — we try to make it

> loving — it could be hating and bitter you know and be strong and creative too — it is in some people like Hitler, but in us it must be loving. Isn't there a lot to think about?

The next morning she adds: "that complete surrender to the creative spirit, that freedom from the shore and rushing down stream — is genius."[48]

She said something of the same thing in a letter to her friend, Helen Kergin: "and suddenly one day as I sat here writing a letter the light broke. I realized that the thoughts came to me if I made myself receptive… I still have much to think about — I've just started really living and there's so much to learn but I love it and am greedy for it."

Chapter Five
Neil's Harbour — The Beginning of Everything

Edna returned to Nova Scotia in August 1945 to drive around the Cabot Trail with Earl Bailey and his brother, Don.

It was a disaster. Bailey had entirely misread Edna's long letters, not understanding that she loved him merely as a friend and intellectual companion. He believed she was his "girlfriend"; he wanted to kiss her, but she was having none of it.

They were supposed to stay at the Keltic Lodge in Ingonish, but the inn was filled and the only place they could find was a dirty cabin they all had to share. It was not what Edna had in mind, and she insisted they pile up the luggage in the middle of the room to give her privacy.

Things were worse later when she and Don took a walk to the nearby beach to talk to fishermen and children; Earl raged jealously. That night, he "strafed" Edna, calling her names. He'd told her about another woman he was involved with — supposedly she'd even had his child, although Edna didn't see how that was possible — and he referred to that lost love as a snake. Now Edna was in the same category. While he raged, Edna lay sleepless behind the barrier of suitcases.

In the morning, Don began packing up the car. He and his brother were returning to Lunenburg, and would drop Edna off at Ruby's in Halifax.

Nothing doing. She wasn't spending any more time with Earl, and impulsively she insisted they drop her at the next village, which they did, and that was that. She never heard from Earl Bailey again.

She was thirty-nine years old, a slim woman wearing a playsuit, and she was stranded in this tiny village of weather-beaten houses rising above the Atlantic at the northern tip of the Cabot Trail. No hotels, no phones even, only one small store, chickens scratching in yards, and she did not know at first that she had finally found that special something to write about. By the time she left three weeks later, she had two hundred pages of notes.

The place was Neil's Harbour, a small fishing village of a few hundred people, most of whom were from Newfoundland. Edna's presence there that sparkling day in August was the beginning of an enduring, lifelong love affair. She would spend years writing a book, in various forms, about the place, and return often to visit. The people became close friends; she even spent Christmas with one family and would package up books to help stock the new library. In the fifties, Keith said he knew she felt more at home in "the Harbour" than anywhere else.

Maybe she did. This was not prim and proper Kitchener where she had to behave a certain way in front of her conservative friends. She felt like a different person beside the ocean, the fishing boats, and the friendly people who did not lock their doors and welcomed Edna like family. The city was grey, dusty, and noisy. Neil's Harbour was all clean air, wind, sunshine, children laughing, men at the dock, women pegging laundry to the line, knitting socks, hooking mats, baking bread. She was not Mrs. Staebler, but "our Aidna" who had arrived like a gypsy and stayed to become almost one of them.

Her first published article, in *Maclean's* in 1948, was about swordfishing in the Harbour, and she would write other articles about the place. Her book about the village, *Cape Breton Harbour*, was not published until 1972, twenty-seven years later, when she was already known for her first *Schmecks* cookbook.

Cape Breton Harbour is a sparkling book that perfectly describes a time and place in a glowing, magical, poetic way. It never sold the way the cookbooks did and made little money, but it remains Edna's favourite book.

And it all started with the Bailey debacle and her strange impulse to be left at the side of the road.

Without that first article, would she have gone on to publish other things? Without Neil's Harbour, would she have found something or somewhere else to write about? Who knows? But this impulse changed her life.

At first she did not even know the name of the village, or what would happen to her. There was no phone in the village, and she got a room with Captain and Mrs. Pearl for the night. The next day she moved in with Christie and Annie Montgomery, two "spinsters," and their elderly mother.

She was dismayed at first. What had she done? And how long could she stand it in the village?

"There isn't a tree — only sun and the sea and about 80 people in little weathered houses. The people I'm with are nice and considerate and curious … [but] the dinner was old boiled potatoes and over fried mackerel — I don't know how long I'll stick it here," she wrote Ruby (whom Edna called "Mike") in 1945.

Maybe she'd go swordfishing.

But what would Keith say? Would he want her to come home right away? She wrote to him on Tuesday, her first day in the village.

> Oh my darling,
>
> Am really shaken. Now at the moment I'm sitting in the chaste bedroom of Captain and Mrs. Pearl in a little fishing village at the northern end of Cape Breton. I don't know the name of the place — won't ask. I don't expect to stay more than a week, if that … I'm ALONE. Thank God. I've never had such a fiendish time as the past 3 days. The country is the most beautiful I've ever seen and I could be happy just being in it … and I've been very happy when I've not been with Earl — but he was mad because I didn't give him my constant attention — he wanted me to kiss him and all that — and I couldn't — naturally — so this morning they decided to go home and I didn't — so I asked to be put off here. I felt pretty queer about it when they drove off leaving me but I'll get my sea legs …
>
> Earl was furious because I went for a walk with Don… Earl threatened me with… I don't know what if I spoke to Don. I didn't fight back, I just let

> him rave. He's a complete egotist, talks and thinks of nothing but himself. No fooling darling. I hope I'll come home a wiser person for this experience … You've no idea how relieved I am to be free of him — completely — I won't even be writing to him any more. Cheers.

If anyone asks about the change of plans, she can say Ingonish was filled up, she adds.

And, poignantly, "Darling, could you please love me terribly well and completely when I come home? On my honour, there is no other man in the world so perfect for me as you are — you know that."

She'd like to leave right away, but it would "look queer." Now she'll rest. "It's so quiet … all I can hear is the surf and a cowbell and the chickens in the front yard. I'm going to really try and write something here."

She felt relieved when Keith wired her to have fun and to bring him back a swordfish sword. "So I feel better now," she wrote Ruby. "[He said] good luck — he loves me — so on the strength of that I may cruise around a bit longer."

She felt grateful to Keith for allowing her this vacation. Edna wrote loving letters of gratitude to Keith whenever they were apart until their separation: he was the best husband ever to allow his wife to spend time away from him, she missed him terribly, and was the housekeeper she had hired feeding him well enough? She never mentions their problems; she thanks him for "putting up" with her because, really, wives going off on their own was not the normal thing. "I think you're the wonderfullest man in the world for letting me have this lovely adventuresome holiday," she assures him in 1945. She's "NUTS" about him and everyone "all over Cape Breton knows it because I've told them I'm married to the most wonderful person in the world and they're all envious."

It's as if she dark secret doesn't exist; she doesn't mention it, even in letters. Obviously, she's told no one.

Still, she's not shy about telling him about men she meets, such as the Halifax artist, Ray Zwicker, who was in Neil's Harbour in

1945, and who gave her sketching lessons — she'd taken a few art classes at the Homer Watson Gallery and School the year before with Fred Varley, who didn't like her attempts ("Terrible, terrible, terrible") and with Ralph Ashton at evening school.

Then there was Tom Glover, a young teacher from Sydney who was also vacationing in Neil's Harbour. They talked for an hour or two on the beach and agreed to write to each other.

The week in Neil's Harbour stretched to three on that first visit. There was so much to do and see and record and she wanted to go swordfishing but had to wait for the weather to be calm so a boat could go out.

People thought she was twenty-two years old. She carried her writer's notebook everywhere with her, making notes for the book she knew she would write. She had never been so happy, she wrote Keith:

> Hello darling. How's my ever-loving husband?
>
> I am so happy that I'm almost nervous about it. I love this crazy little place. I hate to leave it. That's really sort of silly, you know because I've made no intimate friends here — except perhaps Ray Zwicker who was here only a day — but everyone is so nice.
>
> I hitchhiked to Ingonish (15 m) on Monday. Was picked up by the RCMP — late of the Imperial Army …
>
> At night the village had a do for 4 boys who have returned — it was so much fun — I've written about it in my notebook — I felt shy but was taken under the wing of Mrs. Dick Budge whose husband is the plutocract of the town … No fooling dear I'd like to be writing every minute I'm here about everything and everyone. There is so MUCH and I feel so close to it all — but still there is a restlessness in me — you know it so well that makes me want to learn more and more and I don't have enough time.
>
> Yesterday I decided to hitch-hike to Cheticamp (58 m). I went out to the fork of the road and sat in the

> shade to wait until a car came but a fisherman spied me and talked. He said the people of the town hadn't felt like I was an outsider — I "be one of theirselves like." That was PRAISE I can tell you. … He said he believed if people be "koind and 'as their 'ealth that's the best loif can give us." Darling you'd love these people. They're so simple and sincere and strong — it's an education in living to be amongst them.
>
> Anyway his two little daughters came along and he took their hands and went off to find his cows which had been missing since the day before. I opened my book but another fisherman came and sat with me — a Newfy. You'd have a hard time not smiling at their expressions. "He do" and "does" is always "doos." A long "it" is "oi."
>
> Anyway Dick Budge gave me a ride a ride to Dingwall, telling me all about his business. I stood for a while and then a truck came and stopped and took me in. I want to write up that ride. It's priceless. As we went along I said I'd like to do it but Norman (RCMP) said people wouldn't believe it and then the climax came when we reached Pleasant Bay and heard the war was over.[49]

The end of the war doesn't appear to have affected Edna very much. There is just this comment before she continues the yarn about getting to Cheticamp:

> They picked me up at 10:30 and we reached Cheticamp at 4:45 — the six hours home was even crazier. … There were 4 of us in the truck — Norman, a short little man with glasses, a one time bank teller, now RCAF, Mr. Doucette, a little Frenchman who insisted on riding in the back so I could go in front …

The real world of war, Kitchener, and Keith, of committee meetings Mrs. Keith Staebler attended wearing a hat, seemed far way in this enchanting new place by the sea. Instead of a hat, shorts; instead of civic meetings, fishermen met at the side of the road. She felt like a different person — a writer who now had something to write about.

"One morning I woke up and I knew this was it," she says.

This writing would be different, unlike the wooden attempts of the year before. "I've been doing some writing during the past year," she'd written Fred in February, "but there's something not right about it because the rejection slips come back with my work as regularly as I send it out. You have to collect at least 100 before you sell anything. I think I only have about ten so far."

Now, this new world of Neil's Harbour opened before her with passionate possibility.

Back in Kitchener more than three weeks later, she began working on the book immediately. She had two hundred pages of notes to draw from and started writing something that seemed to be a novel. Sometimes she forgot what time it was as she typed away.

She had no experience with a big work, the Newspaper Institute of America was no help, and there were no writers who might have given advice. *The Writer*, an American magazine, gave constructive advice and tips, but the only writer she knew was Mabel Dunham, who brought out another book that year, but she didn't consult the librarian.

Edna had met Margaret Millar a few times, and Millar's first book was accepted while she and her husband, Ken, who would later publish mysteries under the name Ross MacDonald, lived in Kitchener while Ken taught high school, but Edna hardly knew her. Anyway, Edna didn't care for mystery novels.

From housewife to writer was a transition, and Edna faced the problems of many women who did creative work at home. There were interruptions. Fred was soon back in her life, staying at 51 Simeon: Edna even washed his dirty clothes after Keith got him a job in a rubber factory.

Friends liked to drop in, and the neighbourhood kids, especially the Hutton twins, were often at the door. Saying she was busy made Edna feel guilty. She now knew that she was a writer, and she felt like a writer, but how to explain this difference to people who had always seen her as Keith's wife?

She was still doing the Gallup Poll and was active on the library board. Being president of the Canadian Club took time, too, and she frequently invited the monthly guest speakers back to 51 Simeon.

John Fisher of the CBC was a guest that fall, as was a Miss Arnold (Edna would see her again in Ottawa 1996 when Edna received the Order of Canada) who discussed Canadian literature with Edna: there were so few writers.

Keith didn't comprehend what it meant to write a book, but he was often out all the time, sometimes not coming home until the early hours of the morning. When he was around, he expected Edna to accompany him to the parties he enjoyed so much.

He didn't understand this new passion. He wished Edna would go to the hairdresser and have permanents like other women. He wished she'd play bridge and golf and not pick up magazines or books whenever they went to someone's house.

He must have been puzzled by her sudden commitment to this new project. He was not yet resentful, although he would be, telling Edna that a person wasn't a writer until she was published, but he probably had no idea, then, what this change would mean for their lives.

Edna's mother wasn't encouraging either, saying it takes talent to be a writer; obviously she felt Edna had none.

There were still meals to get, laundry to do, the house to tidy. And maybe her thoughts about the meaning of life and love intruded, too. The long letters to Bailey had been exchanged for letters to Tom Glover, the Cape Breton schoolteacher she'd spent an hour with on the beach at Neil's Harbour, although the letters to Glover were shorter.

"It must be the constant quest that keeps us alive and young and eager," she wrote Glover in 1945 without going into the pages of rumination she had sent to Bailey.

But the letters to Glover gave focus to her writing: he was someone with whom to share memories of Neil's Harbour. In November she wrote:

> The clouds over the sea were low, mouldy, deeply shaded with purple, blue, grey and shell pink. There were a few narrow rifts and the rising sun shone through them — making separate paths of gleam on the quiet water. A big black steamer moved slowly across the edge of the sea and the little silhouette of the fishing boats seemed to stand still.[50]

They were poetic words about this shining place, but what form should the book take? What would happen to the manuscript? Should she use first person or third? Should she be factual or introspective and philosophical? Was there a plot? She had images and her notes, but all she knew really was that she had to continue writing. It was that special feeling all writers recognize: the compulsion to write the special book, the knowledge that here exists this private entity that demands to be put on paper.

A fortuitous accident had led her to Neil's Harbour, and now a person appeared at just the right time to provide the next step in the creation of herself as a writer.

On November 15, Dr. John D. Robins, a professor at Victoria College at the University of Toronto, spoke to the Women's Canadian Club on "Some Aspects of Humour." He was the author of *The Incomplete Anglers*, which won the Governor General's Award.

Edna would call Dr. Robins her mentor. Their friendship lasted until his death in 1952 and is documented in a series of letters Edna tried unsuccessfully to publish as "Dear Edna, Dear Friend."

The correspondence is fascinating, showing the growing confidence of a new writer. Dr. Robins would read her versions of the manuscript and give valuable advice, telling Edna, for instance, that there was a difference between being factual and being honest; sometimes her dedication to the facts got in the way of storytelling.

It was through Robins that Edna realized she was writing "creative non-fiction," the genre she has championed over the years with the award she gives in her name for creative non-fiction, which is administered by Wilfrid Laurier University.

Dr. Robins was the perfect friend at just the right time. He was much older than Edna, a well-respected academic. He was not some faraway pen pal, like Earl Bailey, or a soldier she could fantasize about, like Geoff Henson, but a real person who lived in nearby Toronto. He was married, and she knew little of his family life.

There was no question of romance, imaginary or otherwise; there was only a firm friendship with great respect on both sides.

Robins delighted in the mentoring, Edna in the receiving. They saw each other from time to time: Edna went to Toronto or Robins stopped in Kitchener, sometimes staying overnight, on his way to a speaking engagement. He was someone Edna could go to, and she did as their friendship deepened, with her personal problems, but her letters to him remained focused on writing. Unlike everyone else, he took Edna seriously, and saw her as a writer. He wrote that he was greatly interested in her projected book and that he felt she would succeed if she projected her own personality into it. She was writing at a good time, he thought, because Canadians were becoming aware of their writers, especially those writing about Canadian scenes and people.[51]

Edna needed to hear those words. And as for her worry about how the book would be received: "However, as you and I have both felt, the writer is hampered by too great awareness of a public."

And he recognized and reaffirmed Edna's way of looking at the world: that of looking outward and finding beauty in the world around her, of continuing to be enchanted by life and people and nature.

It was hard, though, to always hang onto this idea of enchantment and happiness. As she focused on her writing — "This book is forcing me to live the life of a hermit," she wrote both Henson and Robins in January 1946. "The only social life I have left is my correspondence."

Problems with Keith continued. He was still out at all hours, didn't want to discuss her ideas, and sometimes he drank too much. He wasn't an alcoholic — not yet — but Edna found his drinking worrisome. She didn't drink much herself, a cocktail or two was enough, and she felt bored at the parties Keith loved so much.

Talking to Fay helped. She lived on Frederick, just up the street, and here was somebody to whom Edna could pour out her frustrations with her marriage. After several miscarriages, Fay gave birth to a daughter, Rebecca*, just before her husband went overseas. With Howard away, Edna and Keith tried to include Fay in their activities.

Edna and Fay discussed all kinds of things — spirituality and religion and love and likely their marriages. Howard had sent a coat home for cleaning and Fay found a condom in the pocket.

In the spring of 1946, after Howard was back home and they were having a sort of second honeymoon in Niagara Falls, Fay wrote to Edna that the falls reminded her of Edna's theory of cosmic energy.

It was a theme Edna tried to keep in mind as she wrote and rewrote her manuscript in 1946, sending completed sections to Robins for critique. Dottie might be encouraging, but Robins gave expert, technical advice. It was all right to tell the story simply, he advised, but the narrative could provide a way to convey profound reflection, a philosophy of life and man and nature. He praised her "amazing combination of nice fastidious femininity and quite dreadful vulgarity." Using "damn" and "hell" was all right, even if, as Edna said, her mother-in-law and Kitchener "ladies" would not approve.

"Edna, girl, you get after your book," Robins told her when she felt like giving up, "and get it done and put away."[52]

It was hard. Sometime late that fall, Fay confessed to Howard that she and Keith had been having an affair while Howard was overseas.

What? No one had guessed, or found out, but here was the reason for Keith's late nights, all those lonely nights Edna had discussed with Fay. Howard was furious — there he'd been overseas risking his life, and safe at home his good friend had been having sex with his wife.

Fay must choose, Howard said. She could leave on generous terms and be with Keith, or she could stay with her husband.

Fay chose Howard, who confronted Keith and made him tell Edna, who would — what? Rant and rave or kick Keith out?

That wasn't Edna's way. She had forgiven Keith for his earlier infidelity and perhaps become used to the way things were. Or claimed to be used to it.

"You and I are perfect together in a different way perhaps from most people but then we're not like most people, are we?" she'd written Keith on her way back from Neil's Harbour.

Now she forgave him for Fay, too, trying to understand her point of view, the loneliness of a woman whose husband was away, the upside-down world of wartime. She truly loved Fay and naively hoped the friendship would continue.

And just as naively, she was grateful that Keith was not impotent after all. Maybe now they could get back to normal, after about seven years of not having sex. But that was only wishful thinking.

And what about the betrayal, all those confidences she had shared with Fay? The hours she had spent moaning to her about Keith being out every night? She had even made a nightie trimmed with rosettes for Fay when Howard came home, "a glamorous nightgown for a friend whose husband was overseas," Edna wrote Fred in April.

Fay was not the only woman who'd had an affair while her husband was away, and Edna understood loneliness and temptation, but while she longed to be intimate with her own husband, he was having sex with her very good friend. It was more than plain old adultery; it was a betrayal of another kind.

One expects a flash of anger, a thunderbolt of wrath. One wants some pots thrown, dishes smashed, or at least tears and recriminations, lamentations, scenes, confrontations.

Instead the two couples had meetings; Fay and Edna talked privately and Edna said she wanted to remain friends as before.

Christmas was always Edna's favourite time of the year. She loved buying gifts, decorating the house, trimming the tree, and baking hundreds of cookies. The Staeblers always had a Christmas party with carolling and Edna spent days getting ready.

But Christmas 1946 was not a happy one.

Early in the month she fell, hurting her back. Keith took her to the doctor, but went out that night, not returning until 5:40 a.m. Her head throbbed, but she lay awake, worrying he'd drink and drive and have an accident. The next day he phoned and said he'd be home for dinner in twenty minutes, but arrived home two hours later, drunk, and with a drunken friend in tow.[53]

Christmas brought not gifts from the Adamses, but several letters. The letters are moralistic, angry, and make painful and sad reading.

Howard wrote on the seventeenth and again the following day that he could forgive Fay but never excuse her actions; that there was only shame in the affair and that his wife had given something to Keith that wasn't hers to give. He speaks of cowardice, lying, deceit, hypocrisy, evil, and theft. Their friendship is finished forever and he doesn't care what people will think of him for supposedly abandoning the good friends who looked after Fay while he was away. He doesn't understand how Edna and Keith can expect things to go on, how they can excuse Keith's behaviour and understand the reasons for it.

Fay followed with a pathetic note written in pencil, (was her husband standing over her shoulder?) saying how ashamed she was that she gave something that was not hers to give. She compares herself to Fred. Her behaviour was "despicable" and "inexcusable." She, who'd been having sex with Keith for years, didn't see the irony of lecturing the Staeblers on the nature of good and evil.

Both wish Edna and Keith a Merry Christmas.[54]

The letters must have hurt, condemning not only Keith's actions, but also Edna's tolerant acceptance. She thought Howard was self-righteous and she felt sorry for Fay and wrote about her and the concept of sin to Dr. Robins.

Robins did not agree with Edna that sin was a human concept, but said that "Evil is ignorance … evil is a cause of pain, because certainly whatsoever a man soweth, that shall he also reap. The Wheel turns."[55]

Did she secretly think about leaving Keith? Many of Edna's early letters to Robins have not survived, but she appears to have written to him in December about a longing to escape.

Robins advised her to stay where she was. At least physically. He thought the best thing Edna could do was to erect an internal retreat — "a spiritual Algonquin Park" — to which she could flee.

Although such advice could be dangerous for some, Robins was confident that Edna was too interested in others, too involved in life to fall into idle self-absorption. "Escape you need," he wrote, "but it must be into inner objective joy, not into introspection."[56]

Look out the window, he advises, watch the sky, the cat; imagine the sound of the sea. These things are "healing… restorative; they are tonics."

Edna did not seriously consider leaving — not yet, anyway. It would have been a drastic move. The house was in her name, but how could she support herself? Keith was generous with money and gave her a good allowance to run the house and to buy things for herself. Did she really want to disrupt the world of being able to write at nice 51 Simeon Street? She was a married woman, living under one roof with her husband, who was not inclined to leave her, either. What would people say if she left? Divorce was rare and only granted for adultery, and it would have made for one big scandal. Edna and Keith still both cared about each other. And they also still cared about the opinions of their friends and worried about the public rift with the Adamses.

But the public image was so different from the inner reality. Robins's advice helped, and the day after receiving Howard's letter, Edna wrote to Tom Glover. Like many of the letters to Henson, it was unsent, but it helped her define how she wanted to think in the midst of this crisis: "Being a loving person is like having a light inside you and as you look at people it shines on them and helps you really see them — so loving is not a part time thing or a personal thing — but something which you are."

Being loving: it was a way to survive.

Chapter Six
More at Home in the Harbour than Elsewhere

The friendship with the Adamses was over.

It was awkward. The couples had many friends in common and shared similar interests. After the Adamses moved to another city, they became prominent art supporters. They did not keep in touch with Edna and Keith, but Edna never lost her affection for Fay.

While Edna tried to be loving and understanding, Keith was devastated by the rupture with their friends. Howard soon became an obsession for Keith, who started drinking more and more. He was still fond of Howard and still loved Fay, Edna realized, but sometimes he hated them, too, because of their self-righteousness, and that feeling of hate frightened him, Edna thought. The only time he found release was when he was drunk.[57]

Here was something new. Keith had always enjoyed a drink and it was true that he sometimes got a bit tipsy at parties, but now his drinking brought out his mean side and he said awful things to Edna. It was a pattern that continued until the end of their life together. Keith would be drunk for days. Sometimes at night he took a bottle to the office; his employees found him passed out the next morning. Sometimes he was so drunk that Edna had to spoon-feed him.

Over the years, he was hospitalized many times, joined AA, fell off the wagon, tried to be sober again. There were new affairs; he even paid for one woman's divorce and went on another drinking binge when she found another lover. He did not hide his amours from Edna, but left love letters from other women where she would find them. But he did not want Edna to leave and threatened to kill himself if she did. Several times he took pills, and Edna had to call an ambulance.[58]

Edna tried to understand, and continued to feel that if only she loved him enough, unconditionally and uncritically, he would stop drinking and be the man he really was, generous and kind and wonderful. He helped so many people, particularly after his involvement in the John Howard Society and Alcoholics Anonymous, finding jobs and rooms for them, giving them money and paying for lawyers. Sometimes he let down-and-outs live at 51 Simeon Street. He gave a lot of his time to the music community and was so talented, so creative, so entertaining when he wasn't drunk. He was also a good businessman who worried about his clients. He was generous with Edna, giving her a good allowance with which to run the house.

At one point, probably in the late forties, they tried to adopt a child but were turned down because of Keith's drinking.

Through it all, Edna continued writing, and as she started publishing articles for *Maclean's*, she was often away. She felt like a different person then, away from Keith, who was often drunk upon her return.

Edna wasn't a saint and she became discouraged, depressed sometimes, about Keith, but it is a wonder that she managed to retain her positive attitude, her belief in herself and her work, that she was not filled with self-pity and continued finding joy in the world around her and in her inner life of thinking and writing.

She poured out her thoughts and fears on paper in unsent letters to Tom Glover. Her letters to Robins were more disciplined, more lofty and philosophical, but these unsent letters to Tom provided a perfect vehicle for expressing these new worries. Writing cleared her mind.

The letters show a marriage of two people so far apart: one wretched and miserable, the other trying to cope and to understand. There seemed to be no solution to the misery.

> Tom, what is the answer? I know I must love him, but it's so hard — I want much of the time to run away — to find again the joy I had when I was at Neil's Harbour … but leaving would be cruel — kicking a man when he's down but staying makes me feel like a martyr and that attitude is fatal. I must want to stay because I love Keith, but I live in con-

> stant fear because I know that I so often resent him and his way of life.

She feared her thoughts because: "At times I'm afraid I almost hate him — then I feel guilty and afraid my negative thoughts may be destroying him — that it is all my fault but he is deceitful with me — he doesn't lie perhaps but he keeps things from me."

Her family felt she was "too soft" and that she should be firm, even angry, and that she spoiled Keith — "but if I am and I've tried it — he is furious — determined more strongly than ever to do as he pleases — yet that makes him more miserable and he says his deepest worry and fear is that he makes me unhappy."

It must have been easy to feel hate. When Keith was drunk he said "things that utterly defeated" her and when he was sober he was "so depressed and unhappy" that she felt like "a helpless failure." Worry about Keith sometimes kept her from writing. "That's why I don't get any writing done — because I'm always convincing myself, justifying my right to live as I want to live — as I feel I must live."[59]

She goes on in her letter to describe the turmoil Keith's alcoholism was causing:

> When drunk he is jealous of everything and everyone I love — the children, Neil's Harbour, my reading, all my living — everything. I do [what] I want to do — my intelligence, my attitude towards life — he says a woman should do what her husband wants to do, that she must go 95% of his way and give up her own way — that she would be glad if she really loved him. That is what hurts me and makes me feel guilty — I can't go Keith's way — I've tried, for years I've tried and it is impossible. He is not interested in things that interest me — things that I love best of all — I don't know what the answer is. I only know that I must go my own way. I shouldn't tell you things — I feel a lack of loyalty to Keith in doing it and yet you have a right to know so that you can better understand.

> Really Keith is a kind and wonderful person and far more generous with me than I have a right to expect him to be and he is thoroughly ashamed of his attitude when he is drunk — he says the untruth comes out but I still worry and I wonder if there is any truth in the awful things he says about me. It takes me days to get over his outbursts. I am determined now to ignore them — he says I must forget them.
>
> But Tom, I can't bear to see Keith suffer but I don't know what to do about it. I suppose I don't love him enough — he rouses so much bitterness and resentment in me that I have to force myself to be loving at times —isn't that awful?
>
> I feel sorry for him — but sympathy is negative and makes him more sorry for himself. I can tell him nothing — that makes him think I am self-righteous — superior — I can't speak to him of things that give me joy — that makes him jealous. [But] I find joy so constantly in so many things — that is what I must do — that is my way.[60]

Life went on at 51 Simeon.

Writing helped. She continued working on her book about Neil's Harbour. She also wrote other things — a short story for *True Confessions*, for example, which was rejected. She wrote poetry. She read writers' magazines, and found inspiration in books by David Seabury: *Help Yourself to Happiness*, which she recommended to Tom Glover, while admitting the title was stupid and that he might want to shelve the book with the title facing inwards, and *How To Get Things Done*, which she typed out, all 119 pages, in order to have a copy for herself.

Seabury compared creative imagination to a chemical process, like melting metals in a crucible, and felt listening had become almost a lost art.

She'd already discovered *If You Want to Write* by Brenda Ueland, which was published in 1938, in the library. Edna wrote to the publisher for a copy but it was out of print. Ueland said everyone was creative; you just had to be honest in using your own voice because there was no voice like yours in the whole world. Edna typed two copies — one for lending, the other to keep. (The book became a classic and Edna "almost jumped for joy" when it was reprinted in the eighties, according to Tricia Siemens of Words Worth Books in Waterloo.)

She continued corresponding with Dr. Robins, writing to him not only about her book but also about her way of looking at the world. He went on advising her. Writing about an author he met, he lamented the man's stuffiness in writing, but said he could teach Edna something. He had a startling, wonderful way of describing his thoughts and feelings, something Dr. Robins felt was a weakness in Edna's writing. Although she wrote very well about impressions and reactions, she did not express deeper emotions nearly as well; she often did not think logically about the latter. She should write the way she tells stories aloud, he says, and also, she had to "be completely withdrawn from the preoccupation with things around you now."[61]

It was easy for Robins to say this, but Edna tried.

And life at 51 Simeon was not always gloom and doom. Around this time, Philip Knowling was a guest speaker at the Canadian Club. He was a dashing Newfoundlander, handsome in his British naval uniform, with connections in England where he had been educated; he was related to David Lloyd George, and his family in Newfoundland was prominent: his father was a well-known merchant in St. John's.

Knowling had been involved in intelligence during the war and travelled all over the East — cycling through Indonesia and Singapore, going all over Europe. He was a poster boy too, having been the model for a poster for the British Navy. And he was a bachelor; women wanted to marry him and yearned to look after him. He was the kind of man who came for a week and stayed for six months, a heartbreaker, a bit of a grifter who died poor in England.

Edna kept in touch with him over the years and stored some silver and family porcelain for him. She also saved his personal correspondence — a mouldy box in her garage — and there's poor Dylis, a young Irishwoman who quit her hairdressing job in England on the strengths of Knowling's feelings. He didn't reply to her telegrams and she returned to Ireland after some kind of breakdown.[62] Usually Knowling preferred wealthier women "who had enough money to let him to do he what wanted."

You could say he was a writer, too, on the strength of a few articles about history and politics in British magazines.

Edna was attracted to him: he scoffed at the pretensions of bourgeois society, and in the years ahead, he visited 51 Simeon Street frequently. He and Keith were pals, Keith taking him to hockey and baseball games and to cocktail parties where he "insulted some women." One hostess indignantly told Edna that Knowling was barred from her house.

He flirted with Edna. "Edna, if we could only meet in Spain. I've really thought of running away with you."

But "if I said I'd do it, he would have backed off."

It was a lot of fun, and Edna said Philip "broadened my horizons — he was a man of the world and I was all Kitchener-Waterloo." He urged her to go to Europe instead of Neil's Harbour. What did she want with that small fishing village anyway?

But Neil's Harbour was the one place she really wanted to be, and Edna returned there for six weeks in August 1947. It was a long time for a wife to be absent, especially in these nesting years when men came home from the war to set up housekeeping and start families. Edna knew people would say she was a neglectful wife.

"Don't worry about what people say about your missing me," she wrote to Keith, "if I thought you were sitting there moping I'd have no peace of mind at all. I want you to be happy there."

She knew being away was not conventional. "I feel sorry that you have to do so much explaining about me but maybe some day people will accept me as I am. Actually I don't give a damn if they do or not — but I know you do and I hate to embarrass you."

She was going to Neil's Harbour to work on a story about a swordfishing boat, the *Aspy*; maybe she could sell that. She wanted to finish her book, but perhaps, too, she needed to think about her marriage. Keith had a girlfriend in London, and around this time

Edna secretly consulted a lawyer about a divorce. The lawyer wasn't hopeful and advised her that she'd have to get Keith to leave.

There was a woman in Keith's office, too, and now he humiliated Edna in public, dancing in his stocking feet with his new girlfriend and gazing into her eyes while Edna and everyone else watched. Finally, Keith would have so much to drink that he'd pass out and Edna would drive him home.

Keith had been seeing a psychiatrist, Dr. Harris, in London, and Edna had hoped things would improve after his sessions, but Keith said he'd only sober up if Edna got tough and left him, which her lawyer had advised her not to do. Arriving in Neil's Harbour must have been a great relief.

And here was happiness. Her letters to Keith about her stay shimmer with joy and wonder at what she saw and felt. These were not the convoluted unsent epistles to Tom Glover or the thoughtful ones to Dr. Robins, but a narrative of observations that radiated happiness. They make happy reading: here was Edna finding pleasure and contentment at what she saw — children and kittens and wash blowing on the line and boats in the harbour. The language sparkles:

> I could see the faces of the houses in the cold white light — all looking in one direction at the sea on the bay side where the boats come in… Just as one does not look at the sun to enjoy the effects of sunlight, so in Neil's Harbour one does not look at the moon becoming absorbed by its gleaming on the living water, its dimming of the yellow flame above the shining white slope of the lighthouse, its cool brilliance on the stages. … Sometimes I look at the village and I wonder why it holds me so but last night I knew the answer as I really know it all the time — it's just so God damn beautiful.[63]

She felt like writing poetry at the Harbour, and living by the sea, she was able to see the bigger picture of the book as a whole. She'd written in "such a desultory, patchy way at home that I've lost sight of the composition, the big pattern, the framework, the development."

The people at Neil's Harbour were glad to see her again and remembered her hanging around the wharf and talking to everyone. She was overjoyed to be back with them.

She stayed with Clara May and Henry Ingraham, the parents of a large family. Henry was a fisherman; some of the kids were grown but they kept returning home to sit in Clara May's kitchen while she baked bread and blueberry pie, did the laundry, knitted socks and mittens, and hooked mats. Neighbourhood kids were always underfoot. There were twelve in the house — "I'm not sure of that number. Annie and Maggie were trying to count us up the other day and I think that was the final figure."

She loved the feeling of warmth in the house. "Most of them have blue eyes that shine as they look at each other. They are all so fond of the children. It's good to see the boys — [ages] 14-12-9 carry the baby, Lillian (4), around with such affection. I feel there is so much love in this house."[64]

The family would become close personal friends and well-loved characters in Edna's future writing; she would write a story about Maggie, a daughter, in an article for *Maclean's* in 1951. Clara May said Edna would always have a place to stay as long as she was alive.

Clara May gave her a small working space next to the dining room: "a silly little space … about five feet square, a bit of linoleum on the floor, wooden slanted ceiling, wooden walls that have a bit of old water soaked paper clinging to them, three doors and two windows with cheese cloth curtains. But I never see anything but all that is in front of the windows and that is always beautiful."[65]

She wrote about Charlotte and Archie at the store and Cecil and Tassie and Annie and Charlie and all the Ingrahams "who are a wonderful crowd. I love every one of them and I think they are fond of me — in a way. I never worry or wonder what they say or think about me [and] I never feel that I need to make any explanations. They let me feel that I am what I am and what I do is my business."

This longer visit was giving her much more insight into the village. "I realize just how superficial my reactions were last time I was here ... Last time I had to overcome so much in myself and so much shyness in them I think, or was it all just my inability to see beyond the surface at that time?"

She went to a ladies' do to raise money for the Red Cross, to "toimes" at the Legion, on a drive to Dingwall, out fishing early in the morning to catch cod:

> They didn't let me fish at first — said I couldn't haul them up — too heavy — would hurt my hands etc. but I persisted and they let me try and, dear, I caught more than they did (13) until my hands were so blistered and bleeding that they made me quit and I did quit because I knew to keep on was sheer bravado — tho' it was so darn much fun and I hated like hell to stop. Gee it was good tho, the line went out seemingly for miles — actually 50 fathoms — 300 feet to you, landlubber — then I hung on to it till I felt something move — then I pulled and pulled...[66]

But she spent most of her time writing in her little nook overlooking the sea.

"What you doin' wi' yerself? I never sees yer round the shore loike you used to," people said. Her friends hoped she'd stay or come back for the winter and took out the catalogue to show her what she ought to buy for the cold weather.

There were changes in the village after only two years. Men returning from overseas were drinking more, and a fellow from Sydney had bought a house and installed a movie projector to show films.

The biggest change was that there was another writer, John Anderson*, who lived in a cabin. Oh no, Edna thought, another writer. He'll write a book about Neil's Harbour before I do. But she soon met John and went to his cabin every night to read and talk. There were no electric lights in the village and she couldn't read in bed because the lantern had to remain on the dresser. John had an Aladdin lamp for reading, and Edna spent most evenings with him.

John gave Edna the one thing Neil's Harbour couldn't: a link with the outside world. He came from a wealthy Ontario family, went to Upper Canada College and to school in Switzerland and had travelled all over. He'd lived in Mexico, fished the Grand Banks, and been in the army. He was a music lover and city sophisticate, but here he was in Neil's Harbour, thinking of writing stories. Well, he told wonderful stories and he had everything in his head, ready to write down. In the meantime, he critiqued Edna's work, advising her on form and so on.

Edna wrote Keith that John didn't seem interested in her as a female (might he be a homosexual?) but he was interesting company and it was good to drop in at his cabin to "sit across the table from him and read his books in the glow of the Aladdin lamp of which he is so proud and which cost him seven dollars."

Soon they went walking together on twelve-mile hikes along the cliffs in the evenings, each lost in thought so that they ended up walking on opposite sides of the unpaved road. Edna invited him to go to a dance at the legion with her. She wore a dress and "embarrassed John by telling him it was the first time in my life that I had ever stumbled over a cow path, gone through a fence and called for a man to take me to a dance. Our relationship has been so completely casual that I think he was quite surprised by the thought that I could wear a dress and receive the attentions due a woman."[67]

John offered her a ride to Montreal. He planned to drive through the States, and then Gaspé, and Edna didn't know what to do.

"I wonder if I will?" she wrote Keith. "Since I have been here — at least since the last few days I have been learning again how to relax and love life and everyone and everything in it, including you, my friend. I have again the feeling of my life being directed and not a thing for me to worry about if I have enough faith to let it work itself out."

She knew now that she could write and that she would write for the rest of her life, she wrote Keith. John said any doubts would be dispelled once she was published.

Her letters are filled with John, and despite her statements to Keith about the casual nature of their friendship, Edna was falling in love with him. Why not? She was forty-one years old and had not had sex with Keith for eight years. He didn't even want to kiss her, stiffening up when she approached him. Keith didn't care if she had male friends; he even pushed men at her, and had even suggested it would smarten him up if she left him. He humiliated her in public and verbally abused her in private.

Edna never considered leaving Keith for John, however. John didn't seem interested in marriage and later Edna found out he was divorced, but they were attracted to each other and he treated her like a woman. It wasn't so much marriage she needed, but a relationship with some meaning, as she wrote John the next year.

There's more distance, now, between Keith and Edna. She addresses him as "Staeble" and is of course grateful to him for the freedom to be herself, but the passion and longing in the letters of two years ago ("love me well and completely") are missing. Instead, she admits that she has been silly about the "loving me business." She knows now that her happiness is "dependent on my attitude towards life, not other people's attitude towards me. Why should other people try to make me happy — they have enough to do to work out their own problems — as I must."

Still she stresses that she loves Keith but she knows she has to stay here for a while. She begs him to understand: if he loves her he will understand, and "only through loving do we gain understanding."[68]

Keith would later admit that Edna felt more at home in the Harbour than elsewhere. But did he understand? Did he care? He minded the gossip about Edna's trips away, but they were on opposite paths, almost living different lives.

Edna dreaded returning to Kitchener. She wrote her old friend Helen Kergin from university days that she fell in love with John Anderson in Neil's Harbour, but that she returned to Kitchener "reluctantly and to develop my character" and to help Keith prepare for a concert the following April, when he would perform "Rhapsody in Blue" for the Kitchener Philharmonic.

Driving back to Ontario with John, they stopped at Gaspé, where she saw a derelict boat hauled up on sand. The boat reminded Edna of herself and her marriage.

Keith was drunk when she got back to 51 Simeon Street.

Chapter Seven
Publication

In May 1948, Edna, wearing her "new look" outfit and gold lace straw hat with flowers across the front, drove to Toronto and went to the office of *Maclean's* magazine on University Avenue. She had a twenty-four-page manuscript, a story on swordfishing, with her; she'd spent six weeks working on it.

She was forty-two years old, but looked much younger with her slim figure, reddish hair, and lively face. The new look with its defined waist and flattering mid-calf style suited her, so much more feminine than the boxy style of the war years. She liked her new hat, although she'd given up wearing hats when chairing Canadian Club meetings and been criticized for it.

She'd thought of sending her story to *Holiday* magazine in the States, along with water colour illustrations, but *Maclean's* was closer, and as she was going to visit Dr. Robins anyway, it was worth going against the advice of the writers' magazine (mail your manuscript, include an SASE and a brief letter listing your credits, etc.). As she'd written Fred, you probably could count on receiving one hundred rejection slips before you broke into print. Edna hadn't had that many, but she'd had her share, and here she was, in person, wearing her hat and spiffy new dress.

Maclean's was probably Canada's favourite magazine. It was nothing like the news magazine of today, but printed in a large format with original art illustrations. The magazine published fiction as well as non-fiction by writers like Farley Mowat, W.O. Mitchell, Bruce Hutchison, and Morley Callaghan, names that have become Canadian icons. Edna was aiming high, but many of these writers, including W.O. Mitchell, were just starting out, too.

She had likely never heard of Pierre Berton, one of the editors who would read her first submission to *Maclean's*. He would become associate editor of the magazine in 1952, and he would be for Edna an important mentor, teaching her how to cut and stressing the importance of the first sentence ("Put everything into the first sentence and don't lose any of it"), for instance.

"Pierre would never let anyone change my stuff. My style was so distinctive; no editor was going to write into it."

He would later write that Edna was one of the most graceful writers ever published by the magazine. "She wrote so beautifully … she was so eloquent …"

Might she see the editor? she asked at the kiosk upon arriving at the *Maclean's* office. Sure, that would be Scott Young, on the sixth floor.

Young, "young and very sure of what he wants," looked at her hat and thought, Damn not another little cutie from the Pen Guild, but he was pleasant and said he'd read her work. He'd let her know in a week or two.

Edna was hopeful, but not actually too concerned; she was "too busy thinking about her book," which she was rewriting yet again. She didn't like the beginning, thinking it was too stiff and slow-moving with a flashback to "the girls" (she wasn't mentioning the Baileys) at Ingonish.[69] She'd already spent about three years on the book and had written hundreds of pages.

She'd learned so much more on the second trip to Neil's Harbour. Now the manuscript was changing once more. She hated all the "I felt" and "I thought." She squirmed at all the "nice, kind, goody-goody comments." Would she ever be finished?

After leaving *Maclean's*, she meandered over to Eaton's and discovered a new Cape Breton book by "Somebody Walworth." The two pages about Neil's Harbour were all wrong; the picture wasn't even of Neil's Harbour. Walworth wrote about the poverty of the place and she was furious, she wrote Robins the following weekend. So, she'd better hurry up and finish rewriting her book. "People who write books based on fleeting impressions made me mad — they are the kind who condemn people on a first meeting — exactly what I am doing to poor Mr. Walworth, isn't it? I guess he hadn't time to go to the Harbour and didn't dare leave out a place that is printed on a map."

To Edna's surprise and delight, *Maclean's* wrote her a week later that they wanted her swordfishing story for their summer issue. They'd pay $150.

Pretty hat or not, she wasn't a cutie from a writing club; she could really write.

"Duellists of the Deep," as the story was called, was lively, funny, personal, and astute for its observation of the people and the details of the fishing trip. Here was a fresh voice, and one writing not about celebrities, but very ordinary people who became special because Edna found them fascinating and real. Edna would become known for writing about these ordinary folks. Others might overlook them, but Edna, with her curiosity and interest in how people lived and thought, and her conviction that everyone was part of the big picture, made readers feel as if they knew these people too.

Yes, she could write, and she had obviously something different to say that people wanted to read.

"I needed to do that," she wrote Helen Kergin in June. "To sell something — it helps my morale ... and most important it has given Keith and other people confidence in me and that gives me freedom to work. K. has always said I'm not a writer till I'm published — so in the August 15th issue I'll break into print." (Actually, the story would appear in July.)

Edna sounded casual about it all, but she had no way of knowing even after the acceptance that the sale was another life-changing event and that the traipse to Toronto in her new clothes — how she liked them — and the meeting with Young would lead to years of productive writing for the magazine and to travel assignments, that the articles would lead to the cookbooks that would make her a household name across Canada.

Cookbooks? She probably would have scoffed at the idea then.

But for now she was still immersed in her life of coping with Keith, and in the spring of 1948 she was thinking not only about the book, but also about John Anderson.

Anderson had asked her to sail with him from Neil's Harbour to St. Pierre and Miquelon, the Magdalen Islands and Newfoundland on his yacht, the *Alicia*, and she had said yes.

It was a scary prospect: she knew nothing about sailing and John wasn't an expert, either. But it was an adventure, a respite from Kitchener and all the troubles with Keith. She always felt like a different person when she was away, carefree and light-hearted. The idea of sailing to different ports where she knew no one with John was irresistible. They'd write when they weren't sailing, cook on a Primus stove, and share the work.

John was eleven years younger than Edna, who was forty-two. People assumed she was fifteen years younger than she was and she didn't enlighten anyone. She had no intention of running away with John, who was somewhat of a snob, or of leaving the house she loved, but here was a chance for adventure and happiness.

Keith was all for the trip; they'd tell people she was sailing with friends.

Keith had spent the fall and winter practising his piece for the symphony and Edna had taken art classes from Ralph Ashton (sometimes she wondered whether she should be a writer or a painter). Keith managed to stay sober until after his performance — it was a great success, but he was drunk for a week after.

In May 1948, he began attending Alcoholics Anonymous meetings.

Edna kept her real feelings to herself.

She was "proud and pleased" and "would not have minded" staying home all summer,[70] but Keith urged her to go; he wanted to beat drinking on his own.

"Opportunity doesn't always come so attractively," she wrote Helen, downplaying her interest in John, saying he was "the most impersonal man" she'd ever met. And what was she doing, going sailing? She had no experience, and the boat was so small there wasn't even a toilet or a place to store clothes. She'd be just like another man to John, and furthermore, Edna had just read the new *Kinsey Report* and mused to Helen that John might be gay.

She had lots to learn from this trip though, and she was living the life of a hermit in Kitchener, just walking downtown to the library and going out with Keith occasionally. She was like Katherine Mansfield.

"I mustn't let myself go soft and afraid to go on difficult voyages. I worried terribly about going with John — people will talk if they find out — but I'll have to take that too."[71]

Dr. Robins didn't approve of this new adventure.

And how did John really feel about her?

She wrote about how she felt in unsent letters. "I must be honest — I am not a sexless person but I have a certain decency and dignity — I cannot change. Sex for me must have a halo around it. By that I don't mean marriage but I do mean Love. If I am not loving I cannot be free or unafraid."

He was tender, sometimes, in the intelligent letters he wrote: "The lamp is lit but there is no one coming up the path with love and laughter and lightness of heart."

They shared ideas about writing, recommended authors and lent each other books.

Like a lovestruck teenager, she dialled his number when she was in Toronto. She was nervous about it, because he'd made her feel that, unlike in Neil's Harbour, in Toronto she'd be like "a bad, poor and dirty little boy peeping through a knot hole in a fence at the king's coronation." His mother answered, chatted about "her favourite subject" and invited Edna to visit.[72] She didn't — not that she wasn't curious — but John wouldn't have liked it.

It was hard for people, for John, too, to understand her situation at home. It was a terrible dilemma. She was cemented in an unhappy and unfulfilling marriage, bound to a man who spurned her but who threatened to kill himself if she left. If she left him in the house, she might lose it. And how would she support herself? She had no money, no job. It was seventeen years since she'd taught school.

One wants Edna to leave. Divorce was possible — Nort and Helen had problems, too, and would separate the following year when Helen left and married someone else, even though they had a daughter, Linda, who was brain-damaged from birth and in an institution.

Edna was never afraid, loved adventure, and was not conventional, but she never took the initiative or risk of saving herself from the misery of life with Keith. She was only forty-two, still young enough to have a child or two. Keith's threats of suicide were real:

he had swallowed pills twice, left notes, and once Nort had to keep him from jumping out of a hotel window in Montreal.

But what of self-preservation, concern for her own life? Would she really have lost the house? It was in her name; her father's estate had funded the mortgage. She loved the house, yes, and everything in it, but was it enough?

Edna didn't ask about John's feelings or intentions, but wrote longingly, poignantly, and poetically, imagining she was back in Neil's Harbour. The letter, although fanciful, left no mistake about her longing as she imagined Neil's Harbour:

> I've just been down to the dock with some of the old men and a mess of codfish that they've brought in and of course from there it was no trouble at all — much too little trouble really to run up the road to your path. That's bad, you know. I shouldn't do that in day-light — if you found out I was there your work would be interrupted and my work would be neglected.

She quotes his words to him:

> In your letter you said you were lonely. "The lamp is lit but there is no one coming up the path with love and laughter and lightness of heart." And perhaps even as you wrote it I was on the path — perhaps I was at the window tho I think not — not that night — I didn't see you when you were writing to me. But very often I have looked in the window. I have seen you writing… I have seen you reading… I've seen you bang a book down on the table… I've watched you light your pipe while you've been thinking about your work. I've watched you shaving — rubbing your hand over your chin after you finished, looking a bit wistfully at the top of your head in the mirror; I've watched you washing your clothes, making toast, drinking coffee.

> I've often had to duck behind something so you wouldn't bump into me on the path when you went down to the Dowlings or the Rideouts.
>
> I've always been at the window when you come back and lit the lamp. This is the time I've liked the best — felt most secure... every time I came in the daylight I knew I shouldn't be there, that I should be working... But in the evening I came joyously — as you said, with love and laughter and lightness of heart. I don't know how many times you've let me share your lamplight with you, and the warmth of your fire and your heart, your books, your music... I have come every night but I have knocked only a few times...
>
> I don't want to trouble you, John. I think your work is good and fine and important. I respect it and love it and I love my own. It is your reason and my reason for living...
>
> Together, perhaps this summer we will be doing it on the *Alicia*. Oh I love to think, to dream of the *Alicia*, though sometimes she frightens me a little but that's because for a moment I forget that you are there in charge of her — and of me. I trust you completely.[73]

It was hard to concentrate on the book as she waited to fly to Halifax in July to join John. She sewed curtains for Keith's bedroom, pyjamas, and dresses. John said to bring the minimum of clothes — just a sweater, an extra pair of slacks, running shoes, heavy socks, and only one dress. He told her there wasn't a lot of room to store stuff, so she shouldn't bring a trunk. One or two books only, please, and she could use his typewriter.

They'd leave Halifax on Saturday, July 26, and sail down to Hubbards where they'd anchor and go dancing at the Shore Club. They'd buy the last few things on Monday and Tuesday and then be off. John was as excited as Edna was: "Dammit... how can I be practical when I'm as excited as you?" he wrote.

Edna wrote John in June that she'd just sold a poem to *Poetry Canada* and that she'd applied for a passport.

She was to leave on Monday for Halifax. On Saturday, she had her holiday clothes laid out on the bed in the guest bedroom, ready for packing — "so close I was to becoming whatever I would have been if I'd gone with him, a thoroughly pleasant person although not quite conventional" — when the telegram came: TRIP IS OFF. MOTHER IS VERY ILL AND I MUST COME UP TO BE WITH HER. LETTER WILL FOLLOW. LOVE JOHN.[74]

Edna was shattered. "I feel now as if a wonderful vista which I have been contemplating for months had suddenly disappeared and left a void. I was all set to go," she wrote Tom Glover.

Keith wanted her to go away anyway.

"Keith wants me to go immediately to some other place — I've thought of Greenland or Ireland — but getting there would be a problem that can't be solved quickly. I shall wait to hear from John before I do anything."[75]

Anyway, before she could decide what to do, she had to entertain two of Keith's AA friends that same afternoon. There they were, in the house since breakfast, with all "their restlessness and frustration and bitterness." She was so tired, but she had to feed them — alcoholics, drunk or sober, "kept long hours." She wished the strengths of their program could help her, but it was hard not to doubt John's honesty, hard not to feel broken-hearted and to concentrate on everyday things. The men must have seemed like monsters out of a bad dream as she scurried around preparing dinner.

Was John telling the truth? Was his mother's illness just an excuse?

He wrote, apologizing that the trip was never meant to be.

His mother had lost one eye to TB as a girl; now the other eye was threatened and he was called home. But his sister was home from England and staying with her until the end of August. There was talk of an operation — but later — and John was soon returning to Nova Scotia to sail the *Alicia* on his own. Why couldn't Edna come? Because he had to have the boat hauled out of the water at the end of August, and in the meantime he was determined to salvage something of the trip, which meant sailing day and night, in all kinds of weather, and he didn't think Edna was up to it.

So there. He was still going to Newfoundland, but without Edna. He felt as if he'd ruined her whole summer, he wrote.

John didn't want her, and Keith (who wouldn't even kiss her) wanted her to go away — somewhere, anywhere. But she couldn't get a passage until the late fall. She could've gone to the Harbour, but seeing the *Alicia* there would be too sad.

She felt disappointed and frustrated. What should she do? she wondered, as she contemplated her new clothes. All those tender feelings, the poetry of her letters, the anticipation of the trip reduced to shorts and sweaters, to deck shoes and sandals piled neatly in the spare room.

The friendship with John was not over yet, however. Letters continued, and sometime the next year she met him in Toronto when she accompanied Keith to a conference. She asked John to take her dancing and they went to the Palais Royale. Edna wore a brown taffeta dress with black braid she'd bought at Holt Renfrew.

After the dance, they were in the hotel room when Keith came in. Edna introduced them. Keith didn't mind, but John obviously did because although he and Edna were supposed to spend the next day together, he didn't turn up. To save face, Edna told him she'd met someone else who made her feel like a princess. It was a lie. The someone was John Craig, a handyman, and only a friend, from England who belonged to a writers' group in Kitchener.

In 1949 John Anderson sent a brief, handwritten note that he'd met someone in the Bahamas and was getting married. Around the same time, Tom Glover wrote and said he was getting married, too. Glover died a few years later, and she only spoke to John one more time, when she called him on an impulse to tell him that Cecil Rideout from the Harbour, whose cabin John was renting, planned to visit him in Toronto. John wasn't pleased at the prospect.

After the letdown about the trip with John, Edna somehow coped. Many women would have been severely depressed, but perhaps Edna thought of Robins's concept of "the spiritual Algonquin" and the idea she'd shared with him about "the inner lamp" — a glow inside that spread to others — but it must have been hard. Go or stay? She was still tempted to flee — anywhere — but she didn't know what to do.

On July 21, she drove to Toronto with Norma and her husband, Ralph, and saw Mr. Anglin at *Maclean's*. She was upset because they'd cut nine pages out of her twenty-four-page manuscript and she saw the editing that had been done on it.

"We had fun," she wrote Robins.

> Mr. Anglin — the assistant editor is a darling; he wants me to send him more material on Neil's Harbour or anywhere. After I left him I felt very excited and sure that I'd be a regular contributor to *Maclean's* — but since then I've done nothing but think of three stories I want to write but I've written nothing — except an opening paragraph yesterday morning when I went out to Homer Watson Memorial Woods — I must take you there some day. The trees have straight trunks that go up and up to a ceiling of filtered green. The ground below is covered with a rosy beige carpet of old leaves. There is a stillness and grace and beauty there that I have found in no other place.[76]

Here was "the spiritual Algonquin" — a peace that found resonance in the observation of the world around her. Heartbroken, she did not pull the bedcovers over her head, but gazed outward. She never lost this ability; she had trained herself in this, she wrote her mother years later, during the divorce from Keith. The world was wonderful and it was better to cast her eyes at the beauty than to dwell on her inner misery. Doing so involved not only logical thinking, but a resolute will.

Edna did not put away her holiday clothes until August 21. She had finally decided to stay at home and "work like hell."

A strange new person had helped make up her mind: Walter, an ambulance drive imbued with Culture, who had a part-time job cleaning for the Staeblers. He almost pushed her onto a ship for

England or Ireland, and when she wavered he suggested she get out a map of Canada and pick any old place.

When she hadn't picked a place and said the stories she wanted to write "troubled [her] more than the trip," he said, "Mrs. S. You have made up your mind, you and your typewriter are going to spend a happy summer together."

She wanted to enter the *Maclean's* short-story competition; she had three stories she wanted to write, one about the "Wurchels" (really the Georges), the "disreputable family next door … the idea behind it will be that childhood prejudice and blind spots cling through our lives"; another about a bachelor, Bill, at Neil's Harbour; and one about the love affair of twins.

She really did seem at peace and marvelled at the dew on the grass: "individual sparkles; it seemed that every blade of grass had blown a tiny bubble at its tip." On the way downtown she noticed a funny old lady: "she wore grey lisle stockings and the whiteness beneath them couldn't have been anything but long underwear … Then I saw a woman with a bouncing bosom that looked as if all her belongings had been stuffed down in front of her bright purple dress." She admired the flowers at the market.[77]

"I should try to balance all this glory with solid work on my story this afternoon." She was writing about "Laura" — "so terribly innocent and trusting and eager… Creating a character is like being in love and I think now that quite a bit of my beings in love have been creating characters — the made-up ones are safer. Perhaps now that I've made a start I'll be able to stick to them and not let myself become entangled with live people who don't always act the way I dream they would — but still experience is rather fascinating, isn't it?"

And perhaps it was fate that she had not gone with John. "But what the hell? Why am I talking about it?" she wrote Philip Knowling. "It's over and it didn't happen and I stayed home all summer and worked on my writing. I decided if I am going to be a writer I have to make myself learn how to write — then go on a trip… but not till my Neil's Harbour book is finished."

Chapter Eight
She Knew She Was a Writer

Publication made all the difference. She knew she was a writer, that she had been a writer for years. She had sent stories out, collected rejection slips, written bits and pieces about the ideas and images that filled her head. And all those letters, sent and unsent, exploring her feelings — was there anything more vivid than the letter to Anderson about walking down the path?

She had found her passion in Neil's Harbour and started writing the book, typing and retyping, arranging and rearranging, returning to the Harbour physically and in her mind and writing and publishing poems about the sea:

"Moonlight" (*Saturday Night*)

To enjoy the sunlight
So in Neil's Harbour one does not
Look at the Moon
But becomes absorbed by its gleaming
On the living water.[78]

"Prelude" (*Canadian Poetry* and *Montreal Gazette*)

The sea is gray as the cloudy sky,
gulls fly over the land
rises then falls behind the waves
fishermen sit idly
on the grass in the lie of stages
women walk with arms and fingers
modestly straightened against their thighs
as skirts cling and billow

children like leaves blown across a common
run gaily down the road;
chickens resent the twisted feathers
giving them fan-shaped sails;
cows lie unperturbed by fences,
flicking flies with switchbroom tails.[79]

The poems weren't as strong as some of her letters, but Dr. Robins had praised them. No one else paid much attention — maybe because poetry didn't pay? She tried to write *Cape Breton* like poetry, concentrating on each line and choosing images carefully:

> Close to the eastern horizon soft folds of cloud were shaded with purple, saffron and slate; through narrow slits the rising sun made paths to the water; fishing boats crossed the spots of gleam like phantom silhouettes; the sky overhead was the blue of heavenly morning glories; coming swiftly from the mountains tattered masses of mist joined the clouds above that were gold.[80]

But the book was private — no one had seen it except for Dr. Robins — unpublished, but demanding hours of work. Was this when Keith said, "You can't call yourself a writer until you've been published"? And when her mother made the comment about a writer needing talent? People who weren't writers did not understand. John Anderson understood writing, but he had let her down, and Dottie Shoemaker at the library loved books, but Dr. Robins was the only published author she knew personally.

Probably all that writing (typing) in her room mystified Keith and the neighbours who came calling. Edna never turned anyone away; she never said, "I'm busy writing, come back later." People were more important than art and she didn't want to hurt the neighbourhood kids, especially the Huttons, who came by to make cookies and play games.

Around this time she even took on a piano student, "Little Jesus,"[81] whose mother was poor and couldn't afford proper lessons. Then there were the convicts and alcoholics who came for talk and encouragement and meals. Fred was often there — he was writing too and wanted Edna to read his story.

And sometime during these years Louise Cress moved into 51 Simeon for a year while she had a new house built on Albert Street in Waterloo on the lot John Cress hadn't wanted her to buy.

Edna turned none of them away. She was a writer, but there were meals to get, people to entertain, curtains and dresses to be sewn. Perhaps it was inevitable that family and visitors saw Edna's writing as a hobby, a more eccentric one than sewing, but still a pastime, something for her spare time.

But here was publication, and in a national magazine, too. And she was paid $150, a lot of money in 1948, more than a month's wages for an office worker. The solitary trips to the Harbour — such an unusual thing for a married woman to do in the forties — hadn't been self-indulgence, then. Keith and her mother could no longer say she wasn't a writer. Not Virginia Woolf or George Sand, but a member of the small group of Canadian writers who wrote for magazines. And maybe, soon, she hoped, author of a book as well. Only about 150 Canadian books were published yearly in Canada.

Cape Breton Harbour remained her real concern. She did not want to be a journalist, she wrote Dr. Robins, although she sent a story to the *Maclean's* competition.

It was hard to maintain discipline though, she wrote to Dr. Robins:

> Every night I'd come here to my room and think, Now I shall write, but I'd feel too dull, too sleepy. I've been in bed at 10 every night except last, when Keith entertained — and every day I've been working and couldn't let myself indulge in anything so pleasant to a friend. I'd better stop talking about it or I'll be making excuses… you know there are none.
>
> I started earnestly working on the book after I sent my story away. I have no hope at all by the way.

> It needed more thoughtful care than I knew how to give it when I wrote it.
>
> I started again at the beginning of the book, and have now, in 3 weeks, rewritten 112 pages — too quickly I'm afraid because I am too eager, and too determined to finish it. I have a tendency to want to spend as much time and thought on almost every paragraph as I would on a poem. The result is a lack of unity. I'm afraid still that what I have done is meager, a thin surface, and yet I think I want that. In the beginning that is all I saw. Only time could give depth to the experience — or could it? Should it have been there at the start?
>
> I have gotten rid of the artist. I have not yet naturally been able to introduce another man to talk to. I must be lonely as I was lonely. I am no longer afraid of the book — it will grow somehow, I think. I'm still not sure of its form: it is not a novel, nor is it factual; it is rather like an album of snapshots taken on a holiday.[82]

Dr. Robins was encouraging, but didn't think she should introduce another man; she wasn't writing a romance. He thought for sure she was on her last draft. He advised against too much reworking.

"Get it off your chest and [get] on to something else."

In January Edna went to Toronto and saw three publishers. Macmillan was among them; she knew W.O. Mitchell from *Maclean's*, and with his wife, Merna, he had come to Kitchener to speak to the Canadian Club and suggested Edna take her manuscript to his publisher.

The editor, John Gray, and Bill Mitchell took her out for lunch. Edna referred to Gray as "God."

> I told Mr. Gray I had never imagined God looked like him and he said publishers were not that important but I assured him that to writers they must be.

> He was very nice and Bill Mitchell of course was darling. Mr. Gray said he'd heard only very nice things about me — from Bill, of course, and that made me nervous — like a movie that's had too much boosting. Anyway, I called for Bill and we went down to the King Eddie for lunch at 12:30 till 2:30 — all that time we talked about the book and art in Canada and writers' agents … I'm afraid I was too anxious to be very bright. And I won't know until JUNE if they want it or not … If I hadn't had Bill's help and gotten my book to Gray himself … it would have taken at least six months … Gray seemed quite keen at lunch because Bill kept saying the nicest things about it that roused his interest.[83]

She and Robins were both hopeful. His faith in the book was justified, he said; there was "flesh on the skeleton and a good blood circulation." He was anxious to see the book published so Edna could write something else. She had so much material, and just as importantly, Robins wrote, she had the ability to breathe vitality into what she wrote. Furthermore, the writing and rewriting of this book had been like an apprenticeship, and she had taught herself a great deal, learning lessons that woudn't have to be repeated. "And that's something, let me tell you."[84]

A few months later, Macmillan turned the book down. Canadians weren't ready for regional writing, and they feared the book would not sell enough copies — and their standards were high.

Dr. Robins commiserated. Look around for another publisher, he said — another "taxi stand. In my judgment still, the You in the book is the most valuable part of it."

It was disappointing.

But then Bill Mitchell introduced her to "Mr. Berton," a gangling six-footer Edna felt a bit in awe of, at *Maclean's*.

Berton proposed an article to Edna: a story on the "horse and buggy" Old Order Mennonites. Did she want to write it? Edna demurred; Yes, but she really needed to work on her book.

Didn't she understand that *Maclean's* was assigning the story? Mitchell asked. This didn't happen every day, especially to a new writer.

Edna, a bit reluctantly, accepted the assignment.

She knew little about the Old Order, despite a shared ancestry, beyond what everyone in Kitchener-Waterloo knew from seeing them at the market where the women sold *Kochkase* and summer sausage.

How could she write about them? She had written "The Departure," but she knew she had many facts wrong; she had just made things up.

Maybe she could live with them for a bit? It was a novel idea and one that set the pattern for all the articles that followed: she lived with Hutterites, miners, Italian-Canadians. Not everyone would want a stranger living with them for the purpose of a tell-all story, but there was obviously something about Edna that inspired trust and a wish for friendship.

It was the same quality that drew neighbours, friends, alcoholics, and ex-cons to her door: Edna knew how to listen, she was non-judgmental, and she made people open up. It is the way she still is, forgetting herself and recognizing that everyone is part of the same spiritual force. This is reflected in *Cape Breton Harbour*:

> Being alone, I was afraid to be friendly when I arrived here. Now I tell myself: "They are people, they eat and sleep and wear clothes and are afraid and lonely and angry and shy and curious just like me." If I keep remembering that, I seem to understand them; if I look at them and listen to them, if I am completely absorbed and aware of them, I feel natural and happy and free, and they laugh with me and accept me and I am fond of them.[85]

The result was not, strictly speaking, objective journalism, but rather a view of the world through Edna's eyes: a sharing of the wonder she saw and felt, a result of "deep thinking" that came after

Edna wrote pages and pages of notes about the people others didn't think of writing about.

She would write down everything, and even develop a system of listing hobbies, religious beliefs, work, food, and so on — everything she thought pertinent. Often she would start writing longhand as she thought through ideas and themes; finally she would use the typewriter, going through many drafts before she was satisfied. An article might take months to write, and although she felt free to rearrange events and tell a true story with fictional techniques, and names might be changed, she was a stickler for accuracy (still is; a journalist erred in calling her big living room window a picture window; it is not a picture window!). She took hundreds of pictures on assignments, not only to go with the article, but to remind herself of small details.

She was always afraid of hurting people's feelings. "Pierre told me, 'If you're so afraid of hurting people's feelings you won't be an honest reporter.' … I knew I had to think deeply enough [about people I was writing about]. I was so careful. I was able to go back to any of them twenty-five years later," she says.

The folks at the Harbour hadn't been put off by Edna's notebook and she hoped maybe the same might be true of the Old Order, even though the horse and buggy people kept to themselves; being separate from the world was a tenet of their faith.

She made enquiries at the general store in St. Jacobs, not yet the touristy place it is today, and they told her about the nearby Kraemer family who lived on their ancestral farm.

"Salome and Livvy were in the kitchen and I told them I wanted to write about the Old Order. They said people said things about the Old Order. I told them I'd let them see the article first. They checked with Dan, who was in the barn, and they agreed I could come on Monday.

"I had a room with a straw mattress on the bed. Dan said, 'I think you'll find out about us, but we'll find out about you. Edna, you got a lot of old Mennonite in you yet.'"

Edna lived with them for a week.

She called the Kraemers "the Martins" — Martin was a popular Mennonite name — and the story she wrote about them has the charm of a Christmas card:

> Prosperity smiles on the Martin house from its great painted barn. Beauty surrounds it: gentle hills form its horizons; its fields slope to the maple woods along the curving Conestoga River. On the day I arrived, fruit trees beside the house were snowy with blossom and daffodils bordered the neatly fenced yard.
>
> Bevvy, the mother, and David, the father, live with their three children, Salome, sixteen, Lyddy Ann twelve, and Ansey, seven in the big house; the grandparents lived in the attached "doddyhaus." They have electricity but no car, radio or telephone. The house had no ornaments or pictures and they wore the standard Old Order garb of black collarless clothes for the men, long plain dresses and bonnets for the women. Children quit school at around fourteen. Everyone works hard, the men farm, the women bake, cook, preserve the bounty from the garden, sew, quilt and look after the children. They find strength in their beliefs and family and are pacifists. They take no money from the government, attend church services regularly, and look after their own. They are always prepared for visitors on Sunday; any number might drop in and expect to have dinner, but the cellar is filled with rows and rows of preserves.[86]

It was a different world from Edna's messy personal life and her writing life, too — a big sin for Mennonites is pride — *Hochmut* — and Old Order members must follow the dress and living regulations (for instance, the girls admired Edna's red apron; she offered to lend them the pattern but they wouldn't be allowed to wear it, they said) — and Edna's desire for book publication and recognition was not something an Old Order person would aspire to.

She honestly portrayed the restrictions in the Old Order way of life, but at the same time she shared the quiet contentment she found among them as they sat on the porch after supper, for instance, with "the scent of honeysuckles and blossoms, the sound of frogs near the river."[87]

Her Old Order friends added a lot to Edna's life, sharing their appreciation for small, everyday things. Their obvious contentment appealed too. She never changed her clothes or interests to accommodate them, and as Nancy Martin, Edna's longtime friend, said, "Edna has been a wonderful friend."

The Kraemers obviously liked what they read (and Edna had glossed over the subject of bundling, a sensitive issue). After her assignment, she visited the Kraemers for dinner every few weeks for years. If Livvy didn't see Edna for a while, she'd contact her, asking if anything was wrong.

These dinners led to a later article about Mennonite cooking, which eventually led to the *Schmecks* cookbooks.

Edna had no way of knowing this then, of course. If she didn't want to be a journalist, she certainly didn't have the remotest idea of writing cookbooks, although in these busy years she joked to Robins about writing a cookbook for people who were too rushed to cook.

The article, published in the April 1, 1950 issue of *Maclean's*, was well received locally and elsewhere. She received "quite a procession of fan mail — mostly from farmers in Saskatchewan or somewhere who used to live around here and who told me their whole family history."[88]

Her father-in-law, Leslie Staebler, wrote a letter of congratulations in Pennsylvania Dutch: "Ich hab dye G'schichte gelazed wass doo gescriva hasst fer selly mackascene *Maclean's*. Ich habs so feel geglicha daws Ich hab my awlte frynd, da Eph Weber g'schriva." (I read your story in *Maclean's* magazine and liked it so much that I wrote my old friend, Eph Weber).

Ephraim Weber sent along praise via Leslie: "She has made a delicate job of her delicate material. Will you … please give her my jolly congratulations upon getting the article to read so genuinely that the editor of *Maclean's* couldn't resist it."[89]

Edna's personality must have seemed engaging to readers, too. In the biographical information accompanying the article, she comes across as a breezy, tongue-in-cheek sort of person who doesn't mind making fun of herself — and one who knows how to promote herself, too:

> After I graduated I worked in a library, in a bank, a newspaper office. I taught in Ingersoll for a year, was fired. I operated my late father's spring factory till I sold it because I was too busy by that time getting meals for F. Keith Staebler and myself as well as planning and building a house, braiding a living room rug (10' by 15'), making my clothes, knitting, playing with our dog and talking a lot.

After detailing all her committee work she goes on:

> Four years ago I fell in love with Cape Breton and started to write a book abut it. To convince my friends and relations that I wasn't crazy because I sat in front of a typewriter instead of going to afternoon teas I rewrote a few paragraphs and sent them to magazines as poetry. Some were rejected but a couple of them sold. I wrote an article on swordfishing and *Maclean's* published it in the issue of July 15, 1948.
>
> I have a cat named Minnie, my husband sells insurance and has played the piano part of Gershwin's "Rhapsody in Blue" at a Kitchener Symphony Orchestra concert. He has hundreds of friends and our house on Simeon Street is usually alive with them and the neighbours' children.[90]

"How to Live Without War or Wedding Rings" had the highest reader interest of any *Maclean's* article that year. The writing was vital and fresh, and the contents must have appealed to Canadians who had just gone through a war. Here was another way of life, a life of calm contentment, a life without fighting.

By the summer of 1949 Edna was back in Neil's Harbour after a side trip to the French island of St. Pierre. She wanted to write about St. Pierre, but thought she'd try the *Saturday Evening Post* before *Maclean's*. The *Post* would provide a bigger audience for the island "so badly in need of something that would give it a lift … I don't want to be tied to *Maclean's* nor do I want to be a journalist — except to defray expenses I might have in travelling around. *Maclean's* doesn't seem inclined to do that for me — (But I'll be very happy to let them have my St. Pierre story if the *Post* says no). Aren't I being cocky? But damnit it, I think St. Pierre deserves the best," she wrote to Robins.

She loved St. Pierre and Miquelon, islands near Newfoundland that are owned by France. St. Pierre was not yet the tourist spot it would become, but it was lively with the engaging French and with foreign fishing ships. It was another country, foggy, rocky, and treeless, but there was dancing; red wine appeared at meals and shops sold French perfume liqueurs. Her article, "Isles of Codfish and Champagne" would appear in the November 1, 1950 issue of *Maclean's*.

She travelled to St. Pierre via St. John's, Newfoundland, and had an exciting trip back from St. John's in a heavy sea. The food was terrible, Edna was seasick, the captain and chef were drunk; the chef terrorized the crew one night and kept them in the wheelhouse with the threat of a straight razor. She was glad to be back in Neil's Harbour, "shabbier and friendlier than ever."[91]

Back in Kitchener, Keith, not drinking now, had found religion. There were Bibles and tracts everywhere, and it was hard for Edna to get to work. The John Howard Society sent a troubled young man, John, to live with the Staeblers; Edna's cleaning woman, Mrs. Turtle, fell down her cellar steps and broke her neck just before Christmas; Nort, divorced from Helen, stayed for the weekend with a new girlfriend. There was Bill, another protegé of Keith's, who broke into their house and stole Keith's clothing. He was released into Keith's custody but stole money and watches at his boarding house.

"Keith's soul-saving activities involve me rather completely and not unpleasantly," Edna wrote Robins. "I like the men who come here; they are so earnest, so eager, so interesting and their hopes are happy. It is wonderful to see them growing from the sodden, despairing people they have been to the truly vibrant, creative ones they will be."

Edna still wanted to save the world. But it all took time and concentration away from her work. Writing the St. Pierre piece was difficult:

> I've been acting like a stuttering stage struck temperamental actress. I've made hundreds of starts — all of them seeming to be good to me when I made them but the moment I reread them I drew back knowing that I'd have to begin again, till I developed such fear and loathing of the thing I must do that it was agony for me to even try to think about it — my neck was stiff, I had a headache, I woke up feeling tired. And why? I know now it was my attitude towards my work was not right — I was trying to force it. Then I'd tell myself I must let it come to me — just relax and let it come. I'd pretend I was in a boat in a fog — knowing that St. Pierre was not far away but hidden from me and I must just rest quietly till the fog cleared and it would appear and I'd go straight towards it without any effort at all — just sail it. And that is where I made my mistake — I wasn't willing to make the proper, relaxed effort that was needed to get to the island. I didn't want to row. I wanted the wind to take me there without me moving a muscle and so with my writing — I must make hundreds of starts perhaps till I find the right one — but I must make them with a happy feeling that I am going in the right direction and will eventually arrive — that only by trying with the enthusiasm that first prompted me to want to write about it. If that enthusiasm is lacking, I might as well give up. I must write from a full heart — because it is fun — like doing a puzzle — finding exactly the right word, phrase, the right way of putting them togeth-

> er. It is not hell — it is wonderful and thrilling to be able to do it. Amen.[92]

This wasn't a journalist doing a snap-up travel article, but a writer who considered her work wonderful and important; she agonized for months over "Codfish and Champagne."

It was March before she sent the story to the *Post*. Berton of *Maclean's* asked her for something; she sent him a few outlines of ideas. "I don't know if I should turn him down altogether to write my book and try some short stories but it seemed kind of smug and high hat to turn down what most writers dream about — being asked to work."[93]

The Post rejected "Codfish and Champagne."

The rejection made Edna feel she should be writing fiction "instead of trying to be journalistic. I'm not good at organizing factual material."[94] She also worried about hurting people; a fisherman in Neil's Harbour had objected to something she said in the swordfishing story.

She was rereading the *Cape Breton Harbour* manuscript. Now she felt there was too much self in the book — she was always "butting in." Should she introduce a lost love? Love of place could be a substitute for romance. She could fictionalize herself, make herself younger with "cloudy black hair and wearing red sweaters."

She asked Robins if she should leave it the way it was and try another publisher.

No romance, no strange man, Robins advised.

It was discouraging when *Maclean's* returned her St. Pierre piece, but a note suggested she rewrite it in the first person, like her Mennonite article, she wrote Helen Kergin.

She was tempted to chuck it and get on with the book. She was reading Sean O'Faolain and W. Somerset Maugham's *A Writer's Notebook*. Fred was causing problems, and she was tired of 51 Simeon Street.

"Everywhere I turn there are Bibles and books about how to be a saint and I try so hard and feel so guilty because I know any suggestions of wings I feel are completely phony."[95]

Religion or not, sober or drunk, Keith was still impotent with her. If only she could get away — Ireland or England or back to Nova Scotia and Newfoundland, or to the West Coast or Mexico — but not until the book was finished.

But she had to make a couch cover, sew pyjamas, make a gingham dress, see about shoes, buy a wedding gift, lengthen four dresses, wax the linoleum, mend sheets, plant geraniums. She listed the chores for Robins, and on the other side, like a ledger page, she wrote: WRITE WRITE WRITE.

Why had she inflicted upon herself the agony of writing a book? she asked.

"So I write nothing but a stilted, stumbling story about Neil's Harbour."

But she finally took another draft of the St. Pierre story to *Maclean's* on June 16, 1950, and actually shook hands with Pierre Berton. *Maclean's* accepted the article in August. The story was in the first person, the way most of her future articles would be written.

The Staeblers had gone to Round Lake up north and Edna planned to leave for Neil's Harbour, but her back had been bothering her and the doctor insisted on taking x-rays, which showed that a bone in the sacroiliac region slightly overlapped another. It was troublesome, not serious, but the following week the doctor sent her to the hospital for a "slight female operation" and insisted on doing a hysterectomy.

Why? "He said I needed it," she says.

Edna did not seem unhappy about the surgery, being observant and friendly after the first day of post-operative pain. She entertained her visitors and enjoyed "Miss Lily Wisdom," a practical nurse who told her wonderful stories that Edna wrote in her notebook. She was dying to put down new ideas she had for stories and recorded cards, flowers, and gifts. Glads from the girls in Keith's office and the Presbyterian Church; rosebuds and vase from Dottie Shoemaker; two pounds of Laura Secord chocolates from her mother… The list was long[96] and Edna did not seem at all unhappy when she wrote to Dr. Robins about her hospital stay. "The sad thing" was that her cat, Minnie, broke her front leg.

Now she could never have a child of her own, but she was forty-four; it was eleven years since she and Keith had had sex and they hadn't been able to adopt because of Keith's drinking. She had nieces and nephews she loved, and the neighbourhood children, and her writing life had finally begun. Had she had young children, she would not have been able to go alone for weeks to Cape Breton, or anywhere else. But if she felt disappointed or sad, she kept it to herself.

Any secret sorrow she may have felt must have been eased by the thrilling news in September that she had won the Canadian Women's Press Club Award for best story for "How to Live Without Wars and Wedding Rings."

Aggie Brubacher, who had been the maid at Spetz Street, had come to look after Edna after her hospital stay. Edna was in the bathtub for the first time after her operation when Aggie brought her the envelope. She received a two-hundred-dollar prize and had won over Mavis Gallant, Marjorie Wilkins Campbell, and June Callwood.

"Isn't it amazing?" she wrote Robins.

Winning was wonderful for Edna, giving her the confidence in her own work that had been lacking. Years later, when she endowed the Edna Staebler Creative Non-Fiction Award, overseen by Wilfrid Laurier University, she would remember just how much the award meant to her.

Canadian Press, *Maclean's*, and the *Record* sent photographers; people wired and telephoned congratulations, and suddenly she was a star, feted at a luncheon in Toronto and interviewed about her writing.

A Toronto paper called Edna a "Kitchener housewife who writes in between household chores."[97] The *Record* forgot about the household chores and quoted Scott Young, one of the judges, and the man who'd accepted Edna's swordfishing story, but who was now a freelancer: "I feel that Mrs. Staebler did a remarkable job in getting the feel of the Mennonites' home, showing that humour and wit and girlish pride and a certain saltiness of the soil can exist simultaneously in an environment which most people would not consider warm enough for these elements. Mrs. Staebler wrote with wit, warmth and insight."[98]

She is grinning with happiness in the photo. And why not be happy? Keith said he was hiring a housekeeper. Her mother phoned all her friends and called Edna's writing a good hobby and thought she should drive down to Mexico and write about that (but advised Edna not to tell reporters she'd been fired from her teaching job in Ingersoll, a fact already shared in the bio in *Maclean's* a few months earlier).

Keith was impressed with all the photo-taking. The only way he ever got his picture in the paper, he said, was when he paid for an ad.

"Anyway, winning an award certainly kept me excited for a while and was the most wonderful way imaginable of forgetting about an operation."[99]

Maclean's was so pleased about the award that they were rushing the St. Pierre story into their November 1 issue. They wanted more of her work and proposed a story about a barge going through the Chambly Canal to New York.

Edna still didn't want to become a *Maclean's* writer but "still, if it hadn't been for their publishing my work I'd have had nothing published," she wrote Robins, and she packed to go.

Her real interest remained her book. She was going back to the original beginning:

> Golly… I think working at it again is really going to be FUN. Every time I have any sort of literary success I feel as if I've earned a bit more freedom to write more and be more myself, not in an assertive way, but just less fearful, more confident, and yet I wonder if I'll ever feel SURE of anything. Life fluctuates in such an alarming but interesting way. Today I feel as if I'm being swept along on a tide — very pleasant. But I know tomorrow I must make an effort again to get some real work done.[100]

Chapter Nine
Bursting to Write

The fifties was the last decade of Edna's marriage.

It was a busy ten years. *Maclean's* sent her on more assignments; she returned several times to Cape Breton; she went to Europe three times by herself for months at a time.

Here she was, a new woman, consolidating her career as a journalist (but she didn't want to be a journalist; she wanted to publish her book, and she dreamed of writing fiction). Talent vindicated, her name recognized by the 450,000 readers of *Maclean's*, she attended the Canadian Authors' Society convention, where she met writers from across Canada — Farley Mowat, Thomas Raddall, and Vinia Hoogstraten.

But still.

Two photos: the happy, grinning Edna Staebler, winner of the Women's Press Club Award, and another, a couple of years earlier, a most unhappy woman. In the earlier picture, Edna and Keith are at the Leisure Lodge nightclub in Cambridge, started by Helen Waimel's brother, Olaf. Keith, handsome and laughing, has his arm around a smiling, unnamed woman with dark hair. Helen is chic, very European, in her fashionable coat and styled hair.[101]

Edna sits apart, hugging her elbows. Has she made that blouse with the nice little collar herself? There's no promising writer here, only a sad wife trying to go along with things. There's no inner lamp or sparkle; her face is pinched.

Did she often look like this with Keith?

Here she isn't the woman who chaired committees or introduced speakers at the Canadian Club; she isn't the spunky lady left on the side of the road in Cape Breton, or the woman imagining herself moving hopefully along the path to John Anderson's cabin. She isn't anyone's fairy princess, and she's not the cheerful U of T student with a million ideas in her head; she's not the girl with the filled dance card, just a sad, dowdy wife.

At home she continued entertaining and looking after the house. She was chairman of the library board and still with the Canadian Club. She accompanied Keith to AA meetings, joined a group of women whose husbands were alcoholics, cooked for his friends, and had an ear for anyone who came to her door. She loved hosting her annual Christmas party, baking the familiar cookies, decorating the house with pine boughs and lights.

When she was away, she hired housekeepers to cook for Keith, and their relations and friends had him for meals; she wrote him long, descriptive letters from wherever she was and continued to express her gratitude to this most understanding of husbands for allowing her to travel and work.

But her absences caused talk. What had happened to Edna? They already talked about her because she refused to wear hats to Canadian Club meetings and now she left her husband alone.

All of it was pretty unusual for a middle-class wife in the proper fifties when women stayed home to raise families while husbands worked to provide the money.

And then there were her three trips to Europe— a woman unescorted, not even travelling on a proper package tour but taking off on her own. Keith went to Florida in 1954 for six weeks while Edna sailed to Europe.

Some gossiped that it was because of Edna's relationship with Philip Knowling that they had separate vacations. Knowling often visited the Staeblers, who took him around to cocktail parties where he misbehaved, getting high and insulting. Might Keith be jealous?

At the time of the award Keith was not drinking, although the respite was only temporary and the years ahead would bring breakdowns and hospitalizations. Now he "looked wonderful and except for occasional lapses when he is overtired he is like a different person," she wrote Helen Kergin in June of 1950, but Edna and Keith still did not have sex and they were no closer except occasionally in letters.

"I always feel that I fail you miserably ... [but] I have my work to do," she wrote Keith in 1951. "That I must love more and more all the people and things that come my way in the world, all the strange and not understood or explained people I must learn to understand them ... [but] there will always be that conflict for me. I don't know how to resolve it. I must do the best and just accept it."

The tenets of AA helped: one day at a time, trust in God — "God is love." She was also determined to choose thoughts that were "kind and loving and true" rather than being glum and worried about Keith.

"Put up or shut up," a friend, Mardi Robinson, advised Edna when she lamented about her problems with writing.

She clung to the idea of being loving in the years ahead. "I really believed in the power of love and loving. I wanted to be a loving person — God is love — I would meet some people who would be naturally loving — I wasn't naturally like that — I had to learn it — I tried hard to learn... I'd be in despair and write through to the belief that love was the important thing... thinking about people and seeing them from their point of view."

It was this spirit that made her writing so different, and she tried to see Keith that way too and overlooked love letters from other women she found in his clothes, under his pillow. One woman, twenty years younger than Keith, had a three-year-old child and lived in Vancouver. Keith paid for her divorce and fell apart when she found someone else; he ended up being hospitalized and Edna was sympathetic. Would he leave her? She didn't really think so. He said he'd kill himself if she left him, and they had a kind of arrangement: "Keith realizes more and more the need of letting me live my life as I know it must be lived," she wrote Knowling in 1951. She put up with Keith's drinking and affairs; he "allowed" her to go away by herself. He told people he was proud of his talented wife.

All she could do was love him unconditionally, not nag, and be supportive. If only he would stop drinking, she fervently wished. He would go to AA, then tell himself he could handle a few drinks, and soon end up on another binge. Fellows in his office sometimes found him passed out in the morning and drove him to the hospital.

And yet, he was still helping so many people, and being so generous with Edna. His letters to her when she was away were affectionate; he missed her, worried until he heard that she arrived safely. He praised her descriptive letters.

But it was all ending, this familiar life of being Mrs. Staebler.

The "life as I must live it" was her writing.

She finished the canal barge story and sent it to *Maclean's* in December 1950 — it hadn't taken that long to write — and was happy that *Maclean's* asked for only a few small changes.

It was a tragic trip; two sailors fell overboard and drowned. She was unhappy, however, when the editor, Eric Hutton, wrote, "The Captain wept," making Edna's story seem much nicer.

"It made me so mad. I was there, I knew what I was doing when I wrote about the two men being drowned. … I didn't say that [the captain wept]. He was a short, stocky little man, proud as anything. After the two men drowned, the others wanted to be promoted right away. It was really quite nasty on the way back."

Edna was anxious to return to the book, she wrote Robins, but wondered if she should try a short story for an American magazine; it would help to sell her book.

Forget the story, Robins replied, and get back to the book; if she waited too long she'd have to rewrite it because she would be changed — she was growing all the time as a writer.

Edna listened, although she worried about disguising the people, remembering the fisherman who hadn't been pleased with the swordfishing story. She had learned to turn facts into story in the articles, but if she changed names in the book who knew what else would end up being different? "Honestly, I'm bursting to write fiction — but scared too — like stepping off the earth into space."

On earth, she was becoming known.

In February she gave her first paid speech to the Burlington Arts and Letters Club for ten dollars and expenses. She talked for an hour and loved it.[102]

Later that month, Gerry Anglin, formerly of *Maclean's* and now the new editor of *Chatelaine*, asked Edna to write for the magazine. He wanted her to do a story a month, go and stay in people's homes and write about them. Bill Mitchell thought she should do it, but Edna told Anglin she was "adequately provided with a living by my husband so I can be more interested in trying to do good work than a lot of it; also if I am in Simcoe or Sydney I'm away from home and I'd rather see some of the country. So he asked me where I'd like to go and I said Prince Rupert — and the east coast. He said he'd try to arrange it… but we'll see. I like to do a bit of tripping around — but I want to finish my book first."[103]

Berton wrote too, wanting a new article for *Maclean's*. "Aren't I popular?" But she really wanted to work on her book.

In March she went to Florida with Keith and their friends Charlie and Marnie Henderson. It was fun, but she felt they saw only "the surface" of things and it was a different Atlantic from the Atlantic at Neil's Harbour. She was heading that way in July to work on another story for *Maclean's*. She longed to be alone and to write.[104]

In the meantime, she wrote to Macmillan to see if they were still interested in the book; Gray wrote back cautiously: they were still interested but market conditions had deteriorated and they'd had to curtail the number of books they published, but please do send it.

As always, she was glad to be back in Neil's Harbour with the Ingrahams. She wasn't sure what her article would be about. Berton had suggested making a comparison to city life, and that was a possibility: the Ingrahams were the way they were because of their environment. She fiddled with the idea, writing a few pages, and enjoyed herself by hitchhiking around and visiting the Buchanans, who were Scottish and, unlike the fishing families, subscribed to the *Atlantic* and enjoyed discussing literature and religion — they wanted Edna to write about the Scottish people of Cape Breton, going to the wharf with the children when two boats came in, she wrote Keith.

Keith hoped she'd be home in time to go to a party at the Hallmans. Could Ed send him a wire about her plans? He didn't know if he'd be invited on his own or not. Isabel, the housekeeper, was looking after him and Minnie, the cat. But he understood Edna's need to be in Neil's Harbour, saying he thought Edna could probably be more herself there than anywhere else.

He wrote sadly about the funeral of his friend Peter, who died estranged from his wife. He cried a little at the cemetery; the grave looked so lonesome. Peter's wife didn't come to the funeral. It was hard for him to understand such coldness in the face of death.

Affection was still there, more easily expressed in letters than while they were together.

Edna replied, "I'll love you lots when I come home and always I am really grateful to you for letting me be here and be myself — and not having to worry about it — too much. The family notices a big difference in me."[105]

She couldn't make it home for the party. She wanted to be there when the photographer came to take photos for her story. Clara May was "scared to death" and wanted Edna to stay and it would be "mean if I didn't."

Edna had found her story at last. Clara May's twenty-year-old daughter, Maggie, was moving to Toronto.

Keith was right: Edna was happier at the Harbour than anywhere else, and the story she wrote, "Maggie's Leaving Home," shimmers with happiness and joy. Here was Edna's genuine voice, one of wonder and love for the people and the place she was writing about.

The story is simple. Maggie, the twenty-year-old daughter of Clara May and Henry Ingraham, the fifth youngest of their thirteen children, wants to leave her small village for the wonders of Toronto. Maggie's married sister, Eva, is already up in Toronto and writes about the pleasures of city life. Naturally, Maggie dreams about Eaton's and Simpson's and the "warm and rich and exciting" city life. There are no big stores in the Harbour, there's no electricity, no newspaper delivery, and outside news comes by way of a battery-operated radio. Maggie works as a nurse's aid in the small hospital, the only job she can get if she doesn't want to clean lobsters. Most of the girls her age are married and some even have babies. There's little for young people to do in the village except walk up and down the road and go to the dances.

Naturally, Toronto beckons. But home, as seen through Edna's eyes, is rich too: the hundred little houses beside the sea and the cliffs and the Ingraham house in the centre of a rocky field. Everyone "likes to gather in the enormous kitchen to be with Clara May, whose heart is as warm and crackling with affection as the fire that burns in the shiny black stove. There is always someone sitting on the rocker or the wooden lounge … there is a grandchild begging for a cookie."[106]

Maggie's a cheerful girl, full of life, and oh, she's looking forward to the city. Maybe she'll learn hairdressing. She can hardly wait to order whatever she likes in a restaurant and maybe she'll tell people her name is Marguerite. "'Oh, Maggie, don't talk so. I don't know how we'll get on without you,' her mother laments."[107]

> On the morning of Maggie's departure the sun shines — on the prairies, the highways, and all the quiet places where venturesome youngsters leave home. It shines bright in Neil's Harbour. Lines from lobster traps are hanging over the fence rails to dry …
>
> Two brand-new travelling bags labelled TORONTO are waiting in the Ingrahams' front hall. The family is in the kitchen round the breakfast table. Henry sips his tea and says, "It was quite a family when all thirteen was at home. We used to need twelve barrels of flour a year, now we'll only need four."
>
> "Ewart thinks Maggie will be home again, don't you, Ewart?" Clara May says hopefully.
>
> "Lots went away and came back to Cape Breton," Ewart consoles her.
>
> "I won't till I get a car," Maggie says. "Unless I come home for Christmas."
>
> Good-byes are casual, but Clara May's eyes fill with tears as she stands by the window. That night, when Ewart came home for supper, he said, "It seems like a fall day, don't it?" And Henry, when he came, said the same.[108]

Edna catches all the poignancy of young people wanting adventure despite the love of family and home. It's an intimate and tender telling and Edna's affection is open and candid. As good as she was at describing a place, the sense of wonder was just as strong, maybe stronger, in observing and showing the powerful, tender bonds of family.

It was all so far removed from her own arid life with Keith. Is it any surprise Edna did not rush home to the Hallman's cocktail party?

In September Edna took the train to Alberta. Pierre Berton had suggested a story about the Hutterites; he'd heard there was very little mental illness on Hutterite colonies. Could Edna look into it and write an article for *Maclean's*?

Edna was a natural for the story. The Hutterites had similar Anabaptist origins to the Mennonites, but followed the teachings of John Hutter and lived communally. Each family had its own sleeping and living quarters, but they ate, cooked, and worked communally.

Edna wanted to live on a colony while she did her research, the way she'd lived with the Old Order, but she had no idea if the Hutterites would have her. But she'd never been to Western Canada and going to Alberta would give her a chance to visit Bill and Merna Mitchell, who were living in High River. She loved the Mitchells' company and enjoyed all the writerly talk with Bill.

"You've no idea, Bill, how talking to you peps me up about writing and makes me feel the urgency of sticking at it and not worrying about not doing all the things that everyone else seems to expect of me," she wrote the year before. Mitchell understood her desire to write fiction; he wanted her to write *Cape Breton Harbour* as a novel. And she felt less intimidated by him than she did by Berton, confiding, "Don't tell Berton but some of the anecdotes I used were created in one way or another but I composed them to show certain facts."[109] She hadn't been too pleased how Berton had rewritten some of her first story, particularly his use of "I."

Edna and Keith also had friends, the Bells, who owned a lodge at Waterton Lake, and Edna stayed with them for a few days before getting on a bus to McGrath, a small town near the Old Elm Hutterite Colony.

How was she going to meet the Hutterites? She had no idea, but on the bus she overheard a young woman talking to the driver about the colony.

Edna wasn't shy.

"Excuse me for eavesdropping, but do you live on the Hutterite colony?" she asked.

The woman did. Nadine, a young Mormon, had family in McGrath but lived on the colony, where she was a teacher. Sure, Edna could stay with her until her husband returned from his two-year mission in a few days' time.

Things just happened, she wrote Keith:

> Hello dear, I'm sitting here on a little quilt out on the grass beside the school teacher's house. It's one of those lovely clear but hazy summery days. I love it here on the colony. Everyone is kind and eager and curious. Of course the children are adorable … There is a little boy standing here, his name is Benny and he is eight years old but only three feet tall. He is very cute. He is wearing a mauve patterned flannelette shirt with green buttons, a black cap and trousers. When Nadine calls the roll at school all the children answer "Here" but Benny says "Dere."[110]

This is the voice of wonder observing telling, enjoyable detail. Another person might have found the colony dull. Edna did not enjoy some of the food, in fact, and how they ate greasy duck with their fingers, and she found the idea of lifelong communal living restrictive, but she delighted in what she saw: the bright clothes. Like Mennonite women, the Hutterite women covered their heads, but their clothing was more colourful. After work everyone dressed up and the men shaved. People pressed wine on her (even for breakfast) and everyone wanted Edna to visit. She sang for the school kids (including a German song, "Du, du liegst mir im Herzen" — You, You Are in My Heart) who quizzed her about her life. She enjoyed the ducks and geese, which "formed a convoy going south, just like ships in a harbour." She liked the old maids, "ages twenty-five and twenty-eight," she roomed with, although she was smothered by a feather bed and wool quilt. The preacher had warned her against taking pictures — this was forbidden — but everyone pestered her to have photos taken.[111]

As with other people she wrote about, Edna formed lifelong friendships, and one Hutterite, Joe Wurtz, now an old man, still writes to her once in a while. "I've become a vogue," she wrote Keith, and when she visited years later people remembered her at once, even though she had spent only a week with them.

The article she wrote, "The Lord Will Take Care of Us," paints an immediate picture of the colony and also of Edna's enjoyment — and involvement.

> They asked my age. They asked dozens of questions about where I had come from. They gave me a carrot to eat. They posed while I took their pictures and begged me to take more, although picture-taking is supposed to be sinful.
>
> They showed me around the colony. We went first to the building with the dining room, the bakery, and the cement-floored kitchen with its propane stoves, then to the wash-house where the women take turns doing their own family's laundry. We went to a pond to watch a thousand snowy ducks. ... They showed me a pen for hundreds of pens, a model barn where thirty cows are milked by machine, a spotless white dairy ... The little ones reminded me that the smallest member of a Hutterite colony is an owner of all its wealth.
>
> In the shade of a long white building two couples with babies sat on little painted stools. The women's faces were plain, their eyes bright.[112]

"Ike" drove her back to McGrath; people tittered at his homemade suit — many resented the Hutterites and their prosperous farm — but, she writes, back at the colony:

> He laughs as he helps the carpenter build a new chicken barn, is proud as he watches the erect, measured gait of the colony's women, the waddle of the fattening geese, the combines that cut through the grain of the colony's acres. And when the lamps are lit in the evening and his folks gather for conversation and singing he settles on a bench in the corner and enjoys the peace of his homely retreat from the bewildering world.[113]

Edna knew she could never live on a colony — what about her wanderlust? — but it's obvious she has experienced wonder: look, look at this, look. John Gray, the editor of Macmillan, recognized Edna's special talent, too, but he was still unable to offer a contract when she met him for dinner with the Mitchells in Calgary. He had just decided against her submission of yet another version of *Cape Breton Harbour*, but said Edna could come and see him when she got back to Toronto. He thought the provincial government should establish a trust fund to help publish regional non-commercial books. He told the Mitchells it was "heartbreaking to turn down a book by Edna Staebler."[114]

Edna stayed with the Mitchells for five days and she was exhausted at the end of them. Bill liked to stay up until three in the morning, telling stories and yelling, "Damn you, shut up!" if anyone interrupted. He slept till noon and couldn't understand why everyone was so tired the next day.

The Mitchells wanted Edna to return the following year and write about Bill for *Maclean's*.

The Mitchells pepped her up. She wanted more than ever to write fiction, and surely all those who read her articles in *Maclean's* must want to read more by her. Being published by a big magazine in the U.S. would help, too.

In November she and Keith flew to Philadelphia to visit religious friends he'd met in Bermuda, and Edna dropped into the office of the *Saturday Evening Post*.

The *Post* never published her, but she had the "germ of at least fifteen stories that are bursting to be thought about and written about and it takes time and solitude and tranquility to work at them."[115]

It was another dichotomy: the practical business of being a writer. She had the practical advice given by all those writers' magazines on one hand, and the solitary pursuit of a passion that was not a business at all but a way of life on the other.

Chapter Ten
Europe

Dr. Robins died on December 18, 1952. His death was a great loss to Edna. On the first anniversary of his death she wrote in her journal:

> I've switched the light on at the foot of my bed; on the wall behind my bookcase is my photograph of Dr. Robins, smiling his quizzical smile. But to me he is as vividly alive as if I had seen him yesterday. Still I have missed him many times. I have wanted his confidence and his gentle admonishings. I have sometimes forgotten that I never lacked his affection and faith in me, that I have his spirit always to guide me.
>
> He wanted me to think for myself, not be dependent on him. He wanted me to feel that I have the intelligence and ability to do my own thinking and to make my own decisions, to take the consequences of them — right or wrong. He made me know that I must write and work hard at my writing and that I can do it and must do it extremely well — not because I am wonderful but because I've been privileged to experience wonder.
>
> He has made me know that I must never stop looking for magic and beauty and love. And I must share what I find in my writing.
>
> He has said I was the most unafraid person he has known. I must make that true.[116]

Here was the marriage of wonder and writing, not the glib advice handed out in writing magazines about markets and sales. He encouraged her work for *Maclean's* but never lost faith in her book, despite all the setbacks from publishers.

The book: it was still the book, well into the fifties. Lippincott expressed interest and an editor came to speak to Edna; sometime in the fifties she and Dottie Shoemaker took a trip to New York and Edna went to the Lippincott offices. But they wanted drastic changes: an unhappy woman who is transformed by the Harbour.

Macmillan didn't think it could sell enough copies and suggested Ryerson Press, which also turned the book down (someone there asked why Edna didn't write about what she knew). Edna sent the manuscript to a contest at the *Atlantic Monthly*, and *Cape Breton Harbour* was a finalist but did not win.

"I've seen and heard nothing but Christmas cards from Ian [Sclanders, the new editor at *Maclean's*] and Pierre since the last time I was in Toronto — September 27th," she wrote Philip Knowling in January 1954. "I'm rather glad they haven't asked me to do anything for them because if they did tempt me with something I couldn't resist the book would suffer. I turned down the Cheese piece and maybe they didn't like that. But I'm not worrying. They'll probably be writing me one of these days and if they don't, so much the better for the book."

She finally put the book away, but never lost the hope she and Dr. Robins had for it. His picture still hangs in her bedroom and she often thinks about him, just as she did in the months following his death.

"I read [the letters] over and over to make their thoughts my own, just as when I was troubled about something I would try to think how you would answer my question about it and act accordingly. I hope that I know you so well that I would have few doubts."[117]

In March 1954 *Maclean's* sent photographers to 51 Simeon Street to take pictures of Mennonite food for Edna's story, "Those Mouth-Watering Mennonite Meals," which would appear later in the spring. Edna cooked the food herself. The photo shows her in a frilly, flowered apron, looking serious as she butters a baking dish. White collar and cuffs, ruffled curtains: she's the cozy homemaker, but dinner of red pickled beets and soup and sausage over, she was leaving for a vacation in Spain.

The editorial accompanying her article mused that Edna would soon have a Spanish story for them; they joked that she had some Hemingway in her.

In May 1954 Edna went to Europe alone. Not the aproned housewife, but a jaunty traveller with a sturdy tweed suit for all occasions. She planned to stay for two months; she was away for three months.

Why not? Dr. Robins had said she was the most unafraid person he knew, and she had been wanting to go overseas for a long time. "One day at a time," a friend told her. Another friend, Dr. Reaman, author of the *Trail of the Black Walnut*, "an old boy" who used to drop in to see her to discuss writing, had long advocated travel for Edna. Knowling urged her to go, and Keith didn't mind; he was off to Florida for six weeks with his friend Archie.

The year 1954 started badly. Keith had often been drunk in the fall and around Christmas Edna discovered a lump in her left breast, but luckily it turned out to be benign. On her birthday, January 15, someone called her from London to say that Keith was "spending his nights with a girl who is 25 unmarried and greedy to get a man with a big car who would take her on trips to Florida." The caller wanted Edna to put an ad in the *London Free Press* telling what had happened.

What was she supposed to do? She could either accept the situation or get a divorce. She knew she couldn't stop him from philandering and she couldn't demand that he love and caress her, but she also didn't want to lose her home and the life she'd built, although sometimes she longed to escape 51 Simeon Street and the golf club crowd.

The answer was to put her faith in God, to keep on being loving, to not feel sorry for herself. She must be "grateful, grateful, grateful, for a billion things — the stars in the sky, warm blankets, good food, kittens and children and snow and my car [she bought her first car that year], and Keith who is really a darling and fun and kind and bright-eyed and warm and affectionate and clever and full of compassion and deep understanding for so many sad and lonely people who ask him for help. God save him."

She was taking the high road, but she only slept for three hours on her birthday night. And then Knowling visited and the gossip was hurtful to her: Betty[*] said "she couldn't stand being in the same room with Knowling and they all said he needed a bath and his hair needed cutting and his clothes were awful and they all hated him and called him my boyfriend and everyone said Keith was going to Florida because he couldn't stand the situation in his own home any longer and it was time someone told me what people were saying."

Everyone seemed to think Edna was the guilty party; no one knew about Keith's affair with the twenty-five year old.

Gossip even reached Edna's sister Norm, whose "stitch and chatter club was buzzing and virulent and poor Norm had to defend me… I wish I'd simply ignore the whole business and females and get at my work and not bother with petty bickering and small opinions."

Keith was mad when she wanted to leave a cocktail party. Edna was "so bloody damn sick of a lot of things and people that I'd like to leave tomorrow on a long trip where I could see mostly nothing but sea and sky and birds flying and boats."

Edna booked passage on the *Queen Elizabeth II*, sailing out of New York on March 6. She planned to return May 6.

Away at last from the gossip of Kitchener, away from Keith and his drinking and infidelity. Almost fifty years later, Edna still talks enthusiastically about that first trip to Europe and remembers everything about it. Eyes sparkle, and new memories come: had she told me about the gondola ride in Venice?

Europe was wonderful, and an eye-opener. Edna said later that before Europe she was "strictly local." She'd never had wine with her meals before (and still doesn't know much about wine; later she failed the wine section of the Stylish Entertainment course she took at Rundles Restaurant in Stratford), for instance.

She had just turned forty-eight but looked much younger with her slim figure and reddish hair. She had $1,500 with her — her own money — and a big black wooden suitcase, heavy to carry (she bought a brown plaid one in Spain and filled it with the straw hats, among other things). She had no plans, no itinerary, just freedom, and who knew what would happen?

She toured most of Europe in the three months she was away, going on a tour of Spain, travelling to Greece and along the Mediterranean coast, visiting the major Italian cities, Germany, Switzerland, England, and Scotland (which she toured with Kath Reeves).

She didn't keep a journal, but wrote long letters, sometimes on lavatory paper, and sent them home instead. There was so much to wonder at, to describe.

She started writing down her impressions and mailing them home, sometimes to Keith, sometimes to all the family ("Dear Gang") even before sailing from New York (where, she reported, she purchased pyjamas at Macy's). Edna asked Keith and her family to save the letters for her.

She wrote all the time.

"If only all my time everywhere could be doubled so that I could write everything I see and everything that happens to me immediately after I experience it."[118]

The six-day crossing was rough, "no party on board, people just sitting there." Edna started in a cabin with three other women, but managed to get a room to herself. Rough crossing or not, Edna found the ship exciting. A drunk took her up to first class, where she met Max Aiken, who was going to England "with his mother who was married to a Frenchman, Boris des Boulonges."

The ship docked in Cherbourg, where a lighter took passengers to the boat train for Paris.

Excited? "I could hardly believe I was doing it … I remember seeing mistletoe in trees. I was in the train compartment with a German woman and the French woman who lived in America, and… Alphonse."

Alphonse was a Swiss chiropractor who'd spent four years studying in the U.S., a slender man who spoke French and didn't like speaking German. Edna didn't recall him from the ship, but he remembered Edna and said later that he fell in love with her aboard the *QE2*.

Here was romance — and serendipity, coincidence. And Paris; was she actually there? It was raining in Paris and a man they thought was a porter took off with their luggage. Alphonse chased him and put a hand on his shoulder. "You turn around and take us to a hotel."

Alphonse invited Edna for dinner:

> Bhyrr wine — made from elderberries — and Brie cheese and steak [Edna described the meal in *Schmecks Appeal*] and then we walked along Montmartre where a barker stood outside the Pink Cat. So we went in and sat at the table against the wall and there was a young guy in leopardskin on the stage… we were the only audience. Alph held my hand and kissed me goodnight at the hotel. He looked at the bed and I said, "No, I'm married."

The next day, Edna's back hurt and Alph wanted to treat it. He was leaning over the bed when a cleaning man came in and said, "Get out of here!" But they were dressed.

They walked to l'Église de la Madeleine, the Champs Élysées, the Arc de Triomphe, all those places Edna had read about and seen in pictures. Was she really here, in Paris, with this pleasant Swiss man who found her attractive? It must have seemed unreal and exotic and a million miles away from 51 Simeon Street.

In letters home, Edna called Alphonse "a shy sweet Swiss man." He was slender, with a serious face, dark hair, and a philosophical expression. "Lots of love and don't worry. I am very careful," Edna said, ending her letter.

The afternoon Alph had to return to Switzerland came. "I walked him to the train station at two p.m. and we kissed goodbye. He gave me his address and phone number."

For the rest of her time in Paris, Edna went sightseeing. At the Café Flore, she ordered an omelette every night for dinner, accompanied by a carafe of wine, and wrote in her notebook; she bought French books. At noon she ate a roll on a park bench. She also contacted a Texan, Walter; someone from the boat had given Edna a message for him.

Walter took her to the Lido, then to his hotel, and wouldn't let her leave. Edna asked to have a bath; luckily he passed out while she was in the bathroom.

"A nasty experience… I took such chances."

But it was all writing material. She fictionalized and expanded upon the incident and used it in "Molly," a novella she worked on when she returned from Europe.

After going through Spain (where she met a woman from Brittany, Francoise, who would become a lifelong friend; they would visit each other over the years) and travelling along the Mediterranean coast, Edna contacted Alphonse, who invited her to Switzerland.

It was taking a chance and making a stab — did he really expect her to call? — but it was a chance for… something. Edna, lonely and betrayed by Keith, deserved some happiness and she was unafraid in pursuing it.

Alph picked her up at the station in Lausanne and took her home to meet his parents. Edna and Alph kissed — "it was very, very pleasant" — but Edna left for Lucerne. It was Easter and snowing and she called her mother's house. Keith was there for dinner, and Edna suddenly felt lonely in the foreign restaurant.

She phoned Alph. Flowers were blooming in Lausanne, big beds of pansies. He said, "Come back."

Edna took the train on Monday. "I was wearing the same suit every day so I had it drycleaned. It wasn't going to be ready till Thursday. In the meantime, he drove me around and decided he was in love with me. It was lovely, but it was just a couple of days…"

The romance that started in 1954 was just that, a romance, conducted through letters that have continued to the present.

Edna saw him only in 1954, 1956, and 1958, and only for a weekend or two each time, and he married someone else in 1960. But every Christmas, even now when they are old people, Alphonse sends her a Swiss calendar, reminding Edna of the days she spent with him in the Swiss Alps where they sat in fields of crocuses and drank wine and ate *Brötchen* together.

It was an idealized relationship, and Europe and Switzerland added to its charm and beauty. It was all part of being away, of drinking wine and eating omelettes in cafés while she wrote, of driving through the mountains and taking trains by herself. Edna never contemplated leaving Canada and marrying Alphonse: they were too different — he was too Swiss and she was realistic. "I know the limitations that will always be imposed on our relationship. But I can't help, I don't want to stop remembering and hoping, hoping for more of the joy we have had in companionship and affection," she wrote him when she was back in Canada.

But the glow of being loved by a man who thought she was wonderful was so different from Keith, who stiffened when she tried to kiss him (and there had been a pathetic scene in 1953 when Keith played the piano and Edna danced and danced and then kissed him and kissed him but he did not respond).

"Mon Cheri, I want only to tell you that I love you… and want you and so often wish that I were with you and want you. Darling, when people ask me to tell them the thing in my trip that thrilled me most of the many wonders and beauties, I say, I can think of only one man and one place and every moment we were together and I can't tell them anything at all."

When Alphonse, widowed and in his eighties, wrote Edna and suggested he visit her in Canada, she thought it was better for both of them to remember what had been. Alphonse agreed.

Edna was still in Europe when her *Maclean's* piece about Mennonite cooking came out. Keith sent it to Alph's address — most of his letters went to the man Edna described as "the shy, sweet Swiss"; Keith even kindly mailed her hormone pills to Europe when her supply ran out.

Edna didn't hide her friendship with Alphonse from Keith: "It's been good to stay here and make friends. … Alphonse … who has been so kind but he said people were kind to him when he was alone and a stranger in the U.S. It makes him happy to return a bit of it. He is so shy and inhibited — completely unlike one's idea of a Frenchman."

She wrote assurances to Keith:

> Mme. Thim said last night she thinks I must have a wonderful husband to let me come so far and so long alone and I said he had great understanding of my peculiar needs and temperament. Darling,

> you've no idea how much I appreciate that. It's wonderful for me to feel so free yet so secure and sure of your indulgence. Norm and Mother both told me that you look wonderful...
>
> I can hardly wait to see Sunfish and the flowers in the garden and especially you and all the gang. But I guess I'd better get going and make my ... exploration of Europe complete.

She was in Florence on April 11, Venice the next day: "Since March 28 I've been nowhere longer than a day," she wrote home. "Still I think I'm doing a good thing, seeing much the first time then a little bit later."

On April 26, she attended the opera in Marseilles, and on April 27 it was off to Heidelberg, then to Kaiserlautern to visit Dr. Braun; by May she was in England. May 6 was to have been her sailing date, but:

> Now that it isn't I have moments of being appalled at another whole month from home. Two months is plenty but I know I'd be sorry if I saw nothing of England and the only other sailing date they could give me was May 14, only 8 days longer which hardly seemed worth the extra $70...
>
> Anyway, the 28th it is now and I think it will be good.[119]

She saw Philip Knowling in London. He whirled her "all over London," she wrote Keith; Knowling took Edna to pubs, where she didn't feel she could go alone, but he was the same old Philip, furious when Edna was late arriving at the National Gallery.

Then it was up to Edinburgh with Kath Reeves. "Here at last," she wrote on May 19; she wished Keith a happy birthday on the twenty-second, apologizing because she couldn't send a cable from the small village where she and Kath were staying.

Four days later she wrote that she had bought a ticket to sail on the SS *Scythia*, which would be docking on June 5.

Europe was another life-changing experience. There was Francoise, a new friend, and Alphonse, who provided romantic memories; she had seen so much more of the world, and she felt more sophisticated when she returned home.

Adjusting to the same old Kitchener was difficult. She wasn't home very long before Kitchener held its Centennial celebration, which involved a re-enactment of Conestoga wagons coming to Canada (but it had been much longer than one hundred years since the first Mennonites had braved the trip to Canada) and Edna was on a committee — right back into it. The *Record* published an article she'd written about the history of Kitchener, and she had her first television interview, which she enjoyed.[120]

But she had her old back trouble again, and "everything's just the same as has always been," she wrote Alphonse, telling him she'd had to "get my house in order," and errands downtown seemed to take hours. *Maclean's* wanted her to write about Canadian cheddar cheese, but after the Champs Élysée, how could she care about cheddar cheese, which only reminded her of Swiss fondue "and sitting across from you at the table and loving you."

Instead of cheddar cheese, she thought about writing about German immigrants. There had been a large influx of German immigrants into Canada after the war, and many of them settled in Kitchener. Ironically, the German culture that had become dormant after the First World War was rejuvenated after the Second World War. German clubs flourished, and once again German was heard on Kitchener streets. However, Edna never followed up on this idea.

She wanted to write about her European trip — Pierre thought she should (and what a trip it must have seemed to Kitchener people, who asked Edna to speak about it; and she did).

But how could she write factually about what had happened to her? Fiction, her old love, was the answer, and she started writing a novel about a character called Molly, an innocent and but man-crazy woman from Inglenook, Ontario. She described her in a letter to Helen in November 1954:

> She is naive, tender-hearted, curious, contradictory, makes excuses and is dominated — to some extent by the platitudinous up-bringing of mamma. She goes abroad seeking Education and Culture — she says — but is much more acutely aware of all the males that come within her orbit, assessing each one as a possible mate for herself — and never finding one who is just right — mostly because they are married or don't fall in love with her. I think I can have fun with her. …
>
> Her adventures can be amusing and not unlike many of my own which I couldn't tell too many people and a few others thrown in for excitement … When I came home I was most excited about Europe and unhappy because I didn't know how to put it down. Now I should be able to get it out of my system.

She started writing "Molly" in the summer, and *Maclean's* wanted to publish it in installments, but it didn't come off. Edna planned a second book about Molly, set in Ontario, but she never finished the first — and what a shame because it is irreverent, sassy, light-hearted, and over the top. Molly comes alive today, a young woman whose adventures with strange men show gullibility and naïveté; the feckless fearlessness of the heroine is charming. It pokes fun at small-town Ontario. Oh, Mamma wants her to marry George of the feed store and Mamma buys her long warm underpants so she won't get sick in cold and foreign Europe and hadn't she better accept George instead of gallivanting around Europe?

Molly has inherited a thousand dollars from Uncle Albert and she won't be dissuaded from her trip to Europe in search of Art and Culture, but is she ever disappointed at first by the lack of eligible men on ship. No dukes or lords or millionaires and the only men who wear dashing uniforms are the pursers.

Stuck in a cabin with three dowdy women, Molly strikes off on her own and comes across Bob Lewis, an engaging drunk and cousin of Sinclair Lewis, who decides to get off at Cherbourg with her. But there's also Lord Alfred, a barmy poet who says he wants to marry her *tout de suite*. Plus there's the nice Swiss man, Andre, whom she meets in the boat train to Paris.

It's all wonderful and crisp with fantastic dialogue:

> "You are not attentive, my deah," [Lord Alfred] said sort of peevish. "Have you no interest at all in iambics?"
>
> I shook my head no.
>
> "Perhaps you prefer the hendecasyllabic? I've never attempted to restrain myself to that extent. Won't you tell me of your experience?"
>
> I said I hadn't had any.
>
> He sat up quite excited. "You mean you don't write verse?"
>
> I said no.
>
> "But you must, surely. Think of Sappho and Christina Rosetti and Elizabeth Barrett Browning. I would hardly have thought your blood ran less swift and passionate. You don't mean your hair is like fine gold, your tresses are gold like the gold of the honey-pot, your brow is like Limerick china, perar-lescant; your eyes..."
>
> I got up and made for the door, but he beat me to it and closed it and leaned against it and wagged his fingers at me. "No no deah, you must never leave me. We'll go straight home to Ballyduff and we shall be married on Monday."[121]

In Paris, "gay, free, wonderful, wicked and beautiful Paris," she dines with the nice Swiss, who like Alphonse orders Bhyrr wine.

After Andre leaves for Switzerland, Molly naively delivers a message to a rich Texan who escorts her to dinner and to a night-club where almost naked girls danced. The Texan is crude and hot and before Molly knows it she is in a taxi on the way to his hotel. "I'm telling you kid, you're with SOMEBODY."

"He slid closer to Molly and put his arm around her, saying, 'But don't let it throw you… I can be just an ordinary Joe. You don't need to worry about bein' out of your class.'" He tried to kiss her "with his shining wet lips." Paris.

"'Dr. Ramsey,' I said, very cool, 'you forget your degree.'"[122]

Luckily, he passes out in the hotel room while Molly has a nice bath in his private bathroom, no such luxury existing in her modest hotel.

Edna knew how to use material.

It's too bad that she did not finish the novella — she did not know how to end it, for one thing: should Molly end up with one of her European paramours or return to Inglenook? Edna didn't like the latter, but couldn't come up with a resolution.

But it's a bright and shining piece of writing, not comforting at all, but showing wonder through Molly's eyes as she sees Normandy and Paris. It's tart, and like *The White Waistcoat* of the thirties, it pokes fun at small-town convention, but Edna had become a better writer and a wiser woman with experience of the world. There's something fey here, in almost the tradition of Irish writing: light but knowing, but told with Edna's own voice. And the dialogue is marvellous.

It's written with gusto and enjoyment and not contrived or tailor-made to suit a particular market. Maybe if Edna had finished and published "Molly" her writing would have taken a completely different path. The sauciness of the voice was unlike the heartfelt voice of the magazine pieces about the Old Order and Hutterites. Both voices showed wonder, but "Molly" is more playful and might have led to quite a different reputation for Edna. And who knows where that would have taken her?

Today she wonders how her *Schmecks* fans would react to the novel. But who knows, perhaps the cookbooks would not have appeared if "Molly" had been published. The prim Edna Staebler wearing an apron in the photo accompanying "Those Mouth-Watering Mennonite Meals" (even if she did tell *Maclean's* she was off to Spain) does not seem like the sort of person who would write "Molly."

Was she being cast as too nice, as in the canal barge story when they'd cut the gritty parts? The article about Mennonite cooking would lead to the cookbooks, but perhaps it was as if the stage had been set, as it was with the 1954 Conestoga wagon business. Waterloo County was becoming, and would be more so, known as a Mennonite place, all warm and cozy, almost forgetting that Anabaptists had once been murdered for their beliefs.

Edna's cookbooks would contribute to the ambience, and to the perception of her as mainly a cookbook author, leading a professor to say, "Edna almost created Waterloo County."

Edna was less successful with "The Blue-Headed Cat," a short story she wrote around the same time[123] and sent to *Colliers* magazine, which rejected it, saying it was contrived.

Katherine, an unhappy wife, has just finished "her routine morning housework" and is reading a story about "an unfaithful husband."

Since she'd come home from Europe three months ago she'd enjoyed reading about infidelity. Sometimes she caught herself almost wishing she'd find "her faithful old Stan guilty of a slight indiscretion: it would ease her conscience about Alfio."

Ah, Alfio. The bright star of the package tour to Europe, as a companion to Stan's old Aunt Bea. Three hours of bliss with Alfio, "handsome, gay, ardent, on the cushioned seat [of the gondola] by her side." He'd called her "Carissmia mia," "his voice like a caress." "'To t'ano,' he had whispered, 'To t'ano, I love you.'"

Katherine closed her eyes, remembering, and when she opened them, she noticed the figure of the blue-headed cat Alfio had given her was missing.

Oh dear. Only Stan could have taken it. "Sudden fear" stabbed her. Had Aunt Bea found out about Alfio and alerted Stan? Stan was always "insanely jealous," but once she thought it over, she realized Stan couldn't have known about Alfio; poor Aunt Bea was asleep that night.

Did Stan have a girlfriend? Had Stan given the blue-headed cat to his new woman?

She accused Stan of taking the cat and he denied knowing anything about it. What the devil would he want with a blue-headed cat?

Katherine says she'll believe he has no girlfriend if he returns the cat. Stan becomes suspicious. Who gave Katherine the cat anyway? She has always hated cats.

Oh boy, he is going to see Aunt Bea and then he'll contact his lawyer. Off he goes.

Katherine is "dazed" and finds — guess what? — the blue-headed cat under a chair, "its white whiskers grinning."

End of story, and except for some good dialogue coming from old Stan, the story *is* contrived and unbelievable.

But "Molly" and "The Blue-Headed Cat" would have surprised a lot of people.

Chapter Eleven
The Last Years as Mrs. Keith Staebler

Alphonse hoped Edna would return to Switzerland in the summer of 1955 — they could go camping in the mountains — but Edna decided to stay at home and "work like hell" to earn more travel money.

Maclean's had assigned two stories: a piece on the Six Nations reserve near Brantford, and an article on a Black ("Negro") settlement, New Road in Nova Scotia.

Sunfish Lake provided a consolation. The year before, Edna and Norma had bought a piece of land on Sunfish, a few miles outside of Kitchener, and hastily had a cabin and dock built so they could go swimming and picnicking. Edna loved the place. It was a "godsend," she wrote Helen, and soon she was able to swim around the entire two miles of lakeshore. It was a wonderful escape from the city in the warm weather. With the big cedars and the forest on the other side of the road, you'd almost think you were in the bush.

She hoped to build a proper cottage there, but Keith wanted a bigger house in town. Kitchener had grown to fifty-five thousand, the University of Waterloo was being built, and there was even a shopping centre, the first in Kitchener, going up just a few blocks away from Simeon.

That year, 1955, had started poorly. Keith was still seeing Dr. Harris in London but working very hard. Nort caused distress. He had remarried in 1954, and a son was born on Edna's birthday. Nort had a breakdown the same day and was well for two months, but in May was committed to the psychiatric hospital in London.

In February Keith went to Florida by himself, and in March Edna attended a Rotary convention with him in Hamilton ("dull as hell," she wrote Helen). Keith, preoccupied with Nort and his problems, was drinking.

"Molly" wasn't going well. Edna had completed sixty pages by the end of February, and was wondering if she should scrap it. "It's no damn good and yet I think it could be." Pierre Berton had just told her that Bill Mitchell had sold "275 scripts of Jake and the Kid to an American TV corporation for $1500 apiece. Multiply that out. And he will continue to write it for the CBC and probably will continue to sell it to TV." A "Jake" book was coming out that fall. "So apparently IT CAN BE DONE," she wrote Helen.

While Edna thought about "Molly," she worked on the Indian piece, digging up background information and going out to the reservation, where she stayed with a couple for a weekend. People were kind to her and she found the history absorbing, although she wasn't crazy about eating corn soup. She was supposed to have the article finished by June.

And then Nort died tragically on May 7, after a few days in the hospital. He walked away from the hospital and was struck by a car at two in the morning after trudging along for eighteen miles on the wrong side of the highway. He had massive injuries and died two days later.

He was only forty-two, and a talented musician, concert master of the K-W Symphony, and an active member of the K-W Chamber Music Society.

Keith felt awful. "Nort suffered so horribly and without sedation because of the nature of his hurts," Edna wrote Philip Knowling. "Poor, poor guy. … We just can't believe that Nort won't be coming around anymore, won't be playing his fiddle or chasing up King Street after business, won't be sitting in our living room listening to records and drinking… God we'll miss him."

It must have been devastating for Keith. Nort was his kid brother, five years younger, and they had many things in common: both were dedicated musicians, both worked in insurance, both had drinking problems, and both had had psychiatric care. Keith must have thought about his own life and wondered if he would end up a similar way.

Such sadness. He and Edna were still young, both were talented, both had promising futures, both were popular and liked people, and yet they were so miserable together.

Edna, trying to finish her Indian piece, had trouble sleeping, she wrote Helen. By August, Keith had "two girls on the go."

Edna spent hours on the phone every day with her mother and Norm and thought about the future. "And one day I'll be old and grey and uncertain of where I should put my feet when I go down steps."

In September Edna and Dottie Shoemaker drove to Halifax so Edna could research the "Negro" piece. She loved travelling with Dottie. "Such a darling gal and we had so much fun and I'll be lonely as hell without her," she wrote Keith after Dottie flew home. "The room seems shabbier and quiet and lifeless with no thought of her coming back into it."

They had a few days together at the Sword and Anchor Hotel in Halifax, and Dottie busied herself meeting library people while Edna did research on New Road and interviewed people before Dottie flew home.

Edna had never heard anything so distressing or frightening as the stories she heard about New Road: men knifed each other, women fought and threw rocks, truck drivers making deliveries there carried revolvers, the houses were filthy and flimsy, and people buried the dead in their backyards. People ate garbage, most were illiterate, drank "brew," and had "visions of Jesus and white horses." A Black census-taker told Edna he was afraid to go there alone: "the women were suspicious … many had fierce dogs that rushed out at strangers."[124]

But the RCMP assured Edna the place was safe.

Edna always stayed with people she was writing about, but she didn't stay at New Road. People at the Nova Scotia Home for Coloured Children, a residential centre and orphanage, offered her a room, and Edna took them up on it, driving the few miles each day to New Road.

New Road was not a nice and friendly Hutterite colony or the Six Nations Reserve where the chief talked to Edna for hours about history. Almost sixty years later, Edna still recalls the hostility she experienced there. Kids threw rocks at her, people thought she was a German spy because of her name and the trench coat she wore. When she went to church, she thought she'd "never get out — there wasn't enough on the collection plate … I dreaded every day I went out there but I had to do it. I was asked to do it … I'll never forget sitting in that woman's kitchen — the stench of that woman's washing machine."

Edna wrote about the stinky kitchen in "Would You Change the Life of These People," which was published in 1956.[125] It was straightforward and didn't take as long as the other articles; it was also good journalism, a piece of writing that told the truth, as seen through Edna's eyes, about pathetic people who'd tried to survive for over a hundred years on barren, rocky ground.

The New Roaders were descended from southern slaves and used to a much warmer climate and a different life. They had survived, somehow, and most of them were proud of who they were and suspicious of strangers. Some children were neat and tidy, while others wore rags. There were a few attractive houses, but many were little more than shacks. Not all the kids went to school; the school wasn't large enough to hold them all, and anyway, lots of parents only sent children in the winter because the school was warm. Both children and adults ran away from Edna's camera.

Where did the people come from? Africa, a resident suggested, but no one really knew the history. Edna had done her research, however, and found out that the people were more or less dumped there by the British, who offered to ship them to Trinidad, but the people were afraid of being returned to slavery. "The British government continued their rations of meal and salt herring till 1816, then left them to their own devices." Soon all the firewood had been cut and the people asked for more land; it was granted and other people joined them.

And then the chilling words: "There is no record of how they got on. It is unlikely that anyone bothered about them. They were there fifty years before the government built them a school."

Some of the young children and a few adults were pleasant to Edna and accepted her ("I say we're all God's children") and said they wanted a better life for their children, but after a few days people grew suspicious — and angry:

> Stones were thrown into puddles as I passed between them on the road. Something hit my chin. Small, angry black faces appeared and disappeared in the bushes wherever I walked. The little children who had been so eager and friendly when I came before, now looked frightened and ran when they saw me.[126]

People thought the German spy was going to "go up in an airplane an' drop bombs that will kill everybody."

Friends in Dartmouth advised Edna not to return to New Road. They'd heard women were drinking and fighting about Edna and that the men would be drunk by the weekend, too.

Edna returned on Sunday. Kids dressed in their Sunday best were walking quietly to Sunday school. A few adults spoke hopefully to Edna about the planned new school and teacherage. "Right now, I tell you, we want to get ahead in New Road."[127]

But the children ran to the bushes when they saw her. "If you take any more pitchers round here you'll git a rock on your head."

It was a hard-hitting piece about a destitute and depressed people, and the editorial in that issue of *Maclean's* was about discrimination. Canadians might be smug about racial problems in the U.S., but Canada was not much better. The Canadian government had, after all, interned Japanese-Canadians during the Second World War. "And, as Edna Staebler points out in this issue, there are a good many Canadians in Nova Scotia still willing to believe the ancient and moth-eaten myths about those people whose skins happen to be black."

Legislation had recently been passed in Ontario to force merchants to give equality of service to everyone. In Dresden, which had a large Black population, one restaurant was still discriminatory. There'd been trouble, and some blamed the Communists.

"But if the Communists did [agitate], then the rest of us ought to be ashamed that the credit went to them by default."

This was heavy stuff during the days of the Cold War. Edna had never been too interested in politics; she had simply told the truth. The article caused a lot of controversy: one reader called the article "racist and badly written," but an official from Northern Affairs offered her congratulations. A reporter from the *Dartmouth Free Press* wrote Edna that the article caused shock; *Maclean's* quickly sold out. The paper was going to send a Black employee to New Road to write his reaction to Edna's article, but a little girl had disappeared there and he was sickened by what he heard and didn't write the article. Another reader offered suggestions on how New Road might be helped (a co-op, for instance) but said people didn't like seeing their limitations in print.[128]

A truly vicious unsigned letter arrived from New Road:

> I heard you were very hard to look at … They though [sic] you weren't up too much … I like to see you place people like you usual have one room to eat and sleep when you make a living like you are. What a live you having. You are going to suffer for every lie you told before you die. And when you are dieing think of the sins you done that if you get sick you might die quick … I remember your face wherever I see you…[129]

The writer went on for six pages and concluded: "When we are all through with you you be fit to go through the washing machine. We have started a lot you hear more later."

Edna's New Road story did, however, bring about some improvements. The NAACP heard about it, and people came from Georgia to work with the New Road residents.

The Native story, "The Unconquered Warriors of the Six Nations," also received some criticism. The people of the reserve had warmly welcomed Edna, and she wrote about their pride in their history and their customs, but someone from American Indian Freedom wrote a long, impassioned letter about Indian history, saying she had only skimmed the truth. The writer felt that Edna did not care for Indians.

But she had 160 pages of notes on the reserve. Pierre Berton thought she should write a book about the place.

Years ago Edna had been upset because a fisherman didn't like something in the swordfishing story and she had decided not to use real names in *Cape Breton Harbour*. She had grown as a writer, and was clearly less afraid of saying what she saw and thought, whatever the consequences.

Edna drove home alone to Ontario, following the beautiful St. John River in New Brunswick. *Maclean's* had suggested a story about New Denmark, a New Brunswick settlement of Danes. The article never came together — there was not enough of a story, it was felt — but Edna enjoyed her visit with the prosperous farmers who kept refilling her coffee cup with their beloved dark coffee. She hated the strong brew, but it was a good interlude, quite the contrast to New Road.

And for once she was happy to get home. "I've never been gladder to be at 51," she wrote Philip.

Edna returned to Europe in 1956. She wrote to Alph on April 12, 1956:

> Mon cheri,
>
> Now it is only two more weeks and a few days. How quickly it passes but I wish it were tomorrow. And I wish I could come straight to you.
>
> K and I went over our itinerary on Sunday and as far as we know this is it: we meet on May the 8th in Chester where I'll come from Ireland, hire a car and go up to Edinburgh and up into the Highlands then down to southwest England were we'll visit our friends in Devon for a couple of days, then southeast England to see our friend who has been in a san for two years, then London for a day — that should be May 22 — then we'll fly to Paris where K will be with me for four or five days. This is a surprise. He had

> had no desire to go there till Sunday when he suddenly decided it would be a good thing to do with me because I know my way round a bit. I'm so glad he's going. I think it will be wonderful for him to see more of the world than Kitchener and Florida's Clearwater Beach. He wants to see Les Folies Bergere and La Moulin Rouge and the top of the Eiffel Tower.

It might have been a second honeymoon with Keith, but they weren't even travelling together. He wanted time alone in London to see a lady friend and Edna wanted to sail again on the *QE2*, but the travel agency goofed and she flew to Shannon by Lufthansa for one week in Ireland where people were nice: a young airport employee, Maeve MacGibbon, took Edna for lunch, gave her a book, and arranged for a car (and for years she sent Edna a shamrock plant on St. Patrick's Day) so Edna could drive around Ireland. She had adventures all along the way. Then over to Chester and Keith (Edna driving north because Keith was drinking) before meeting Alphonse.

Edna and Keith didn't discuss Alph.

"I'll come to you the moment I can… I've read that Fribourg is a beautiful, medieval city. I'm looking forward to seeing it. And you, you, you," she wrote Alph.

Unfortunately, Alph had to work and Edna could see him only on the weekends, but it was enough.

She dreaded returning home, she wrote to Keith. "I dread the adjustment period of my coming home and it's good to know that you'll understand it. The thought of having to listen to Mrs. W's latest ailment and what Norm had to eat at so & so's luncheon and what colour the drapes are in someone's living room makes me feel I'll be coming back to crawl into a box of cotton wool stuffing — Difficult after the glamour of Paris and mountains in Switzerland… but thank God I do have my writing and can escape from the dullness once in a while."

Don't tell her family how she feels, she begs Keith.

Alphonse hoped Edna would return to Switzerland the following year, but she was busy working on a short book about Electrohome.

It was a commissioned work, and Edna spent many hours doing research in the basement of the library, touring the plant, and talking to employees. It was a challenge making "a dull business into interesting reading," she wrote Helen in 1957. She was paid five thousand dollars, a lot of money in the fifties.

She also had an assignment for *Maclean's* about the Amish, a group that had splintered off from the Mennonites and was stricter in its observances, not even having electricity. They weren't as welcoming as the Old Order, and Edna couldn't find anyone who'd allow her to live with them, and by the end of the year she had made five trips to see them.

She was beginning to reread Ruby's letters. Ruby wrote to her sisters and mother a few times a week, just about normal, everyday things and family life. The letters were pleasant, cheerful, funny, and sometimes poignant, and Edna wondered if they might make a book or a series. Edna worked on the project for a few years, but a book didn't appear until years later.

But what took the most time was building the cottage at Sunfish, a project Edna enjoyed. She designed the cottage with the kitchen and living room windows overlooking the lake. There were two bedrooms; she and Keith planned to spend the warm months out there, and Edna was there as often as possible, supervising the workers and even hammering nails herself.

Louise Cress had a cataract operation; Edna stayed with her for the surgery in Toronto. While Edna was out of town, Keith "got drunk and caused quite a commotion among our friends and relations and broke my favourite ruby vase," she reported to Helen.

> However I feel he is really trying and achieving a little, and as long as he does that I can't put him out. That's the way it has always been, of course… and will probably keep on going for the rest of our lives. That sounds horribly hopeless and resigned and spineless and everything I never was and never wanted to be. At times I feel as if I've been ground down and haven't any guts left, other times I feel

> that perhaps I've had to develop more guts than I would have if I'd run away. If I can get some writing down I'll be quite content and sure that I've done the right thing.[130]

It must have been wonderful to return to Europe alone in 1958. From Lisbon to Paris, to Geneva and Alph, and then to Nice and along the coast where she saw Picasso's studio, and up to Belgium to see the World's Fair, over to England and Wales to stay with Philip Knowling and his cousin.

She spent only a few weekends with Alph. She watched la Fête Dieu celebration with him in Fribourg, and had lunch with his mother. He was sad when the train carried her away, and felt like crying, he wrote.

No one met Edna in Toronto when she arrived from New York at midnight. She had only English and foreign currency and phoned home. Keith was in a clinic. Edna had arranged for a young couple from St. Jacobs to stay with him while she was away, but Keith had been drinking again.

Edna took a taxi home.

Chapter Twelve
Divorce

In August 1959, Edna wrote Philip Knowling that "my very good and wonderful friend Helen Kergin has been staying with us for a month and ... her son, a 14-year-old, will be with us later in October. ... I wish you could see our lovely little Sunfish this morning — misty reflections all around and the water as bright and clear as a silver tray. There are ducks flying over and crickets chirping."

Edna loved having Helen with her. Helen had a soft voice — that was what most people noticed about her — was taller than Edna, with soft brown hair, and like Edna, enjoyed dressing neatly but casually.

They had a lot to talk about. Helen had left her husband in British Columbia and spent a year teaching in Switzerland; she was over there when her divorce came through. Edna had even helped her with legal advice, consulting a Kitchener lawyer on her behalf before Helen separated from Bill.

Helen was the only one who knew about Alph, and Edna had confided everything to Helen ("Dearest Nelleh") about Keith. Helen knew about Keith being drunk while Edna's mother had surgery, about his times in hospital and his affairs. Edna had even confided such embarrassing details as Keith saying she was repulsive, and she pondered to Helen about whether she should leave him.

"[I could] accept him as he is and enjoy the rich fantasy that comes from my reading and experience of life and do something creative about it. I stay here and dream and do nothing... I suppose basically I too am afraid of being alone."[131]

Maybe they'd grow old together, Edna suggested in a warm and emotional letter. "I'm looking forward to spending my old age with you, dear, but hope there may be a couple of old boys somewhere around to give us a life. ... Write to me soon. I'm always afraid you'll have moved on and I won't know where you are when I want to."

Edna had even offered to give Helen Alph's address: "I don't think he's a man you'd fall in love with, but if you did I'd give you my blessing. It must be kind of fun to feel free to fall in love if you want to… On second thought I don't want you to lure Alph away from me."

Not since Fay had Edna had such a close female friend. Leave Keith, Helen advised. Live your own life; travel. Sitting by the fire at the cottage they talked about the twenty years they'd been apart, about men and love and marriage. It was almost uncanny how they looked at things the same way and how parallel their lives seemed. In a way, Edna said later, she felt closer to Helen than to anyone else in the world then.

Helen received only $3,600 alimony a year and had two children to bring up: one son remained in British Columbia; her daughter was at teacher's college.

What to do? Edna helped her get a job on a bookmobile at the Kitchener library and found her an apartment. Until the apartment was ready, Helen and her son stayed at Sunfish. Helen commuted to work every day with Keith, and even after she moved to the apartment, she was over at 51 Simeon all the time for dinner and talk.

"A snake in the grass," Edna said later of the woman Keith married after their divorce.

In the late summer of 1960, Edna and Dottie Shoemaker drove to Neil's Harbour for a holiday. It was Edna's first time away from Keith since 1958, and she had a wonderful time with Dottie. Edna mused about writing a novel about Neil's Harbour; there were so many changes since she was there last.

On the way back they stayed with Ruby in Peterborough and learned that Keith was in the hospital in Kingston. It wasn't his first hospitalization that year. He'd worked for only four months and was taking pills along with drinking. Edna felt like turning around and going back to Neil's Harbour.

One doctor said if Keith kept using pills and liquor he'd be dead in three months.

When Edna got back to Kitchener, Keith went on what she describes as "the binge to end all binges," running around the house with knives and threatening suicide with pills. Several clinics refused to have him back: what was the point? Finally, he agreed to go the Hidden Springs Centre, a Christian rehabilitation farm near Brantford, where patients worked on the farm while receiving counselling.

Hidden Springs seemed to be the last chance, but Keith would have to stay until he was better — no going home — and the director suggested Edna go away for six to eight weeks so Keith wouldn't be able to return to 51 Simeon.

Edna agreed, but where could she go? There was Ruby's in Peterborough, but it wasn't far enough. Luckily, Doris Anderson, the editor of *Chatelaine*, had recently asked Edna to write a series for them on how people lived, and Edna suggested Neil's Harbour as the first piece. What better place to write about now, when she needed a haven? She'd be away for Christmas, her first Christmas without 51 Simeon decked out and all those homemade cookies and Keith playing Christmas carols on the piano.

But Clara May was like family, and if she had to be anywhere but home for Christmas, there was no place she'd rather be than in Neil's Harbour.

Chatelaine agreed to pay all of Edna's expenses for a prolonged stay and sent along forty-five rolls of film.

Edna flew to Halifax in early December and took the bus to Neil's Harbour. She was just in time to witness preparations for Christmas. She had never been to the Harbour in the winter, with the sea stormy or sombre, snow covering the ground, and at night lights gleaming from the little houses.

At Clara May's, she typed letters and notes in the kitchen with children hanging around her neck. It was cold, and Edna wore layers of clothing to bed but still shivered beneath the blankets. Luckily, the kitchen was always warm.

Clara May's daughter and son-in-law, Jean and Owen Williams, said Edna could write about them. Owen was a fisherman and it was hard times; money from fishing was tight and Owen lost some fishing gear that winter, but Edna loved their small, contented family. She wasn't sure what her story about them would be, and they did spend a lot of time in front of the new television set, but Edna busied herself making notes, taking photos, walking, picking up the mail, and sitting in Clara May's or Jean's kitchen while the women baked and neighbours visited.

And in the meantime, there was Christmas. Ruby mailed gifts for everyone, Dottie sent Christmas money, and Edna added to it, buying dolls for the girls, sweaters for the boys to wear to the Christmas concert, and small things for the adults.

She bought candied fruit and helped Clara May and Jean make Christmas cakes. She loved wrapping gifts and delivering them through the snow.

Sometimes she missed family and Keith, but she was happy that Christmas at Neil's Harbour. Her letters from December 1961 would make a small, cozy Christmas book.

To Norm she wrote:

> I have tried to train myself to live one day at a time and to know that nothing lasts forever and it won't be long before things are better; I look out of my window or I go outside and soon I am seeing something beautiful that thrills me and all is well again. I can do that here better than anywhere I know because the sea is all around me and it is always moving and exciting to me and all the little houses and outbuildings have such marvellous shapes that they thrill me and there are always funny little kids and cats and dogs to enjoy, and Clara May to listen to and Henry and Martin.
>
> The day before Christmas was the most beautiful imaginable here — all day — great gusts of snow that made it hard to see very far…
>
> In the afternoon I went out delivering parcels — first to Max Fricker who had carried my 44 lbs suitcase up to the house from the bus the night I arrived… I took a gift to his little boy and he gave me

> a drink of apple cider… Then I went up to the Budges on the point with a few things for the kids and they gave me tea and three kinds of cake… Then I called on poor Christie and Annie Montgomery — they are old and lonely and have no one. I took a box of candy to Christie and she was so pleased — I think that's the only gift she got.
>
> We opened all our things here after dinner — Clara May and Lily couldn't wait any longer. …
>
> Christmas Eve here was the most beautiful I've ever known in my life — it was just like Christmas Eve in all the picture Christmas cards with all the little houses in the snow having lights in the windows and the snow like feathers coming down.[132]

It was an enchanting time, and in Neil's Harbour she could lose herself in the goings-on of others. Clara May knew something about Edna's problems and the family commented that she looked tired and strained when she arrived. Soon her eyes were bright, her cheeks pink; she walked miles every day.

There were Christmas parties to go to, and everyone wanted to have Edna for dinner or supper. The problems of the past year must have seemed so far away as she unwrapped gifts of salt and pepper shakers, underwear, and trinkets beside Clara May's Christmas tree.

Keith felt that there was an improvement, but he seemed to be "trying desperately instead of being able to forget himself." He "missed me like hell" and was "full of remorse for many things he's done," but "still very nervous and not working," Edna wrote Norm.

But what did Edna really know in her enchanted winter landscape? At the beginning of January Ralph Howlett, the director of Hidden Springs, wrote to her in Neil's Harbour. Keith had made some improvement, was commuting to work from the centre, and hoped Edna would be back before too long. Howlett wanted to see her when she got home.

Edna flew back to Toronto on Wednesday, January 18, and spent the afternoon at *Chatelaine* looking at the developed photos — nine hundred of them — and took the train home the next day.

Keith met her in Galt, thinner and glad to see her and "full of religious fervour" but not overjoyed: there was still a barrier between them.[133]

Edna had a terrible cold, but they ate supper with her mother, and the next day Ruby and her family came from Peterborough. It was dinner at Mother's again, but Edna went home to bed, still sick with her cold. Keith made breakfast, and later Edna got up to prepare lunch for him.

He had something to tell her, but he didn't have the nerve. Instead, he talked about going to Phoenix on a holiday. Edna worked on her story about the Williams family.

A few weeks later, Ralph Howlett told Edna that Keith and Helen were in love and wanted to get married. This new development stunned her, and she was so upset that Howlett sent someone from Hidden Springs to stay overnight with her.

Here was something she had never expected nor imagined. All the years — twenty-eight years — of an often tortured marriage, years of introspection and worry, years of having found a way — she thought — of being able to live with Keith — and now divorce? Keith had always said he'd kill himself if she left, and although she'd gone as far as to consult a lawyer once, she had never thought that Keith would want to leave her.

But she always told herself she had the option of leaving.

Just six months earlier she had written a friend about her "travesty" of a marriage and said that if she had any courage she'd "clear out and live by myself in Neil's Harbour where I could read and write and go fishing." But she stayed with Keith to "do my duty."[134]

They were toying words. She really expected she and Keith would grow old together and hoped he'd stop drinking and become again the man she married. Being a wife was part of her identity, almost. She still cooked and entertained for Keith, they had a social life with friends and family, and he was generous financially, "allowing" her the independence and freedom to travel and go on writing assignments.

She'd put up with his drinking, his affairs, his depression, his denigrations, and now, when he was sober, he wanted a divorce to marry Helen. At first, Keith's affairs with younger women made her worry that he might leave, but the affairs had always petered out, and they'd stayed together.

At heart, Edna realized that she'd never loved any man more than she'd loved Keith, especially the way she'd loved him when they were first married and so happy. She always hoped they'd find that happiness again. Even today, she says Keith was the love of her life.

And Helen — how naive and trusting had Edna been? She'd been naive about Fay, too, but she'd forgiven her long ago and still felt affection for her. But Helen was different. She'd helped Helen in a big way when she really needed help, had opened her home to her and trusted her. Maybe trust didn't enter into it. She'd never imagined that Helen, who kept urging her to leave Keith, wanted her husband for herself. And in two years, while Keith drove Helen back and forth to work in the summer, they'd fallen in love. They'd even spent weekends together. Edna had been suspicious when she and Dottie stopped in Kingston in the summer on their way to Cape Breton and visited a friend, Bob Inch, where Keith was supposed to have spent a weekend. But he hadn't been there.

Keith marrying Helen? It was unthinkable. He was finally sober again and Edna had told herself that they had a chance for a future. And now this.

She was heartbroken.

What would happen to her? She felt her life was over, that she was old and unemployable, and she worried about standing on a street corner in a blizzard as she waited for a bus to take her to a petty office job. She'd be old and there'd be no one to look after her. Keith would be with Helen, and Helen had kids to care for her, and who would Edna have?

Once she had thought she and Helen would grow old together if her marriage to Keith fell apart. Now she had lost Helen, too. But it was the treachery that rankled. Dottie Shoemaker wondered if Helen had had this planned all along.

But who would want a drunk?

Helen did, and she wanted "permanency" too. She gave Keith an ultimatum: it was marriage or nothing.

Now that he was sober and determined to stay that way, Keith felt guilty about the torment he had put Edna through. Or so he said, and Edna saw Helen's reasoning in this. Might it not be better to get rid of the guilt by cutting the ties between them and make a fresh start with Helen? They were in love; they did not have years of misery behind them.

What really bothered Edna, too, was that they expected her to simply "bow out of his life … without self-pity or resentment or fear."[135]

Edna didn't have to give Keith a divorce. She could have refused to divorce him for adultery, but Howlett advised her to let him go. There was no guarantee that Keith would not start drinking again, and Edna told herself that if she refused to divorce him, he'd simply move in with Helen and he wouldn't have to give her any alimony at all. Then the two of them would try to catch her in an act of "indiscretion." Her family thought she should divorce Keith, too. They were supportive and had her in for meals, but rehashing what had happened only fed her "indignation and suffering."

Edna agreed to the divorce, but she felt angry, displaced, resentful, and hurt. She was soon going out to Hidden Springs herself for art therapy, pouring out much of her "self-pity and resentment into abstract oil-pastel drawing" and group therapy.

Despite her own turmoil, she found the people interesting: "a girl from a burlesque show in Detroit, a very fat young man from New Jersey … a beautiful socialite who had been divorced three times and now has no money."[136]

Edna went to Hidden Springs almost daily, from late morning to early evening. She also gave writing workshops there.

Keith moved out of the house in March and took a motel room. It rankled that he soon bought a forty-thousand-dollar house with a pool and a car for Helen. It was a lot to pay for a house in 1961. Keith estimated that 51 Simeon and its contents were worth twenty-four thousand dollars, but Edna sold the house for far less in a few years' time.

He also changed his will, took Edna's name off their joint bank account, and cut her allowance in half.

Luckily, the house and cottage were both in her name and she kept those, but Keith offered her only $3,600 a year in alimony, exactly the amount Helen received. Plus, one of the conditions Keith wanted was that Edna would receive alimony only if she remained unmarried and "chaste."

Edna fought for her rights. Why should Keith's income be calculated for a year when he only worked for four months? Her father's money had financed Simeon Street and Keith had been able to mortgage it to raise money for expanding his business. Her mother had given them a lot of household things, and because of her connections to the furniture trade they'd been able to pay less for furniture. She'd need money for house maintenance. "My nerves are shot," she wrote, "faith shaken — can't trust people — cry, can't sleep — jittery — work hard at it but I'm so tired all the time. They get everything — together — I'm left alone, lonely, lose my status as a married woman — stigma — divorcee a failure, need money to retain self-respect and status in community and elsewhere."[137]

She pondered the years she'd stayed with Keith, and what her life might have been like if she'd left earlier. "I'd have been able to provide a profession for myself — or a husband — too late now — unemployable — won't be able to live at Sunfish as long as I get older — too damp and couldn't get help or get in and out — must have place in town," she continued.

Where was the ability to lose herself in others and in nature? Where was the "private Algonquin," her "inner lamp"? Flown away, it seemed, as Edna cried in front of Keith. Here was a tragedy, a change of life she had never anticipated, and being positive in the middle of such suffering was difficult.

She was "scared stiff of being sick and old without enough money."[138] It was true she'd earned money writing articles for magazines, but even her editor friends said not to count on that to support herself.

Before Keith left she told him she wanted more alimony than he'd offered and half his estate upon his death. When the divorce came through the following year, Edna received eight thousand dollars a year in alimony.

Edna had to go to court herself — she recalls her brown dress with a tunic, the jade earrings she wore — when she divorced Keith on the grounds of adultery with Helen. Neither protested.

Keith and Helen married as soon as they legally could and went on a trip around the world. Keith never drank again, and they seemed to have gotten on well together, although several friends said everything revolved around Keith, who remained committed to AA. Visiting jazz musicians came for sessions at Keith and Helen's after the clubs closed. Keith continued his involvement with the John Howard Society and went on helping people, including members of AA. He was instrumental in establishing Centre in the Square, Kitchener's splendid performing arts centre.

Before Helen's health failed, they enjoyed travelling and going on cruises. Like Edna, Helen enjoyed writing intellectual letters and corresponded with various people she met on holidays.[139]

It took Edna a year to get over the divorce. Writing and having to meet deadlines helped. She had to finish the Neil's Harbour story, and then *Maclean's* sent her to Wawa to live with a miner and his family. Edna slept in their basement and cried herself to sleep every night.

Also in spring 1961, Edna and Dottie Shoemaker went to a library convention in Minneapolis. Brenda Ueland, author of *If You Want to Write*, which Edna had typed out twice, lived there, and Edna wanted to look her up. She had written to Ueland in 1959 care of her publisher, but the letter had come back. Ueland was listed in the telephone book, and Edna called and received an invitation to visit the following Sunday.

Ueland was an eccentric character who was married for the third time. "She's really something — wild longish black and grey hair sticking up and out all over her head and over her collar — a dark suit and a messy white blouse with a tie collar tied round her neck and one button missing and her slightly fat midriff popping out," Edna wrote Ruby.

They "hit it off," but Ueland wasn't helpful, saying any woman whose husband left her for someone else deserved it: it was her own fault. Edna wasn't at her best, still talking about Keith and Helen, while Ueland told her that four men had divorced their wives for her.

Edna felt tearful when she passed a men's clothing store and realized she would never again buy Keith clothes.

More helpful and cheering were her friends from *Maclean's*, who assured her they were her friends, not Keith's. Pierre and Janet Berton and their children, in what would become a yearly tradition, stayed overnight with Edna on their way to the Stratford Festival.

"Being with you helped me greatly to determine to work like hell at my writing and stop analyzing and talking about K and H. I hope now I've passed through that stage and will now think only — or mostly — of my life in the future and NOW," she wrote them after a visit.

Still, the sadness remained.

There's a newspaper photo of Edna a year or so later, taken when she addressed Jaycettes about Mennonite traditions at the Walper Hotel. Her face looks pinched, as if it's aching, and she's lost weight. She looks fragile and dwarfed by the taller women with their big hairdos.

Edna talked about the Waterloo County traditions of cooking Mennonite food, being thrifty, and having a fetish for cleanliness. She recalled the days when she used a hairpin to clean beneath baseboards and turned the house upside down fall and spring for a thorough housecleaning.

She'd done these traditional things and here she was: a divorcee. For years she'd felt like a housekeeper instead of a wife, and now she wasn't even that.

"Sometimes I'd feel so utterly weary that I'd think I'd have to give up — I couldn't go on any more — couldn't try any more but somehow there is always some compensation — often very small — and I'd be starting all over again," she wrote Ruby.

Part *Three*

photo: Edna Staebler Collection

Edna's parents, John and Louise Cress.

photo: Grace Schmidt Room, Kitchener Public Library

The original home of Simon Cress, demolished in 1974.

Edna, left, and cousin Cora in Seaforth.

photo: Edna Staebler Collection

The former Cress home on Spetz Street.

photo: Veronica Ross

Edna (right) and friend, 1926.

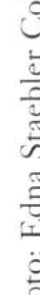

photo: Edna Staebler Collection

photo: Edna Staebler Collection

Edna, graduation day, University of Toronto.

photo: Edna Staebler Collection

Edna and Keith, just married.

photo: Edna Staebler Collection

Edna and Keith, young married couple.

photo: Veronica Ross

51 Simeon Street as it is today.

photo: Endla Loney Collection

Helen Waimel, left, Edna, Keith at far right with unknown woman.

Fred Kruger.

photo: Edna Staebler Collection

photo: Edna Staebler Collection

Edna, 1942.

photo: Edna Staebler Collection

Neil's Harbour.

photo: Edna Staebler Collection

Edna and some young friends at Neil's Harbour.

photo: Edna Staebler Collection

Clara May and family in Neil's Harbour, circa late 1940s.

photo: Edna Staebler Collection

Edna and Keith in the backyard of 51 Simeon Street, circa 1950s.

photo: Edna Staebler Collection

The Cress family during Christmas at Norm's house in 1953. Philip Knowling standing by tree, Keith at his left, Edna, Norma, Ruby, and Louise Cress on the couch.

photo: Edna Staebler Collection

Harold Horwood and Edna.

photo: Veronica Ross

Edna's place at Sunfish Lake.

photo: Edna Staebler Collection

Gerry Noonan and Edna at her Sunfish Lake home.

photo: Veronica Ross

Edna and Tom Allen at a 2003 awards ceremony.

photo: Veronica Ross

Pierre Berton and Edna, April 5, 2003, at the mayor's dinner.

photo: Veronica Ross

Edna today.

Chapter Thirteen
"It Became a Wonderful Life"

The old life was over.

Edna's divorce was final on February 23, 1962. She sold 51 Simeon in May 1964 and lived in the now winterized cottage at Sunfish. Edna resigned from the library board, on which she'd served so many years, when she moved from Kitchener.

"My whole life changed after my divorce. It became a wonderful life. Sometimes people who've had a hard time come out here and they cheer up knowing about my life."

But that was later.

In 1962 she didn't know that a whole new life was just ahead. She'd always dreamed of publishing books, and the sixties would see the publication of two: *Sauerkraut and Enterprise* and *Food That Really Schmecks*. The latter would bring national fame that was cemented with two other cookbooks, *More Food That Really Schmecks* and *Schmecks Appeal*. The cookbooks would make her financially secure; she even dropped the alimony.

She'd worried about being old and lonely, but in the years ahead fans and friends, writers and non-writers, would flock to her door to enjoy muffins and tea and bean salad and, more importantly, the aura that surrounded Edna, a transforming aura of contentment, a mixture of culture and down-to-earth happiness.

She became an example of a woman constructing a new life for herself when she was in her fifties and sixties, the age when many people think about retirement. Here was a woman who didn't publish a book until she was sixty, a woman whose old age saw success and fame and fortune, a woman others sought out and emulated.

But in 1963 she pondered what to do with her life. Should she travel or stay in Waterloo County and write? She had a new car, a Valiant. Maybe she could drive out west? She had enough income to live comfortably if she was careful, and earnings from writing paid for travel. And she had the freedom now to do as she liked.[140] Her mother had wanted to live with her following the divorce, but Edna was determined to be independent. Her sisters backed her up in this decision.

Still, she felt cast adrift. A long marriage wasn't wiped out so easily by a piece of paper. Now there was no husband who came home for meals, no husband to accompany her to social events. She hated eating alone and she hated driving by Helen and Keith's big house.

She tried not to feel bitter and to remember Dr. Robins's advice about positive thinking. But it was difficult. She'd worked so hard for years to have happy thoughts, but now that the reason for the unhappiness was removed, she missed what her friend Alph called her burden, which had restricted her for years.

Still, even the year before, after a meeting with Keith to discuss finances and other matters, she began a letter to him by saying, "I wish you could see the funny little kids eating chunks of dirty snow on our boulevard as I sit here at my window…"

Here was that way of looking at the world outside herself. She tried to remember the quote from Katherine Mansfield: "Accept everything." And: one day at a time. "I'm really trying as I have for many years to take each day as it comes," she wrote her friend Kath Reeves in England.

She advised Ruby, whose husband died of a heart attack in May 1963, and who felt bereft, to make a list of interesting and pleasant people and things she saw and try to think about them instead of her own troubles. It was advice Edna tried to follow herself.

Writing helped in the next few years, typing on a new red portable Olympia typewriter, only eight pounds and ideal for travelling.

The Waterloo Trust Company commissioned Edna to write a history of the company.[141] There were assignments from *Chatelaine* (a story about Italian Canadians and the Wawa piece), *Toronto Star's* weekly magazine (a story on Jehovah Witnesses), and *Maclean's*, which sent her to the Maritimes and Labrador to do a story about Atlantic Provincial Airways, asked for a story on the Kitchener Farmer's Market and another, more controversial, on the British Trust Company in Stratford that went out of business. There had been a few years when she didn't write for *Maclean's* because the editors changed. They'd just suggested she do a series of articles about new Canadians, five or six a year, and she enjoyed living with three generations of an English family, "when the whole editorial staff of *Maclean's* was changed suddenly and unexpectedly. Welll!!!" she wrote Alph.

The new editor didn't like series and the story about the English people never appeared. But her old friend Ian Sclanders returned from Washington and wanted Edna to write for the magazine again.

In the meantime, she worked for *Chatelaine* and stayed "with a lovely Italian family who spoke little English, and ate miles of spaghetti and drank lots of vino," she wrote Alph.

Family and friends, especially Dorothy Shoemaker, were supportive. Her writing friends stood by her. She visited the Sclanders in Washington, D.C., in 1963, and Pierre Berton and his family saw Edna a few times a year. Pierre was BIG now, Edna wrote Philip Knowling; he'd had seven books published and appeared on television and radio. People noticed him when Edna accompanied the Bertons to the Stratford Festival. There were Canadian Authors friends too: Joan MacKenzie, Vinia Hoogstraten, Georgie Hamilton, Max Braithwaite, and Sheila Burnford, who wrote *The Incredible Journey*. Peter Angeles, a philosophy professor at Western University, asked Edna to speak to his class and became a friend; he wanted her to spend a semester at the Albert Schweitzer College in Switzerland.

Evelyn Boyd, whose creative writing class Edna attended in 1962 while she was doing her Wawa story, became another friend. Edna didn't care for the changes Boyd made on her manuscript, but she was someone local to discuss her writing with, especially when she was writing something that was different. Dottie and Joan MacKenzie wanted Edna to apply for a Canada Council grant to write a travel guide to Ontario,[142] but that idea didn't resonate with Edna. In a letter to Sheila Burnford, she wrote:

> I want to do something more personal — something no one else can do — something from my

> own experience of living and loving and understanding and growing.
>
> Could I do that? … Sometimes I feel I am fairly wise. Sometimes I think I've overcome resentment and prejudice and fear and anger and criticism. I long to be compassionate, loving, enthusiastic and eager for life in all its aspects, to feel and be aware of everything sharply and sensitively. To know people, to become people in my understanding of them.
>
> I'd like to do that in my writing. Is it any wonder that I don't even try? Is it really impossible? I'm not at all clever. But I have no desire to write a clever book. I'd like to write one that is beautiful and moving and true and alive. Do I dream wildly?[143]

No, she wasn't dreaming wildly. This book would come soon.

There was a new man in her life, Brian O'Sullivan*, a Waterloo banker, a "very Irish looking" man with dark hair and a square jaw.

She'd known Brian since they were teenagers. "I always envied Lillie* who married him. He was older when we were in high school and he had a Hudson Roadster and we all envied Lillie."

Brian was lonesome after Lillie died suddenly of a brain aneurysm in December 1962. In 1963, Edna's next-door neighbour at Sunfish, Belle Playford, invited Brian, a friend, Mary, and Edna for Brian's birthday. Brian had come with Mary, but he drove Edna home in her car to Simeon Street.

Brian and Edna were friends for thirteen years. In 1962 he was "a lifesaver." It was good to have a regular companion, and unlike Keith, Brian wanted to spend all his time with Edna. There was no question of marriage because he was Roman Catholic and couldn't marry a divorcee. He was "kind, generous, charming, impetuous, reliable, Irish, fun," Edna wrote Alphonse in 1964. "He reads, drinks too much, is ultra-hospitable, helpful and extremely tidy."

He also didn't like to travel and suffered from a heart condition, hypertension, and high blood pressure and liked to talk about his ailments. He and Edna weren't well matched, and after a year of togetherness, she found his attentions "suffocating." Her writing friends found him tiresome and once someone threw him fully dressed into the Bertons' swimming pool.

But he was a companion in those early days of living at Sunfish. "No one comes to see me at all — except Brian my friend. Even my family hasn't been here since Christmas," she wrote Knowling. Sometimes there was only her cat, Willie, to talk to.

Brian did overcome his dislike of travel and Edna joined him and their friends the Eulers in Florida for a week of sun in 1965. Two years later Edna and Brian went to Barbados together, despite Norm's "conviction that I am an immoral woman. I get so ruddy sick of this thought of having to govern my life by what other people MIGHT say."[144] But they did have separate rooms.

Edna went to Europe with Dottie in 1965. It was Dottie's first time on the Continent and Edna enjoyed showing her around Italy and Germany (where Dottie, usually so idealistic that she made excuses for people's behaviour, agreed that the Germans they met were rude and unfriendly).

They also visited Alphonse and his wife, Cecile, in Switzerland. Edna was nervous when she called Alphonse, but he invited them for lunch.

It must have been a bittersweet meeting for Edna. She liked Cecile with "her friendly blue eyes" and appreciated her "generosity of spirit,"[145] but watched as the couple departed arm-in-arm after driving Edna and Dottie to the train station. Alphonse shook her hand on parting. It was the last time Edna saw him.

Edna was glad to get back to Sunfish. "This is the first time I have ever felt happy to come back from Europe," she wrote Alphonse. "Right now I am watching a baby chickadee preening its feathers — it looks as if his ears are tickling him and he'd like to get at them but can't quite make it. He is sitting on the pine tree just four feet from my window. And on the lawn a flicker is finding grubs in the grass; a humming-bird has flown by. These things to me are somehow exciting and I could happily watch them with joy every day."

Edna's first book, *Sauerkraut and Enterprise*, was published in 1966. She was sixty years old and the book was a Centennial Project sponsored by the University Women's Club, who applied to the Centennial Commission for a grant.

The book was not new writing, but a collection of five of Edna's articles that had been published in *Maclean's* about the area: her stories about the Old Order and the Amish, Mennonite cooking, and the Kitchener market (which had just appeared), and an essay on the Twin Cities. Edna designed the book herself, dealt with the printers, and arranged publicity.

"Betty Sims was in charge. The girls would get them and take them to the stores. … We didn't know anything about publishing."

Sauerkraut and Enterprise was a modest book, ninety-six pages, selling for two dollars, with a blue cover and pen and ink illustrations done by local artist Jane van Every. Edna's brother-in-law Ralph was a talented artist and Edna asked him to do the illustrations, but he "didn't follow directions" and kept putting it off.

Club members had a great time putting it together and distributing it to local book and gift shops. The library held a party and Edna went around autographing copies. People sent copies all over the world; fan mail arrived. "All very gratifying," Edna wrote Alphonse.

To everyone's astonishment, it sold ten thousand copies locally, going through six printings before the typeface wore out.

There was obviously something to the book. It made people happy. Maybe it was the way Edna portrayed the local scene, including the Twin Cities: here, do you see how delightful it is? Have you ever considered how peaceful the Old Order are, and how unusual and content are the Amish? Have you ever noticed how colourful and rich the market is? "Kitchener and Waterloo" portrays growing cities with a rich heritage rooted in industriousness and hard work.

It's a highly idealized description of K-W, where people happily snip hedges and trot off to work, and there's little about Edna's personal opinions about the restrictions she found living there, but it's a pleasant look at a place she knows so well.

"The Old Order Amish" ends with a young wife, Catherine, saying, "We're contented just like we are."

The whole book suggests this kind of contentment. It's as if Edna is holding up a mirror to places and people and asking, See this? Look at it, how wonderful and beautiful. This isn't her more realistic journalism, like the New Road story or the one about the trust company in Stratford, but softer and filled with Edna's sensibilities and wonder.

Sauerkraut and Enterprise, with the five local stories under one cover, also set the stage for the portrayal of the area as a very Mennonite place, a portrayal that would grow with the publication of Edna's cookbooks, when people all over Canada came to see Waterloo County as Mennonite country.

"Important, heart-warming, and useful for all Canadians," wrote Dottie Shoemaker on the mail order form.

"I feel as if I was in the Martins' kitchen," wrote a fan, "sitting on the couch, sniffing the cooking odors, or wandering around the market with you. I know that the happiness you are bringing to all who read your book will come back to you ten times over and I'm very happy for you. You have a wonderful talent, Edna."[146] Not only Waterloo County people enjoyed the book.

McClelland and Stewart reissued it in 1969 with a bright blue cover and Pennsylvania Dutch folk art and an introduction by Pierre Berton, who praised Edna's ability to portray people. It eventually sold twenty-five to thirty-five thousand copies.

When the book went out of print, M&S returned the rights to Edna, who assigned them to the Joseph Schneider Haus, which sold it in its gift shop with a foreword by writer and artist Nancy Lou Patterson. Edna gave the Schneider Haus fifty thousand dollars with a gentleman's agreement to keep the book in print. The Friends of the Haus also established the Edna Staebler Research Fellowship.

In 1966, Edna's friend Vinia Hoogstraten invited her to be a guest speaker at the Canadian Authors Association convention in Winnipeg that June.

Edna talked about how she did research for her magazine articles. People loved her.

In the audience was Mr. Flemington of Ryerson Press, which had been interested for a few months in the idea of Edna writing a cookbook after someone who worked for the Kitchener newspaper suggested the idea.

Flemington mentioned the book again.

"If you write that book the way you talk, we'll have a best-seller."

Should she do it? She always made her own bread, and Toronto visitors liked the local dishes she made. The Bertons had already said she should write a cookbook based on local recipes, but she was always busy with magazine assignments and she knew nothing about cookbooks and owned just two: *Betty Crocker's Picture Cook Book*, published in 1950, which Keith had given her for Christmas, and a Mennonite cookbook from the States, which her mother had bought on her honeymoon.

And in the summer of 1966, she was still busy with the galleys of *Sauerkraut and Enterprise*.

The Township of Waterloo was also asking Edna to write a book about the history of local schools.

Still, she'd never had a book publisher before and it would be fun to try writing a cookbook, although there seemed to be no urgency to it.

It was hard to work during the summer, she wrote Flemington. Her friends liked to visit Sunfish to swim. "Almost every week-end is taken and I have also had a week with friends at a cottage … and worked on galleys and page proofs of … my Centennial Book."

But, she reassured Flemington:

> Almost every day I have written a recipe or two in my notebook; I have read cookbooks from the library, analyzed several to get an idea of proportions of recipes in different categories; and I have been making and baking all sorts of delicious breads, biscuits, cakes, and Mennonite-style dishes. Also I have been thinking, making notes, writing comments about recipes and foods, entertaining my Mennonite friends, making lists of Mennonite women to interview and thoroughly enjoying myself.

"I just want to let you know that I am not wasting away," she concluded.

The Bertons thought she should write "informally" and use not only Mennonite recipes, but also old-fashioned ones from her mother and others. It was excellent advice. The Bertons had recently published *The Centennial Food Guide*, an interesting book of trivia, history, old illustrations, food songs, pictures of stoves, as well as recipes and stories about their large family. They had included Edna's recipes for Bevvy Martin's Old Time Potato Salad, Fetschpatze and Bean Salad, as well as an excerpt from "Those Mouth-Watering Mennonite Meals." The *Food Guide* was a good read and far more interesting than how-to cookbooks.

Cookbooks could do well. The Betty Crocker book, with its detailed instructions and photos showing how to, for instance, frost a cake, was a best-seller in the U.S. ("Betty Crocker" actually did not exist, but was pictured as a sweet grey-haired grandmother.)

But a cookbook wasn't the book Edna dreamed of writing. By 1966 she'd given up the idea of having a book published because *Maclean's* sent her all over the place on assignments; she was known and respected for her articles and people asked her to speak. Life was busy and full with Brian and travels, and while *Cape Breton Harbour* remained unpublished, she no longer felt the same urgency about it. It was true that *Sauerkraut and Enterprise* was a book, but it was a compilation of published articles.

Now here was a chance to publish a book — although it was a cookbook — and soon Edna became excited about the project and busied herself trying to get it together.

For years she'd gone on Fridays to Livvy Kraemer's for lunch and dinner, and Livvy lent Edna her small notebook of recipes. Edna's mother and sisters contributed more recipes.

It took her two years to write *Schmecks*, one year getting ready, looking at other cookbooks, trying out recipes, figuring out exact measurements, and another year doing the actual writing.

It was a slow process. She didn't spend hours closeted away, lost in the writing. She didn't take the cookbook too seriously and was more concerned about the township book.[147] The chairman of the board told Edna they'd have asked Stephen Leacock to write it, but he was dead. Edna was flattered, and thought about the old days of Berlin and the games children used to play.

With other writers, she seemed embarrassed by the cookbook.

Working on the cookbook seemed more like puttering, she wrote Sheila Burnford, who'd visited that fall, in January:

> I've actually been working on my cooking book — and enjoying it but finding it is a helluva chore that probably should have been done by a staff of cooks and researchers. Whenever I come across something different that sounds wonderful I want to try it — and I should but if I try everything I'll be eating too much and puttering around with this thing forever. Not that I'd mind — I love doing it — but what about my publisher and my public and my profession???

And there were always so many other interesting things to do. She was still promoting *Sauerkraut and Enterprise*.

For Christmas 1966 Edna baked 1,500 cookies and invited 210 people to drop in at the cottage on December 26 and January 1. Eighty people slid along the narrow, icy road, with a ditch on either side, to visit; luckily they did not come all at once.

In February she went on a three-week tour to Hawaii with Brian, first travelling to Vancouver by train.

She was still concerned with the Waterloo Township School Board book, going to meetings and discussing distribution. But she almost hoped they wouldn't ask her to do it, she wrote Sheila Burnford at the end of March. She wanted "to keep puttering" with the cookbook. "It is so much fun to do and, I think, could be quite good." But she admitted she had never "achieved my great work — or my market."

> The writing I enjoyed doing more than any other was my book about Neil's Harbour; I wrote it because I was so excited about the village and the life there that I HAD to do something about it — but the book has

> not been published. Ever since I started having writing assignments from *Maclean's* I seem to need a commitment to make me work. I deplore this … but what the heck — I can't write any more about this now."[148]

By October 1967 the township book was still more on her mind than the cookbook, which she continued to work on: "I've got to work like mad on my book now because I still haven't started the Waterloo Township one and they're getting anxious," she wrote Ruby.

"I have to finish my book," Edna wrote Clara May and Henry in January.

Food That Really Schmecks was published in June 1968. The launch, held in the Crystal Ballroom of the Walper Hotel, was quite an affair, with roast goose, potato dumplings, red cabbage and apple salad, schnitz pie, and strawberry fritters, all recipes from *Schmecks*, served to guests.[149]

"Dear Friends," Edna wrote to Alphonse and Cecile in November. "*Food That Really Schmecks* is a best seller in Canada and will be published in the U.S.A. as well."

Was it possible? Here was the book she had puttered with, the book that had embarrassed her in front of her writing friends, the fun thing she hadn't taken seriously, and people all over Canada bought it and loved it.

The book sold for $6.95 and had an attractive cover of an old-fashioned table set with a roast goose on a platter, accompanied by a pile of ribs, a pie, and a salad. The title page read: *Food That Really Schmecks, Mennonite Country Cooking as Prepared by My Mennonite Friend, Bevvy Martin, My Mother and Other Fine Cooks*. An introduction by Edna is followed by "Those Mouth-watering Mennonite Meals" and a short essay about the Twin Cities with their "schmecks appeal."

It was a folksy, friendly book, filled with traditional Mennonite dishes like Chicken and Corn Soup with Rivels, *Tzvivelle Supp Mit Kase* (Onion Soup with Cheese on Toast), and Shoofly Pie; German dishes like *Sauerbraten* and *Apfelstrudel*; and modern recipes like Norm's Chicken–Potato Chip Casserole. There are chapters on sweets and sours, vegetables, cakes ("A Cake in the House"), yeast baking, desserts, and "Some Drinks, Wines and Punches."

You could bake Neil's Harbour Bread, or how about trying Emanuel's Dandelion Wine or Black Currant Cordial? But "Drink Net tzu fiel," as the Mennonites say ("Don't drink too much").[150]

You can make a pot roast or fry bologna or whip up a casserole with leftovers, and if your guests don't like sauerkraut, heat up some canned peas for "the miserable deprived creatures."

Busy on wash day? Bevvy Martin makes Wiener Kraut.

You can make summer sausage, sauerkraut, *Schmierkase* (spready cheese) or even Bevvy's Lotion for Chapped Hands, mustard plasters, and your own cough mixture — all from "A Variety of Things."

You can do it: Edna speaks directly to the reader, and if you really don't want to make your own sauerkraut, it's still fun to read about it.

Rave reviews followed from Penticton, Moose Jaw, Kingston, Saskatoon, and Ottawa. By September *Schmecks* was in its second Canadian printing of five thousand copies, and just before Follet Press released the American edition, the *Christian Science Monitor* praised it.[151]

It was the stories that made the book different from other cookbooks. While everyone enjoyed the recipes for their simplicity and old-fashioned heartiness, reviewers quoted Edna's tales about the Martins.

"[The book] is filled with the atmosphere of Conestoga wagons and the philosophy of the simple people," noted Jo Carson of the *Globe and Mail* in a pre-publication article in May.[152]

"Delightful comments and anecdotes make the book fun to read," wrote the *Country Guide* in Manitoba.[153]

Schmecks seemed to fill a vacuum. Edna knew that people who didn't ordinarily buy books would buy cookbooks, but most people enjoyed *Schmecks* for the stories as well as the schmecksy recipes. The stories about Mennonites even attracted the flower generation of the sixties, and several mused about joining the peaceful Old Order. But "they'd never be able to stand the discipline," Dan Kraemer told Edna.

Food That Really Schmecks was, and is, a phenomenon. It is still in print today and has sold more copies than any other book published by McGraw-Hill Ryerson, Edna says.

Sales rose even higher after Carroll Allen wrote a story about it for *Homemaker's* magazine with its large coast-to-coast circulation in the early seventies.

Fan letters came, and continue to come, from all over the world; doctors have recommended it for soothing bedtime reading.

"I feel as though I know you," readers write Edna. "I feel you are my friend." "You have changed my life."

It is a storyteller's cookbook and it's very obvious that the author loves to tell stories.

"We want the book to be like Edna Staebler," Ryerson editors told her when she began writing. She wasn't sure what they meant, but sat down and wrote the book as if she were relating stories about her life, the ways of the Mennonites, and the goings-on of family and friends. To dip into its pages is to imagine you are in Bevvy Martin's kitchen or watching Edna's father roll out Christmas cookies so long ago.

But it's not the recipes that make it special. They are authentic and good, and reassuring to read, and some are even rather casual (Friends coming over? Easy. Whip up some muffins; even concoct something with leftovers), and the tone throughout is sprightly, with Edna's usual apt images.

The author's voice is that of the storyteller, weaving a kind of happy spell, an easy contentment as you flip through the pages. The writer's voice is always there and it is a pleasant, accessible one with a style that is quite different from anyone else's and rather hard to categorize. Strangely, it's just a tiny bit like the upbeat voice in Edna's novella, "Molly" — without the sassiness, however — and the message is to enjoy life; go on, look around you; don't be afraid of mistakes. In the two later cookbooks, Edna would even mention her European experiences.

The books begins:

> Before you read any further I must warn you: I have absolutely no qualification for writing a cookbook except that (a) I love to eat, (b) my mother is a good cook and (c) I was born, brought up and well fed in

> Waterloo County, Ontario, where the combination of Pennsylvania Dutch-Mennonite, German, and modern cooking is distinctive and "wonderful good."[154]

And then Edna tells a story about her mother teaching her daughters to cook local dishes (not quite true, Louise said you could cook if you could read) that husbands enjoyed. But company coming demanded more impressive fare. Finally Edna served bean salad and schnitz pie to friends from Toronto. It was food "designed to fill up small boys and big men."[155]

"Jolly, creative cooking," she calls it, but, "Forgive me, please, if you find some of my directions inadequate. If you test and taste for yourself, you might achieve something fantastic."[156]

You: the reader, my friend.

You hear about Edna's favourite birthday dish: noodle soup. "When our hands were washed clean, our pinneys tied under our chins and we were sitting around the big square kitchen table, she'd fish the meat out of the kettle…"[157]

Breadmaking?

> You need only an eager, experimental approach and the willingness to endure a few failures… Breadmaking is a grand thing to do. Kneading is a kind of reveling; it makes one feel like a primitive, pioneer woman — unstarvable, self-sustaining and joyful. Bevvy sings happy hymns as she works with her yeast dough in the smooth old pine breadtrough her great grandmother brought in a Conestoga wagon to Waterloo County.[158]

Christmas cookies:

> When Mother thought the consistency was right, Daddy would roll out the dough. Mother would shape the cookies with fancy cutters and decorate them with red and green sugar or nuts. If I was quiet

> or good I was allowed to put the currant buttons and eyes on the gingerbread men and to taste the first cookies that came from the oven, before they sent me happy and dreaming to bed.[159]

Is it any wonder Edna had fun "puttering" while she wrote the book? And that other people had fun reading? But there is still something else. She opens the Mennonite world and makes it widely accessible. It's a simpler life but an enjoyable one, and you too can find contentment in simpler things. Stories and food, such an elemental combination and so suggestive of the possibility of happiness, not necessarily in big achievements, but in cooking simple food to share with friends.

Edna was thrilled with the success of the book. In a letter to Alph she wrote:

> Publishing a book — even though it is only a cookbook — is quite an exciting experience. There was so much advance publicity, then a glamour reception for the press, radio and TV people at a luncheon at Kitchener's food-famous hotel. And ever since I've had to do all sorts of promoting things like TV interviews, autographing parties, dinner at the Toronto Women's Press Club, speaking engagements and all the publicity that comes along with being the writer of a best-selling book.[160]

She was amazed at the book's popularity. Even men liked it. "It amazes me that so many men seem to be reading the book, men who don't cook but enjoy reading abut good food and about the nostalgic recollections that the book recalls."[161]

Six years earlier she had been devastated by the divorce and thought she was old, that her life was finished. Suddenly she was an author and a celebrity. She loved it. She had not one book published but two, and both were selling well. An author at last, someone who earned money from books that people bought and read. She looks happy in the many newspaper photos, holding a filled plate and smiling coyly (big corsage on the shoulder) at the Walper, and wearing pearls as she cuts shoofly pie for the *Globe*. She was sixty-two years old but looked younger and happier and more relaxed than in earlier photos.

She was proud of the cookbook — of *Sauerkraut and Enterprise*, too — and was not shy about promoting them or making sure they were prominently displayed in bookstores.

Checking to see that Sheila Burnford's *Incredible Journey* was prominently displayed in Provident Books in Kitchener, Edna overheard a customer asking for *Sauerkraut and Enterprise* in the fall of 1969 after the book had been reissued in the new edition.

Edna's little book was, alas, on the bottom shelf of the Canadiana section. The clerk brought out the copy published by the University Women's Club and the other "a reprint by Ryerson."

Edna piped up, "By McClelland and Stewart," and added that the new edition had an introduction by Pierre Berton. She said she'd be glad to autograph it.

"You mean you're Edna Staebler?"

"And she reached out to shake hands," Edna wrote to Burnford in November. "I'm considering coming in the Provident to sell books until Christmas — my books and yours."

"My *Schmecks* book has been buried amongst other Mennonite cookbooks where no one who isn't looking for it would find it," she fumed to Joan MacKenzie.[162] But in Toronto she was gratified when she went into a bookstore and asked about its best-selling cookbooks and was told, "The *New York Times* one and this other one by Edna somebody from Waterloo."

She had lunches in Toronto with Ryerson executives to complain about the American edition, which sold for two dollars less than the Canadian one; it was cheaper for Canadian bookstores to order from the States. She was losing royalties because of this. Ryerson was anxious for Edna to do another book for them, but Pierre Berton said he wished he'd seen the *Schmecks* contract before she signed it.

McClelland and Stewart wanted her to write a history of Waterloo County in her own style.

She loved the interviews on radio and TV, with Helen Hutchison, Fred Napoli of CFRB, and Gil Christie, who used to be on *Tabloid* with Joyce Davidson.

"Of course I was being lodged in the Park Plaza and taxied all around and fed etc. by M&S and the *Schmecks* (Ryerson book) for far more praise," Edna wrote to Sheila Burnford.

Other pleasures added to the ending of this surprising decade that had started so horribly. She went to Mexico and down east with Brian and introduced him to her friends in Neil's Harbour. In 1969 it was to Europe, including Ireland, where they drove all along the Irish coast.

There were new friendships with writers, too. Margaret Laurence came to speak in Kitchener. Edna picked Laurence, wearing jodhpurs, up at the train station and escorted her to the talk to the University Women's Club. Laurence was so nervous she gripped Edna's hand before speaking and spoke for ten minutes, not the scheduled hour. Later, at a reception, she turned down the liqueur and said, "Make mine a double scotch."

Laurence was still living in England and in the middle of her divorce. She and Edna stayed up until the early hours talking while Laurence finished a bottle of wine. Later, she wrote about her visit in *Heart of a Stranger*. Edna visited Laurence at "the shack," the cottage Laurence bought near Peterborough after her return to Canada.

At Laurence's talk, Edna met Gerald Noonan, a young English professor at Wilfrid Laurier University and an aspiring writer who invited Edna to speak to his class about creative writing in exchange for dinner. Noonan would be a close friend for the next thirty years.

You must wonder what Keith made of his ex-wife's sudden success and fame. He had a heart attack in 1969, and as for Helen, she fell on her face and broke her nose, which had a cast on it, Edna learned.[163]

Chapter Fourteen
Cape Breton Harbour — At Last

Edna's years-long dream of seeing *Cape Breton Harbour* in print was fulfilled with its publication in 1972.

"Maybe it's time we had another look at that Cape Breton book," Jack McClelland told Edna after her huge successes with *Sauerkraut and Enterprise* and *Food That Really Schmecks*.

As she'd written to Sheila Burnford, she'd never forgotten the passion that inspired that book. Dr. Robins had such faith in it, but it had been in her filing cabinet for almost twenty years; it was twenty-seven years since she'd started working on the book she called her apprenticeship, spending half a day writing a paragraph.

Now she got the manuscript out again and spent a year rewriting and cutting, but in spirit it was essentially the same book she'd written so long ago, not the novel she'd attempted, or a love story, but the story of her first stay in the Harbour, honest and true but not factual, with facts, incidents, and the timeframe rearranged to tell the story in the genre she would come to call creative non-fiction.

Names were changed. Clara May Ingraham became Ella May Patson, for instance, and the time period was around 1951 when Maggie was ready to leave home. Edna did not include her later years of visiting the Harbour or her long friendship with the Ingrahams; the book remained the story of one visit: the young woman left in the village (not by the Baileys, though, but by two girlfriends). Her friends are anxious to get back to the city; Edna wants to stay.

It's the story of one woman's enchantment with the folks of this tiny fishing village in a period of nineteen days in August. There's reference to the Korean War, which has passed, but a few young men enlist because there are few opportunities in Neil's Harbour. The narrator is young, not married, although you learn that "George," back home in Ontario, has his eye on a girl visiting from Regina.

Edna/the narrator stays with the spinster sisters and for the next few weeks explores the life of the village, talking to the fishermen, visiting, going to "times" at the hall, walking, hitch-hiking to Cheticamp. She meets Maggie, who is just leaving home, as she does in the *Chatelaine* article. The book concludes with Edna going swordfishing.

The language is poetic, strong, and vivid. The villagers, with their Newfoundland accents, come to life, making the particular universal in its portrayal of a way of life. Edna's passion for the place is obvious and her eye is keen:

> For a long time I looked at the sea, whose blueness flowed forever to meet the paler blue of the sky; on its distance ships were sailing and white birds flew, on its shining face was calmness. I breathed its fragrant air; I watched a rock beyond the rest, with water breaking white all around it; I watched a man riding alone in a yellow dory, gently rising and falling in the swells, oars glinting in the sun; he was moving away from the Harbour, rowing far into the blue, and it seemed a wonderful thing. I wanted to memorize the beauty, to have it become so much a part of me that I could take it back to my narrow street in the city where buildings rob me of a horizon.[164]

This is the place she wrote about so movingly in letters home, the place that stayed with her when she was back home on Simeon Street, losing track of time as she wrote about talking to fishermen at the stages.

In the book, she states her plans to write about the Harbour:

> Oh glorious day! I'm full of zest and zeal and Zion! I'm so excited I can hardly hold my pencil! I woke half an hour ago knowing I'm going to do a marvellous thing — I'm going to write about Neil's Harbour. I'm bursting to talk about it and no one could listen to all

> I have to tell; I've always wanted to write and at last I have something wonderful to write about.[165]

She is soon scribbling away. Old John Clipper says, "You always writing', ain't you? Must be noice to write…"

And here it is, the book she has worked on so long, concentrating on each line to make it perfect, like poetry, Edna says.

The images are startling:

> Wind fills the washing on the lines next door: round bellied dresses jostle one another like fat women hurrying to a bargain counter; pink bloomers are blown up like Siamese-twin balloons; a white flannel nightgown and a man's long underwear cavort with verve that is amazing in such plumpness; towels flick, napkins flutter, sheets strain to be free — and the lean tall woman who hangs them is a mast among flapping sails.[166]

And:

> I walked on the Point in the moonlight. As one does not look at the sun to enjoy the sunlight, so Neil's Harbour does not look at the moon but becomes absorbed by its gleaming on the living water, its yellow Light, its cold brilliance on the stages in whose shadows one feels warm. I could see the faces of the houses in the cool white light, all looking on one direction, all looking at the sea where the fishing boats come in; all but the houses of the doctor, the preacher, the merchants, whose places face the road because they have no men coming into the harbour.
>
> I watched the moonpath on the water, living and breathing, silhouetting the little boats that lay in its wake, and sadly I thought there is no moonpath in the city, there is no moonlight, no soft diffusion of

> blue brightness; there is only the moon, a disc of silver unnoticed above the electric spatters that light the streets in long monotonous rows.[167]

Here is someone who can really write, someone who loves language, someone with passion, someone with feeling for the cosmic, the magic. A few years later she would write about this magic to Harold Horwood when he sent her a passage from his new book.

She is really experiencing wonder in *Cape Breton Harbour*, and it remains her favourite book. It is no surprise that when she received the Order of Canada more than twenty yeas later, she chose this book and *Maggie*, a collection of magazine pieces and follow-ups, to give to the Governor General, Romeo LeBlanc, and not the famous cookbooks that were cited during the investiture. Edna also read from the book when she gave the Margaret Laurence Memorial Lecture at the annual general meeting of The Writers' Union of Canada in 1997, saying *Cape Breton Harbour* was her favourite.

Louise Cress died in March 1972, at age ninety-one, three months after a big birthday party, which postponed publication of *Cape Breton Harbour* for three months. She'd had a bout with kidney cancer in 1960 but recovered and lived alone in her big house on Albert Street. Her money was almost gone when she became ill again. Edna, afraid of being trapped out at Sunfish by bad weather, stayed in her mother's house to be near the hospital, but returned to Sunfish daily, walking in half a mile because ice made the lane inaccessible by car, to feed her cat, Willie. It was a wrenching time for Edna, who was used to phoning her mother regularly and seeing her often, and M&S agreed to hold off publication until June.

Cape Breton Harbour sold nowhere near as well as the cookbooks, and earned Edna only $3,900 in royalties the first year — not bad for a Canadian literary book, but nothing to compare to royalties from *Schmecks*.

There was little publicity, even in Toronto, where only someone giving the weather from a helicopter talked about it on radio, but favourable reviews appeared in *Tamarack*, *Quill and Quire*, and elsewhere. A friend said some people thought Edna was putting the people of Neil's Harbour down and thought they still lived without electricity or telephones after reading Edna's book, obviously not realizing the timeframe.

Some Cape Bretoners thought the dialogue was not authentic, forgetting that Neil Harbour's people were originally from Newfoundland. However, other Nova Scotians wrote glowing fan letters: "a pleasant surprise." "You have done your very best work."[168]

Joe Wurtz, from the Hutterite colony, to whom Edna had sent a book, said reading it was just like visiting with Edna.

The *Globe and Mail* reviewer had wanted to review *Cape Breton Harbour* because she was familiar with *Schmecks*, but found no recipes in the new book. She wasn't disappointed, however, saying that *Cape Breton Harbour* reminded city-dwellers that Canada was populated by ordinary people who could accept a stranger into their lives, and that Edna wrote with obvious joy.[169]

The *Record* [Kitchener-Waterloo] said there was "a Walden Pond quality to the theme but the skillful unfolding of the many Harbour characters gives a dynamic appeal that Thoreau lacks."[170]

Harold Horwood says today, "No Canadian travel book is better than *Cape Breton Harbour*."[171]

It is certainly a different book, and no other book Edna published was written with the same passion, or the same sense of poetry. She enjoyed, she says, work by the Irish writer John Millington Synge, who wrote about the Aran Islands and lived there for a while. Also, she liked Mary Webb, who, like Edna, lived with people she wrote about.

There is that feeling of another voice in *Cape Breton Harbour*, a literary voice, a voice different from the one in the cookbooks. It's as sprightly and alive as the voice in "Molly," but more poetic, more sensitive to the nuances of place interacting with people. Edna wrote several stories about Neil's Harbour, of course (the Maggie one, the story about the Williams, and her first published story on swordfishing), but all her old passion for the place comes together in *Cape Breton Harbour*, and you wonder, once more, what other writing Edna would have done if she hadn't published the cookbooks.

When the soft-cover edition of *Cape Breton Harbour* was published by McGraw-Hill Ryerson in 1990, Edna donated the royalties to Neil's Harbour high school; for years she also sent the school library books from the University Women's Club annual book sale, held at a church in Waterloo. After the book was remaindered, she sent five hundred copies down to the Harbour for the children to sell to raise money for the school.

Cape Breton Harbour reinforced the fact that Edna was not "just" a cookbook author. When *Schmecks* was published, the *Globe and Mail* referred to Edna as a cookbook author, but that was certainly not the way she saw herself.

She made this clear to Carroll Allen, who came to interview her at Sunfish in 1973 for *Homemaker's* magazine. Allen spent several days with her.

"I'm a writer, not an expert cook," she told Allen, who praised the recipes and called *Schmecks* "entertaining in a low key, comforting, soothing way. It tells the reader a little about Edna's mother and three sisters and how they cooked. It evokes homey sounds and smells and is rich with anecdotes and colorful Mennonite dialect, collected along with the recipes for drepsley soup and shoofly pie."[172]

By then *Schmecks* had gone into its sixth printing and she recalled with a chuckle that the mayor of Kitchener had given copies to Margaret Trudeau, W.H. Auden, and "heaven knows what other illustrious people."[173]

It was winter when Allen visited, and the photo that accompanied her article shows Edna by her rail fence, wearing a fur coat and hat. It's snowing lightly, and there she is, a few pages over, smiling broadly in front of open kitchen shelves displaying crockery and dishes and the Quimper pieces she bought in Europe. Add pine walls, the same small stove Edna still has today, and a row of spices: it's all cozy contentment. Like every other winter visitor, Allen watched the birds at Edna's feeder: the chickadees, blue jays, cardinals, and nuthatches that draw your eyes to the big window overlooking the lake. Add a dozing cat, geraniums, magazines, and books — many autographed by Canadian writers — Edna's braided rug, comfortable furniture, and the scene is the same as today, casting enchantment and a break from day-to-day modern life.

Even the distance from town and the country setting added to Allen's enchantment. "If you closed your eyes and conjured up a vision of a perfect little island lake and opened them to find it miraculously spread before you, you'd be at Edna's."

When Allen left, she felt as though she'd been away from Toronto "for a long long time."

Allen became a close friend and visited Edna often, sometimes for a weekend or longer, always remaining enchanted with Edna's company and Sunfish. What was it about this writer that drew people to her? There was something indefinable, perhaps Edna's joie de vivre, her acceptance of people, the friendly way she acted with everyone, her curiosity about people, her zest for life. She was "never mean," didn't say a bad word about anyone. Allen had never met anyone with more enthusiasm, and she thought Edna was around forty when she interviewed her in 1973; Edna wasn't telling her age in those days and was furious when "her cover was blown."

Edna's personality has remained the same since Allen first interviewed her. The *Homemaker's* article for the first time revealed details about Edna's life and essence to readers across Canada and they liked what they read; sales for *Schmecks*, which had been out a few years, jumped again.

At the same time, Allen portrayed her not as a cookbook author, but as a professional writer, an accomplished journalist, and the author of *Cape Breton Harbour*, which Allen described as "an immersion experience," who just happened to have written one cookbook.

> "It's ironic that *Schmecks* would be the book everyone is interested in and wants to talk about," she said ruefully. "I guess even people who don't normally read much must like to read about food.
>
> "But I'm a writer, not an expert cook," she stated firmly and frequently during the two days we spent together. "I make that clear in the book and I just wish everyone would believe it. I love eating and I love food and I wrote *Schmecks* because the publisher wanted a writer to do it — someone who was familiar

> with the distinctive style of cooking that's grown up around the Mennonite and German and Dutch and Swiss population that settled Waterloo County.
>
> "Of course, I'm not sorry I wrote *Schmecks*. It was enormous fun and judging by my mail, it's brought pleasure to a lot of people. A doctor's secretary wrote to say her boss prescribed it as bedtime reading for his neurotic patients. They were to pick a recipe, prepare it and invite someone in to share it."[174]

Edna hinted to Allen that she had other works on the go, but she wasn't saying what they were "for fear of talking it away — the common dread of writers. She does tell me she's been asked to do a history of Waterloo County."

One reason Edna hesitated to do another cookbook was that she feared becoming known as just a cookbook author.

She did have ideas for new books, and while she tentatively began assembling recipes for another cookbook — she had lots of recipes left over after *Schmecks* — she was more interested in other projects.

Three publishers were courting her: McClelland and Stewart, Ryerson Press, and Van Nostrand Reinhold. Edna knew all the editors, and W. Garry Lowatt of Van Nostrand Reinhold had even come out to Sunfish to discuss Edna's ideas. Toivo Kiil of Ryerson wanted to meet with Edna in Toronto to talk about an ethnic book, and McClelland and Stewart hoped to have her write another book for them, too, even though *Cape Breton Harbour* hadn't been a best-seller.[175]

Jack McClelland counselled patience with *Cape Breton Harbour*, which Edna felt wasn't doing as well as it should. *Cape Breton Harbour* was a "minor classic," he wrote, but added that it wasn't the sort of book the market snapped up quickly.

In 1974, at the urging of Margaret Laurence, Edna attended the first annual meeting of the new Writers' Union of Canada, a professional group for authors who had published a book, unlike the Canadian Authors Association, which was more grassroots and open to aspiring writers as well. She'd met Farley Mowat earlier, and now she met his wife, Claire, whose book *Outport People* Edna would love, as well as Harold Horwood, a writer from Newfoundland who would become a close friend, Sylvia Fraser, and other writers.

Edna had met other writers before, of course, but not all of them were authors of books. That first union meeting was the beginning of new friendships with other authors.

Farley and Claire Mowat had recommended *Cape Breton Harbour* to Horwood, who "though not given to praising," wrote Edna that he didn't know when he'd enjoyed a book so much and that she had the "attributes of a first-class novelist." Horwood felt her book would become a classic, Edna wrote Jack McClelland in February.

Hearing that she could be a first-class novelist was wonderful for Edna, who'd tried so long to write fiction, and which remained a dream to her. She had great respect for Horwood and carefully considered his words when he told her that she shouldn't write a second cookbook because then she'd be known as a cookbook author. She admired him greatly as a writer and as a person, and in the years ahead the two would become close friends.

The ethnic book idea was soon dropped; Edna didn't think her Mennonite friends would be favourable to it, and it would have involved a lot of research.

She had two other book ideas: one about Fred, and the other an edited collection of her sister Ruby's letters.

Fred was still in her life, working in a tavern and sometimes taking a taxi out to Sunfish to visit Edna. He called himself a writer now, and had written not only his autobiography but also a suspense novel. Writing had helped him greatly, distilling his anger and giving him perspective. It was years since he'd overcome the powerful urges to steal, and while he still got angry sometimes and wanted to hit people, he managed to contain his rage most of the time. He even lived with a woman for a while.

It was a long time since he'd talked about crazily about building a tank of some sort and robbing banks all over with his friends.

Edna's friendship with Fred could have made an interesting book, and Pierre Berton always wanted Edna to write about him, she says, but Jack McClelland wasn't interested. Nor was he interested in Ruby's letters.

Edna had proposed making a series of the letters to *Ladies' Home Journal* in 1960:

> Are you looking for a new monthly feature for your wonderful magazine? Here are some letters written by my sister and edited by me — they are amusing, unsophisticated, utterly natural, with poor spelling, cliches, and homely philosophy — they would have great reader identification for anyone with a home and children. My sister's buoyant disposition and character are revealed in the writing, her problems with her two children — a boy and a girl — her acceptances of her husband's inability to make money, her irritations, her gratitude to her family who help them along, her independence after she starts working part-time in a store, her day-dreaming, her modest ambitions, her industry, her eagerness, her generosity, her joy in little things, her delightful observation of what goes on in the world outside her kitchen window, her feeble efforts to reduce, her harmless gossip about her neighbours.[176]

The magazine rejected this idea of what was surely an honest but not glamorous portrayal of the life of an average woman.

She pitched the idea to M&S in 1974. She had five hundred pages typed, she said.

> The letters are anything but literary — but that is their charm, I think — they are so natural, naive, the prose has a well-paced rhythm even when things aren't going well. The mistakes in spelling are fun, the strange associations of ideas is surprising, the ungrammatical shortcuts, repetitions, cliches are all exactly right, I think. There is no pretense. The daily

> routine of this very average family becomes — for me at least — fascinating, important, almost exciting.
>
> Though there is no continuing narrative it all hangs together and you wonder what happens next. Even her rug-making, her weight-losing, etc. Though many bits and pieces could be dropped out and not be missed, they do in a way have some significance that adds to the total picture of children growing up in the fifties — the years of war-time babies.[177]

Jack McClelland bluntly told Edna that the readers found the letters boring.

Edna was ahead of her time. She was never political, and she doesn't seem to have been very much affected by the growing women's movement. She told a reporter a few years before, when judging a beauty pageant, that while she'd faced no discrimination in her work because she was a woman (but what about male editors and journalists who said she couldn't support herself with her writing?) she did realize the importance of ordinary women's lives — so different from her own.

The life Ruby wrote about was largely happy and ordinary, unlike some of the women Betty Frieden wrote about in *The Feminine Mystique*, and certainly interesting to women doing their best to raise families.

It would be years before publishers became interested in "women's life writing" and the letters were published by an academic press.

What everyone really wanted was another book about Mennonites, preferably a cookbook, but an ethnic book would be worthwhile as well, and interesting, they felt, to the thousands of readers who had enjoyed *Schmecks*. Already in 1973 Jack McClelland wrote that they were ready to sign a contract at any time for the ethnic book, although Edna reported being reluctant to go ahead because of the attitudes of her Mennonite friends. McGraw-Hill Ryerson also wanted the book.

Tentatively, Edna suggested another cookbook. It was an idea, she wanted another book out, and since the two ideas she'd proposed hadn't been successful, the cookbook was something to think about anyway. She had lots of recipes and the experience from writing *Schmecks* was helpful. M&S jumped at the idea, but Edna was cautious:

> I have typed over 500 recipes for the book. I've made many notes. Some of the recipes may be redundant, I must get others to fill out certain areas necessary to a good cookbook. I have done NO writing but much thinking about the book. I think it could be pretty good. It won't be ready for some time. The other one took me two years — but of course now I've had the experience. I certainly would like to discuss it with someone before I go much farther.[178]

Edna was frank about Ryerson. They made her feel "Ace High" and she enjoyed getting fan mail from all over the world, and knowing that her book was selling all over the world, even in Nairobi. She liked all the attention and was "disgustingly susceptible to flattery."[179]

At M&S she knew only two people, and one was Jack, but she did like the idea of having a Canadian publisher.

On the other hand, she tells Jack that an editor of "another publishing house came to Sunfish twice and spent 8 and 6 hours here chatting; I liked him but told him before he came I would not give him the book — but he keeps working me. Now you know where I stand."[180]

She didn't exactly sound enthusiastic about the second cookbook and told Jack that she'd been to the Bertons for the Binder Twine Festival at Kleinburg and they'd all talked about what Edna should be writing. Pam Berton wanted her to write about Philip, and so did Pierre, "but he also thinks I should write about Fred. Or several other things. Molly. They know me pretty well and know some of the weird and wonderful people and things that have happened to me in my weird and wonderful life."

She wrote this in September and said she was expecting company from Toronto. "That's how it is — 'til the snow flies. Then I'll be lonely and I'll work like hell."[181]

Well, not exactly. It took Edna six years to write *More Food That Really Schmecks*. She kept remembering Harold's warning that she'd become known as a cookbook writer.

"I thought I was violating my integrity," she recalls. "I was supposed to be writing fiction."

The cookbook idea was made more difficult at first because she had no theme in mind, and she worried the book would not be as good as *Schmecks*. "Things have changed. My Mennonites aren't as quaint as they used to be, aren't as young, don't eat as much. They had Colonel Sander's Kentucky Fried Chicken for their Christmas dinner a year ago!"[182]

And no, she wasn't going to be repeating all those meat and pie recipes (seventy-four pie recipes in *Schmecks*). It was easier when she decided to use the market as a theme, based on the article she'd written for *Maclean's* and repeated in *Sauerkraut and Enterprise*. The recipes would contain only Canadian ingredients, things easily obtained.

She'd include some Mennonite recipes, she decided, and friends like the Salters, who lived at Sunfish and sailed around the world on their yacht, and Ross and Lorna Carruthers — he married Lorna after his first wife Helen Wickwire ("Wicky"), who went to university with Edna, died — had wonderful recipes they agreed to share.

She still had a lot of Norm's recipes left over, and initially Edna even suggested to Norm that they write the next cookbook together, but Norm said she wanted to write her own cookbook, something that never happened.

Any excuse not to write was a good one, it seemed, as she worked on the book that would be called *More Food That Really Schmecks*. She went to Europe with Ralph and Norm in 1975 and visited Philip Knowling in Wales where he lived with a cousin, and to Arizona to visit Dottie Shoemaker and her friend Marnie Paisley who had a vacation home there. Visitors flocked to Sunfish, including Edna's friend Kath Reeves from England, who stayed for months and kept the cottage cluttered with quilting projects.

There were speeches to give, talks, meetings with the local Canadian Authors Association, which often had picnics at Sunfish.

She saw Gerald Noonan a lot, visited her Old Order friends, went to the market, attended her book group meetings, and gave interviews. She began knitting mice — toys for cats, which Ruby filled with catnip and sold in gift shops. Norm and her family came out frequently to swim, eat, and play Parcheesi, their family game. She discussed Noonan's writing with him, read his novel manuscript.

"Nothing accomplished… puttering all day," she wrote in her diary. And a few times: "Can't remember what happened."

Just living at Sunfish filled time. She had to walk out for the mail, there were birds to feed and watch, her neighbour Belle Playford to call on. Her nephew, Jim, and his wife, Nancy, had moved into the cabin at Sunfish, making things livelier. Their friends visited. Nancy interested Edna in vegetarian dishes; Edna would include the recipes in the new cookbook.

"As a procrastinator (you said you were one) you will understand how easy it is for me to keep putting off writing," she wrote Jack in February 1977. "I've been working on the cookbook. Slowly, mind you, but every day and like it a little bit more. Good weather for soups."

McGraw-Hill Ryerson was still asking her to sign a contract, but she finally settled on M&S, who sent one in late February, which she did not return to them until July.

It was hard and slow going. Her diary for 1977 shows just how much she resisted completing the new cookbook:

> April 21 — a pub crawl throughout the county with Gerald Noonan… Maryhill, lunch in a tavern spare ribs and sauerkraut, then across the street to the other inn where we played shuffleboard.
>
> April 22 — bought two summer sausages, took Dan and Livvy to hotel in Linwood for dinner
>
> April 25 — Robin Burns (?) of McGraw Hill came at 11, stayed till 3:30, we talked about his cat and my cats… he didn't try to change my mind about the

> new *Schmecks*... later to book group. The girls are looking pretty old but so am I.
>
> April 26 — CAA meeting at Wilfrid Laurier University. I enjoyed it. All of them trying to ... working at jobs and not have TIME to write. I have lots of that and I waste it.
>
> April 27 — Actually sat at my typewriter for a little this morning — not much, tired today, rested, cleaned bookshelves... later to library to hear John Mellor read about Dieppe... Gerry was there, we went to the Valhalla for drinks after, talked about writing.
>
> April 29 — Worked a bit on book, tired... Cocktail party at the Walper.
>
> May 3 — did not work at my book — in town with my car for check-up.

The next week she went to the Writers' Union conference in Toronto, where she met Fredelle Maynard, Ken Mitchell, Peter Such, Andreas Schroeder, and others.

A strange new friend, a depressive named George Dawes, a *Schmecks* fan and would-be writer, called when she got back to Sunfish; he often visited to complain about the world. Carroll Allen came out and on the eleventh there was the Canadian Authors meeting at the university. Marnie Paisley came to stay after an operation and Kath Reeves was over from England.

Where was the time to write?

> July 13 — moved typewriter from living room to bedroom.
>
> July 15 — Stratford with Bertons.

> July 25 — Jennifer Glossop (editor at M&S) there with husband and son. She seemed to agree with everything I suggested… vary stories with recipes, make it personal…
>
> July 27 — Puttered all morning with recipes. Pierre and Janet came after seeing Richard III. Pierre went over my M&S contract…

On July 29, the day she sent the signed contract, checked by Pierre, to Anna Porter at M&S, her entry was simply "Canada Geese landed on lake." The contract didn't seem to make much difference in the months and weeks ahead.

> July 30 — market, typed 2 recipes…
>
> August 4 — Worked on cake recipes, not encouraging.
>
> August 24 — worked on salads today — no writing… watched a TV documentary on the starving people in the world. Makes me feel humble. After it was over I ate ice cream and granola.

Puttering, baking *baba au rhum* for the book group, going to the Wellesley Apple Butter Festival, dashing to the market, mailing one thousand mice to Ruby, judging cakes at Kinderfest, speaking at the Woodstock Library: anything but writing. She even spent time photocopying Dr. Robins's letters, which she still hoped to publish.

Brian O'Sullivan died on October 13. He'd been in the London hospital for months and Edna visited him often. He'd been increasingly weak but hated just lying there with other elderly patients. Edna had not felt as close to him as she once had, but they'd had some good times and travels together and she felt sad when he died, attending the funeral and wake afterwards.

Four days later Edna was at Rundles restaurant in Stratford, where she was taking a Stylish Entertaining course. "We were told about Burgundy wines."

"December 17 — woke at three a.m., have no Christmas recipes right for book."

"I hope 1978 will be more productive," she wrote on December 31.

More Food That Really Schmecks was not completed until May 1978. Edna took the bus to Toronto on the eleventh to deliver the manuscript to Jennifer Glossop. Jennifer called Edna, finally — was the book good or not? — on the twenty-fourth to say the manuscript was "great" but needed cutting and repairs.

"I felt like celebrating," Edna wrote in her diary, but the "repairs" would take most of the year: cutting, adding, then cutting again because the typesetter hadn't allowed the correct spaces between recipes. It was a tiresome business and a nuisance in the busy months that followed.

Edna had tests at the hospital in June to see if her veins were blocked (they weren't) but the rest of the year spun by at a pace that would have tired a much younger person.

Edna, accompanied by Gerry Noonan, attended the Canadian Authors convention in Halifax and visited Neil's Harbour in June — Clara May had died and Edna missed her; Kath Reeves came over from England; Edna hosted a CAA barbecue at Sunfish; in September it was over to Kleinburg to see the Bertons for a weekend. Dinner with Old Order friends, Hannah and Sylvannus ("Such dear people… and a family of black and white kittens in the barn and a family of white goats including a bearded ram who looks like Harold Horwood"). Jim Morris, the owner of Rundles where Edna was learning about wine and "fine entertaining," came for dinner. Edna bought a new car with blue velvet upholstery, had dinner at the Stone Crock, supper at Swiss Chalet. In October she was on the Women's Committee float in the Oktoberfest parade. "Had prominent lace in front beside two huge urns of flowers — roses, mums, glads. People clapping as we went by."

Edna loved all of it.

Loved all of it except working on the manuscript.

She was reading *Wild Geese*, *To the Lighthouse*, *A Casual Affair*, and Emily Carr's journals, which made her feel like writing "bits and pieces" about her own life at Sunfish. Why didn't she, she asked herself, "instead of just keep on reading and feeling tired and glum and unsatisfied doing it?"

I wish she had written a book of bits and pieces about her life at Sunfish, perhaps the way May Sarton wrote about her life, because the diary is charming and inspiring and filled with pleasure about people, nature, and books. Like the Christmas letters from Neil's Harbour in 1960, the diaries make pleasant reading. All this happiness, all these experiences of wonder: it was a shame she did not write about her life.

But *More Schmecks* loomed. On September 26, she learned the book wouldn't be out until after the following Labour Day. The next day Edna was trying to cut "200 pages out of a 600 page manuscript."

"Very slow work on *More Schmecks*," Edna wrote on December 31.

She noted the day before that "Helen Staebler has had a stroke and can't talk. I feel sorry for Keith. They had a lot of trouble."

Helen had previously had a mastectomy, and as noted, Keith had suffered a heart attack. He had been very active in establishing Centre in the Square, Kitchener's performing arts centre, and remained involved in community groups while he continued in the insurance business, but he and Helen had obviously had their share of troubles.

Edna had the alimony stopped the year before and all the old resentment was gone; she hardly thought of Keith at all anymore, but it was ironic that while she had a whole new life and was a household name across Canada, Keith and his second wife were experiencing ill health and the problems of old age.

Chapter Fifteen
More Food That Really Schmecks

More Food That Really Schmecks finally appeared in the fall of 1979. It had the same ambience as *Food That Really Schmecks*, but there were fewer Mennonite recipes and more contemporary ones given to Edna by relations and friends, including the owner of the elegant Rundles Restaurant in Stratford where Edna had taken the Stylish Entertainment course.

It began with a shortened form of "Market Days in Kitchener and Waterloo," explaining changes: the market Edna wrote about in the fifties was torn down in 1973 and vendors moved into two floors of a downtown mall, while another market started in a field in Waterloo.

As always, Edna creates places you want to visit or imagine: "The sight of schnitz at the market on a cold winter day suggests a warm steamy Mennonite kitchen with a couch in the corner, a table set with ironstone china, and a big, black wood-burning cook-stove with a ham bubbling slowly."[183]

You can imagine Edna's life, too, from the book.

Her life as portrayed in the new cookbook is not as busy or frenetic as in the diaries, but buoyant with enjoyment of friends who visit her at Sunfish. She's a woman happy with the simple pleasures of food, visiting her Old Order friends, and remembering eating buttercakes at Child's Restaurant in Toronto when she was a girl.

Harold Horwood, "Newfoundland's award-winning novelist, naturalist, journalist, politician, teacher, explorer," cooks Chinese food at Edna's[184]; filmmaker Lawrence McNaught "slim, with masses of curly brown hair" prepares tomato sauce while Edna chops cauliflower.[185] Niece-in-law Nancy swims in the lake and likes the Meatless Meat Loaf that Edna serves to Ashram members who stay with her — one "offered to anoint my feet with oil."[186] Niece Barbie's old cow, Agnes, slaughtered and frozen, turns up in "Agnes-At-Her-Best" stew.

Edna relates the story of her winter cookie party and provides the recipe for Chicken on a Bed of Rice, which fed the Bertons one night, the Carruthers the next, and finally, Gerry Noonan and his wife, Pam. And muffins. Edna is always baking muffins for friends who eat three or four each.

The Old Order friends are still around, and Edna informs readers that Bevvy's daughter Eva has married Melvin and has three little girls and has time to help at the market, quilt, read to her children, and give Edna recipes. Clara May from Neil's Harbour is present with her pork buns. And here is Alphonse, although unnamed, sharing Swiss fondue at a "candle lit restaurant" with Edna,[187] and escorting her and his mother to a restaurant in Montreux where they ate Crêpes Gruyère.

At the end of the book, she gives her address and invites readers to write to her if they notice any mistakes in the recipes.

No one reading the book would have guessed how Edna had dawdled with the book, worrying it was "violating her integrity." She kept those feelings to herself.

"This cookbook, like *Schmecks*, isn't just a collection of recipes," she told a *Toronto Star* reporter months before the book came out and while she was still fiddling with the manuscript. "It's something to read — a warm sort of book you can curl up in bed with."[188]

Privately she wasn't that keen. She hadn't really done the writing she'd wanted to do all those years ago and which Dr. Robins had encouraged her to do. While still working on the manuscript, she took a day off to read Dr. Robins's letters and to think about using them for a book:

> Beautiful wonderful letters that bring him back to me with all his affection and wisdom and appreciation, generosity and encouragement, joy and poignancy and loneliness, passion, beauty. I'm sure the letters should be shared, should be published. I'm sure they are great letters — or is it because they say such incredibly fine things about me? …
>
> They make me feel so good — so rich for having known and had the friendship of this great man

> — but regret that I have not fulfilled his expectations of me as a writer.[189]

Thinking like this did not help. It had been a busy summer. The index took forever, and Kath Reeves was there on her annual visit from England; Edna rose at five to get some writing done. The family came to swim and eat and play Parcheesi, friends visited, and there was always somewhere to go — into town for lunch, out with Gerry, to the market, or out to Eva's for fresh eggs.

Reading Edna's day-to-day diary of her busy life it is easy to forget she was seventy-three years old that year and aware that her lifelong friends were becoming older and frailer. She must have thought about Helen, too, once her rival and now slowly and only partially recovering from a stroke, getting around with a pronged cane and barely able to talk.

Edna herself experienced some health problems with bleeding the summer before her book came out and made a will in July, worrying about her cottage being dismantled after she was gone, and what would happen to her cats, Cecily and Willie? She'd had Willie a long time, but loved Cecily more than any cat she'd ever had. The cats were always glad to see her when she returned home; "home to my animals" she noted after a busy day in town. Sometimes leaving the coziness of Sunfish took effort, especially when the weather was bad. She kept her age a secret from people who hadn't known her all their lives, and even Pierre Berton was surprised when *EnRoute* magazine wrote Edna was in her seventies; he thought it was a typo, but the future was very much on her mind when she went to the hospital just before the new cookbook came out for tests under general anesthesia.

September 4 was "D-Day" and Norm drove her to the hospital. Luckily, she learned the doctor had found "nothing to remove." She swam in the lake the next day.[190]

Edna forgot about her health when the hoopla started for the new book. The first print run was fifty thousand copies, and M&S expected it to be a best-seller. Edna wasn't so sure. Don't count your chickens, she thought when a friend suggested she'd earn at least one hundred thousand dollars from the new book. *Schmecks* was still selling well, but what if its fans didn't like the new book as well?

Edna's ten free author's copies arrived on October 5, but she'd already seen a copy. The owner of Tavistock Books had phoned and asked Edna to meet him at the stockyards in Waterloo to autograph books, and there was her new book!

The book was lovely, she wrote Alph later, lovely to see the thing finished with the same look as *Schmecks*, but initially she was disappointed with the cover, which showed a tureen of pale orange soup with sausages dangling above. John Visser had photographed her at the market in early spring for a cover photo, but it was too early: there was only asparagus for sale along with last year's apples. The photo was used on the inside of the dust jacket: Edna in a blue coat, carrying a basket of apples. She is barely smiling beneath her flip of white hair.

October 6 was "the BIG DAY," with the first autographing session and local launch at Provident Bookstore in downtown Kitchener.

Edna took her Old Order friends, Eva and Hannah, with her and signed books from ten to three ("time out for lunch," she noted) for "a stream of people" and then headed over to the Stanley Park Mall store. There was already a lineup when she arrived.

Edna was on the move now: to Dundas on the twelfth, Burlington on the sixteenth, and Hamilton on the seventeenth. She was on the *Betty Thompson Show* in Kitchener (where she bought a set of luggage), and in early November she was interviewed on the CBC, but the real tour was ahead.

It was a blitz. From November 2 to 15, Edna, carrying only a flight bag, flew to Winnipeg, Calgary, Vancouver, Ottawa, Montreal, and Halifax. Sometimes she gave nine or ten interviews a day on radio or TV or to the newspapers. Fans lined up everywhere to have her autograph books. Fans of the first cookbook said, "You've changed my life." Men bought the book for their wives. Some called it "a bride's Bible."

Back in Ontario, with only one day to rest, she was driven to Collingwood and Peterborough. A few days later she took the early train to Toronto, where she autographed books at Eaton's. On November 22 she autographed two hundred books.

Edna loved it all and felt great about all the nice things buyers said about both the cookbooks. "I felt like Queen Elizabeth," she said, describing the "beautiful big room [with] a basket of fresh fruits with the compliments of the hotel manager" in Vancouver. Calgary was "the same," but alas, there was no basket of fruit.

"Coast to coast in 11 days — I enjoyed every minute of it — and gained 4 pounds!" She did "15 TV interviews, 26 radio and over 30 press and 43 store autographings."[191]

The tour and meeting so many fans face to face entirely changed her perception of writing cookbooks. *Cape Breton Harbour* was still her favourite book, but she realized her cookbooks gave people so much pleasure.

"I had this guilty feeling but as soon as I started autographing, I thought: What's wrong with that? Here I've written a book so many people have really enjoyed. A woman who moved to England said whenever she felt homesick, she pulled out my cookbook.

"Before, I felt as though I were doing an inferior thing. I didn't think about writing a novel after that."

Chapter Sixteen
Maggie

People wrote from all over the world, telling Edna how much they enjoyed her new cookbook. A doctor even contacted her from Saudi Arabia. It wasn't just the recipes they loved, but the writing and the stories.

The fan letters she received would have thrilled any author:

"Our family has looked forward to its arrival for many months and share with me in the reading of delightful anecdotes and delicious new recipes. Your writing skills are most unique and provide many hours of enjoyable reading," wrote a reader from Mississauga.[192]

A man from Alberta liked the first cookbook and "then when I saw your second book here in the store I bought it … I would really like to thank you for having the inspiration and talent for writing a cookbook like this."

"We sat up in bed reading it and drooling over the recipes until 3 a.m.," said a Waterloo fan.

"Thank you for spending six years on a new book … I adored your first … and can hardly wait to try some of your new recipes," wrote an Oakville fan.

From Texas: "I am very pleased with the cookbook. Tonight I cooked my first recipe from it, the chicken and corn soup with rivels. It was fun to cook."

"It begs to be read from cover to cover. In fact, I rationed my reading to a couple of chapters to prolong the enjoyment."

"Not only were the recipes interesting, but also the anecdotes of Bevvy and her family…"

"I spent Boxing Day reading it cover to cover."

"I thought I'd write to say how much I like your two cookbooks. I really enjoy the stories also."

"[Your cookbooks] are two books that I could not do without in my kitchen. Not only are the recipes most delicious and simple, but the reading [is] very enjoyable. I take them with me whenever I travel to visit family."

"I'm not usually the sort of person who writes to authors (perhaps because I'm somewhat overawed by such people) but your books exude such warmth and friendliness, I feel right at home doing this."

That was it, of course: Edna's personality and enjoyment of life and people created an irresistible spell. Here was this older woman living alone by a lake in a small cottage with her cats — and she was happy. Writers and other friends came for meals or muffins and tea. Edna did not need elegant restaurants, although fans knew she enjoyed Rundles in Stratford, but dinner at the Martins and Chelsea buns with Bevvy were just as enjoyable.

That was the message: you could enjoy life, it was not difficult, you just had to open your eyes wide and see.

Maybe it was more of an aura than a message. It is an aura that holds today, when Edna at ninety-seven says, "I wish you could have been at the lake last night to have seen the moonlight on the water," or "I had six cardinals at the feeder yesterday." "Last night Kevin and I listened to the frogs for hours."

Even today, pending disaster — three feet of snow on the roof of her sunroom threatened the collapse of the ceiling and her books out there were covered with ice — does not preclude happiness: "Today is Mally's tenth birthday." Who else would think of the cat when she could be buried under a falling ceiling?

"Edna never complains," says her friend Wende Gregory-Frei, who met Edna after the first cookbook appeared when she was a new bride. "We considered her cool during the sixties. She's never changed. I'd be visiting at the cabin at Sunfish and she'd visit there, always smiling about everything, asking what was happening. That sense of humour — it's always bubbling up. But she's an intellectual, too. I don't know anybody who's like Edna. And the generosity she extends to people — she never seems to stop giving. There's no BS in there. I took two friends there recently. On the way back, one of them said, 'I want to be like Edna Staebler.'"[193]

Jim Morris, the owner of Rundles Restaurant in Stratford, used to take the bus to Petersburg in the winter. Edna would pick him up and he'd take the bus back after spending the day with her. She was part mentor to him, going over promotional material. "She encouraged a lot of friendships, sort of adopted people. For some people regular visits to Edna were a bit like going to a psychiatrist. She's lived across a range of social circles — some friends are artsy types, others down-to-earth people. I think her greatest message is how to live a joyful life in old age — not to be bitter."[194]

"She does not act old, she's timeless," Pierre Berton says.[195]

"She's always up and wonderful company," says Janet Berton. "I've near heard her say a mean word about anybody."[196]

Edna wakes up every morning, wondering what surprises and pleasures are in store that day and gives thanks every night for her life. It's a childlike curiosity, the bright-eyed anticipation of someone who still sees the world as new and exciting, always changing, just as she did when she spent Christmas in 1960, just before her separation, at Neil's Harbour; just as she began her letter to Keith in 1962: "I wish you could see the children across the avenue…" while she was still traumatized by the pending divorce.

More than twenty years later she told a journalist from the *Galt Reporter*, "A lot of people came into my life and a lot of things happened. Every day had some excitement of discovery or understanding."[197]

"Her warmth, enthusiasm, and genuine interest in people are irresistible," Cathy Williams wrote for *Highlights* magazine in 1984. "A visit with Edna Staebler recharges the emotional batteries and invigorates the intellect."[198]

People still feel that way today.

"I had fourteen visitors on Saturday," Edna will say.

"Laurence brought out soup."

"Kathryn came out with dinner."

Or perhaps a businessman has invited her for lunch. Bryan Dare, for instance, has had lunch with Edna at the Mennonite restaurant in Millbank.

Through the years journalists have continued to write about the feeling of happiness being with Edna brings. Many writers have returned for personal visits at Edna's invitation and become friends. No one seems to remain unaffected.

This effect began soon after the first cookbook appeared. Earlier interviewers were friendly and polite and admired her work, but the people writing about the housewife who won an award or earned money for travels had not felt this aura when they interviewed her at 51 Simeon. She appears prim and matronly in some of those photos, a woman wearing apron and necklace while she fiddles with cookies. This was the woman who wrote long, unsent letters exploring the meaning of life and how to live with unhappiness.

Carroll Allen was probably the first journalist who wrote about the deep contentment of Sunfish and Edna's new tranquility and happiness. After being an idealist who wanted to change the world, Edna had realized she could change only herself. "And I'm still trying to do that," she wrote Harold Horwood.

She had always said in the days with Keith that she was quite a different person away from Kitchener, a cheerful and carefree being people took to. She had made friends easily on chance encounters: Tom Glover in Neil's Harbour, Francoise in Europe, and of course, Alphonse, and all of the people she lived with while doing assignments remained on good terms with her.

Along the way she had learned to focus on others, realizing everyone was part of the same spiritual or cosmic field. She had trained herself, as she wrote at the time of her separation, to look outwards, beyond herself, to forget sadness and despair, but she hadn't always succeeded.

You only have to look at the happy face in the picture of, say, Neil's Harbour, as she smiles impishly sitting on a car, and compare it to her pinched face in the photo in the club with Keith around the same time to realize the difference.

And here she was, in the late sixties and early seventies and beyond: a woman with greying hair and a larky grin, happy all the time, whether to-and-froing to the market, visiting the Mennonites for Chelsea buns, going to a reading with Gerry, or talking to a journalist. This is how people saw her, and the image has not changed.

"She's a lady with attitude," her friend Lawrence McNaught, who has known her for years, says, "and that attitude is to be happy."[199]

Happiness coupled with intelligence, wit, and an ability to focus on others is a powerful combination. She was proud of the cookbooks and not unhappy she had done them.

"No doubt publishers considered them commercial ventures — but I didn't. I honestly tried to give recipes and attitudes and ideas that meant something to me," she wrote Harold Horwood in 1984. "And who knows, those two books have probably added more joy than anything I shall ever write."

Still, she winced when she was called a cookbook writer. She was a creative writer who just happened to write cookbooks. And her cookbooks were more than just collections of recipes, and she proudly reminded people of *Cape Breton Harbour*.

At the same time she knew that if she had written and published a novel, she might only have sold three hundred copies. Margaret Laurence said Edna had made more money with her cookbooks than Laurence had made with her highly acclaimed novels.

Money was important, especially for an older woman on her own. The days were long gone when she rejected the proposal from *Chatelaine* that she write regularly for the magazine, saying she had a husband to support her while she worked on her book — as if she considered earnings from writing pin money.

Now, the money from writing supported her and supported her well. Once she worried about being old and poor, but when she had her will updated, her lawyer told her if she lived another ten years she'd end up a millionaire.

Edna had never cared much about money, had never thought about it when young, and later Keith was generous. She loved her cottage and did not crave the big house she could have afforded in town. She no longer avidly copied styles, as she'd done as a younger woman. The red blazer she often wears nowadays is about thirty years old. She didn't buy new furniture, but is content with her old braided rug and comfortable chairs and sofa. She doesn't even buy extravagant food, but carefully records the price of market strawberries and lettuce in her diary and concocts new dishes out of leftovers. A few years ago she lost a lot of money when her Nortel stock went down — for a while she was a millionaire — but the loss didn't affect her much; she certainly didn't brood about it.

She did enjoy travelling, and in the years ahead would vacation in New Zealand and again in Europe, visiting Francoise Dehlemme, the friend she'd made so long ago in Brittany and who visited her in Canada, but she was just as happy being out at Sunfish.

One thing money did for Edna was to enable her to help others, and she says that although she can be generous, she can't be extravagant (there's the old Mennonite strain), but many would disagree. Over the years she has helped friends with a mortgage, given a young musician eight thousand dollars to study for a year in New York, bought an electric typewriter for a writer friend, paid for friends' trips, covered the cost of chemo drugs, and helped many others whose names she will not divulge.

"Do it when you can and forget about it," is her philosophy.

In 1980, her friend Harold Horwood was writer-in-residence at the University of Waterloo. Edna was glad to have him nearby. He'd visited Sunfish often, and now he had his wife, Corky, and two young children with him. The whole family frequently came out to Sunfish; after Corky and the children returned to Nova Scotia, Harold came for dinner and read while Edna cooked. It was a comfortable friendship, one that Edna wrote about in her cookbooks, not only recalling the Chinese food Harold cooked, but also using the recipe for a casserole made out of leftovers (gravy, meat, and vegetables put into the blender and then baked — doesn't sound too appetizing but hey, here are two writers enjoying each other's company).

Horwood was anxious to see a literary magazine founded in the area.

The *Tamarack Review* folded during Horwood's first year at Waterloo. Writers and editors in Toronto wanted to found a replacement, but "announced they'd start only after they had funds amounting to (I think) about $150,000 pledged or in hand," he recalls. "They never got it and their magazine never came out. I said to my associates at the University of Waterloo, 'We'll publish a magazine without any preliminary funding. We'll just begin it and do it, with volunteer work.' … Edna, Farley Mowat and I donated $1,000 each, and that was the only major funding we received."[200]

The result was the *New Quarterly*, a national magazine publishing fiction, poetry, and essays. The magazine continues to publish and has won National Magazine Awards.

Edna's contribution was the beginning of her official philanthropy to the writing community.

While the fan letters continued to arrive, Edna pondered what to write next.[201] She did not need the money from another book, and she had a full and happy life, seeing her friends, giving talks, and autographing books, but she couldn't not write.

She still wanted to write about Fred.

Once again, Edna approached Jack McClelland with the idea of a book about Fred, but he told her such books were "a dime a dozen."

She thought about writing about Philip Knowling, who had recently died a poor man in England, looked after by his cousin, and whose dishes and silver and papers she had stored for him.

Or she could write a book about cats, she mused in her diary.

Ruby's letters remained a possibility, too, but editing them would take a year and she didn't have a publisher, so what was the point?

There were Dr. Robins's letters, too, which she reread frequently. A young professor at the University of Waterloo read them around this time and thought they should be published "in a limited edition," but McClelland told Edna that Robins's letters wouldn't sell. He wanted "something more about food — make money for them," Edna noted in her diary, and added that he had the idea of small books on individual foods that could be sold in supermarkets for one dollar apiece.

McClelland wasn't crazy at first about another idea Edna had: a collection of ethnic magazine pieces that were good in their day and written "with compassion, great insight, wisdom and style … but they would be damaging to my name as one of Canada's most saleable writers… Damnit…"[202]

Edna rushed over to Norm's for dinner and Parcheesi, which made her feel better.

A few months later, however, Jennifer Glossop told her that she thought the articles book was a good idea, but by the time Jack called in October to discuss a contract, Edna was less than enthusiastic.

Edna, usually so healthy, was beginning to suffer from what would be diagnosed as sciatica. It had been a good year 'til then, with a trip to Brittany to visit Francoise in May, literary dinners in London, Ontario, and Toronto based on *Schmecks* food, visits from the Bertons, trips to the Stratford festival, Janet Berton's sixtieth birthday celebration, shipping books to Neil's Harbour from the book sale, and the usual comings and goings, lunches and dinners with Gerry or Harold or her Mennonite friends or others.

Horwood came out about once a week while he was at the university. Usually he shared space with "a bunch of students" and the cooking was vegetarian; Edna always cooked something with meat, and they drank pina coladas, which she made with creamed coconut extract — "the best mixed drinks I've ever had."[203]

Edna found the sciatica so painful that she didn't attend Barbie's Thanksgiving dinner and even cancelled a speaking engagement in Oakville.[204]

Kath was visiting that fall, but Edna felt thick-headed from the pain medication she was taking. Physiotherapy helped, and by December 14 she was well enough to attend the wedding of Patsy Berton at the McMichael Gallery in Kleinburg.

It was not the best beginning for a new book.

More ill health followed in 1981. She had suffered "tic douloureux," a painful neuralgia in her face, before, and the condition was back by the end of the year. The new book involved not only selecting her articles from *Maclean's* and other publications, but returning to people and places she'd interviewed.

In January 1981 she wrote Jack McClelland that she had about 125 pages done but that the research trip to follow up on the Neil's Harbour story would have to wait until at least the fall.

In April, she was coughing up phlegm and feeling feverish when Maggie, Eva, and Marty, friends from Neil's Harbour, visited Sunfish (where they walked around and saw, through the window, cat Willie happily walking around in the neighbours' living room). Edna managed to take "the girls" to the Stone Crock in St. Jacobs before they left, but a few days later the doctor diagnosed pneumonia.

Her friends rallied. Harold Horwood told Gerry, who dashed out with dinner (roast beef and gravy, sweet potatoes, and the next day "potato salad, spinach with mushrooms, apple cole slaw with pineapple … custard").

In May she had recovered enough to attend the Writers' Union annual meeting at Lake Couchiching, where she sat with Paul O'Neill from Newfoundland — "nice mild man … who has a cat," but later in the month she discovered a lump on her eyelid. It was skin cancer, but it was successfully removed.

It was hard to work. Kath arrived for her annual visit; the Bertons came "bag and baggage" at the beginning of August. Edna was glad to see them — "My life has been closely linked with them for 35 years" — and a few days later it was off to Toronto to visit June Callwood.

In August she managed to drive out to Millverton and Millbank to follow up her Amish story (and visited Vera McNichols, a popular psychic, "such a charmer" — always something new), and found that the Amish couple she'd interviewed years before now had cars in their yard.

Finally, in September, Edna, with Marnie Paisley for company, drove to Nova Scotia to update the down east material: the stories about the canal barge, St. Pierre and Miquelon, Ile-aux-Courdes, an island in the St. Lawrence (the piece had been assigned by *Maclean's* but wasn't published. Edna had sold it to *Canadian Home Journal* but the magazine folded before her story appeared), New Road, and of course Neil's Harbour.

The leaves were changing and it was a leisurely if focused drive along the St. Lawrence River and then on to New Brunswick.

Except for Neil's Harbour, she had not been back to these places since the fifties when she'd been a much younger woman. Did she think about how much had changed? She was a new journalist then, only in her forties. Now she was in her seventies and a best-selling author. The changes must have seemed more poignant when they were in New Brunswick and Marnie called Kitchener and learned that Helen Staebler had died.

Things were different. The barge boat no longer travelled through the canal, there were new hotels on Iles-aux-Coudres, and more cars and brighter houses on St. Pierre, where Edna was received warmly by the folks she'd met so long ago.

And as usual, Neil's Harbour and the Ingrahams were wonderful: "Marnie amazed at their loving enthusiastic greeting of me — such a fine and wonderful family."

She wasn't received so warmly in New Road. Most of the old shacks were gone and there were new houses and two schools, but Edna still found the place untidy and depressed. Memories of Edna's article remained. The principal at the school ordered her off the schoolyard, and a woman at the daycare asked Edna not to write any more about them; everyone had been so hurt by what she'd written.

It must have been a relief to arrive at Harold Horwood's home near Annapolis Royal. After chowder and haddock cooked in wine, they sat up talking until after midnight, and she awoke at six to find Harold making tomato relish.

Back home four days later, after a long drive through the St. John Valley and Quebec, Dottie greeted them with tea and shoofly pie.

Keith, bereft, had a heart attack a few weeks after Helen died. Helen had been sick a long time, and while several people have said that Keith always wanted to be the centre of attention, that things had to go his way, and that it had been hard for him to look after Helen when she became ill, he missed her terribly. Now Keith was alone after twenty-one years of marriage to Helen.

Fred Kruger also died that fall. He'd returned to Saskatchewan after his shoe repair business failed. What had happened? In November, Edna wrote to a trust company in Alberta, asking for details of his death and if any manuscripts had been found among Fred's papers. She was still thinking of writing a book about Fred.

Apparently, Fred had left his Toronto apartment and his effects were placed in storage until news came of his death, when everything went to the Salvation Army for disposal. As to his death, Fred's body was found outside of Webb, Saskatchewan, where he'd been born. He'd been dead for a few days when his body was found, and as there were no assets, Social Services had looked after the burial.

The trust company gave Edna permission to publish manuscripts Fred had written; if successful, royalties would go to the family (Fred had a sister).[205]

It was a sad ending to a sad life, and Edna did not forget her old friend. She must have thought about Fred in the old days at 51 Simeon as she mourned his death and considered his story. So much had changed. Helen was dead, Fred was gone, Keith was alone and ill.

Only Edna was moving ahead.

Whatever Happened to Maggie and Other People I've Known was published in the fall of 1983 to good reviews (but overlooked by the local *Record*, to Edna's distress; she spent a few sleepless nights mentally composing letters to the paper).

The new book was comprised of the down east and Waterloo area stories, as well as the pieces about the Hutterites, the miners in Wawa, and the Italian family she had lived with.

The stories were familiar to readers who remembered Edna's writing in *Maclean's* and *Chatelaine*. The brief updates that followed the stories continued the sagas for anyone who wondered how Edna's subjects, especially the Old Order and the folks at Neil's Harbour, had fared. (They were characters in the cookbooks.)

Learning that Salome and Lyddy Anne now had families and farms of their own, that Bevvy at eighty was still cooking "those mouth-watering Mennonite meals," and that while Clara May had died in 1976, the grown-up Maggie was back living in the Harbour must have seemed like satisfying sequels. Edna's return to the places she'd been brought the stories full circle. She'd even visited the Italian family in a small village in Italy after they left Canada.

But for readers who had only read Edna's cookbooks, here was a different aspect to the author of *Schmecks*. Pierre Berton pointed this out in his graceful introduction, saying the famous cookbooks had grown out of her writing. He wonders if the cookbooks would have been written if *Maclean's* hadn't assigned her to write the Old Order pieces.

Berton praised Edna's ability to convey how people talked. Unlike many journalists, Berton said, Edna was not merely an observer, but "part of the narrative," living with the people and becoming their friend. Edna's "evocative prose" had made the diverse people in *Maggie* — "the Canadian Mosaic" — seem like neighbours you'd be happy to have.[206]

Despite its strength, the New Road piece was not included. Edna thought it should be, she wrote Kath, and writer friends agreed, and Edna was "conscious of its absence," but editors felt the controversial piece would have overshadowed the book. Edna also thought including it would have created legal problems, not because it was libellous, but because even hints of litigation would have held up the book.

The New Road story would have changed the book. Reading *Maggie* is like plunging into the cookbooks or rereading her early magazine pieces. The effect of Edna's affection for her subjects is compelling and she makes you want to know these people too. But New Road, with its shacks and the rock-throwers? Its inclusion would have made the book saltier, controversial, but less of a piece.

Cathy Williams mentioned in *Highlights* that some readers thought Edna viewed people through rose-coloured glasses because of her sympathetic portrayals (the *Globe* reviewer of *Cape Breton Harbour* had mentioned this too).

The New Road piece would have changed that opinion, showing that the rose-coloured glasses came off when the eyes behind them looked at true distress.

"In sketch after sketch we are delighted and indeed, astonished as Staebler's obvious enchantment with the subjects of her search opens windows in our own imagination and we are, quite simply, charmed," wrote Nancy Shiefer of the *London Free Press*.[207]

Would New Road have charmed? Where was Edna's enchantment there? Or New Road's connection to the warmth of the cookbooks? It had been the same thing with the canal barge story, when the editor had deleted Edna's details about what really happened after the two men drowned.

"Her style is spare, original, precise, uncluttered; she gleans the essential in both people and place and brings to these collected sketches the same warm insight and wry wit which made *Food That Really Schmecks*, *Cape Breton Harbour* and *Sauerkraut and Enterprise* such longtime best sellers."[208]

The reviewer added that Edna had what Eudora Welty called "a writer's prime asset, the ability to enter into the mind, heart and skin of a human being who is not oneself."

This was good and appropriate praise, and it would have applied also to the New Road piece. But New Road would not have suited the image of the nice cookbook writer.

The Edna Staebler image was firming up.

Edna was soon off on a promotional tour to Halifax (where she missed Harold Horwood by one day) and on to Ottawa, London, and Brantford. As always, she had a wonderful time.

Chapter Seventeen
Dr. Edna Staebler

What should she write now? She felt she should be writing something after the success of *Maggie*, but she was "floundering," she wrote Harold Horwood in February 1984.

Horwood was back in Nova Scotia, where he was working on sequel to his famous book, *The Foxes of Beachy Cove*. Actually, it was not quite a sequel, as its scope was wider, but a mystical/philosophical book set in the Annapolis Valley. Harold was excited about the book. It was coming slowly, but:

> Now and then again out comes the magic phrase, just as it did twenty years ago. Like this:
>
> > He who flees from the world into the barrenness of the spirit finds not God, but an idol, for the world is the very flesh and blood of God, dancing with the heavenly fire. He who attains truly to the love of God loves not God solely in the unity, but God in the diversity: God in child and man and galaxy; God in moth and leaf and thorn. The world is God dancing, God beside himself.[209]

Writing this made him feel "renewed," he wrote Edna, who recalled similar feelings of cosmic magic she'd experienced in the writing of *Cape Breton Harbour*. She read and reread his letter and felt more hopeful about writing something new.

She has been doing a lot of thinking, and maybe she would sit down one day at the typewriter and "let things come…"

She was proud of the cookbooks, and although she knew the publishers saw them as commercial ventures, she did not, she wrote Harold: "And who knows these two books have probably affected more lives and given more joy than anything I shall ever write. And yet, I want to try to write about some of the people and thoughts and wonderful things that have happened in my life. Only in writing and solitude could they be truly shared."

Harold's letter had made her feel hopeful:

> "Keep the faith," you said, "and keep true to the dreams of thy youth." I'm afraid I've been so involved in the trivia and mechanics of day to day affairs that I have too long not thought long and seriously about my faith and my dreams. Your letter has made me think back. I was such an impossible idealist. I'll never forget the shocking day I suddenly realized that I COULD NOT CHANGE THE WORLD. I could only change me. I'm still trying to do that — without much success. But perhaps a little, at times.[210]

She closed her letter by thanking him for "nudging" her.

She was snowbound when she wrote to Harold, and few came to visit. She had the solitude and time to write, and yet there were diversions: reading, radio, knitting mice, walking out for mail, talking on the phone, watching the birds ("those darling chickadees, nuthatches, juncos, tree sparrows … a ruffled grouse that has eaten all the berries on the high-bush cranberry"), and TV at night.

Soon her busy life resumed.

In April Edna went with Ruby and Norm on a twenty-five-day tour to Hawaii, New Zealand, and Australia. Edna had her wedding ring cut off in New Zealand — she'd worn it all these years so people would know she wasn't a spinster — and replaced it with a gold and jade ring purchased in Hawaii on the way back.[211]

Francoise visited in July, followed by Kath who stayed for five weeks. There were only two days from May to October when Edna didn't have company.[212]

Some of the company included lawyers for Proctor and Gamble and Nabisco who were involved in what became known as "the cookie war," a dispute about a cookie patent; the cookie was very like Edna's recipe for rigglevake cookies in *Schmecks*. The recipe was a Mennonite one, and the lawyers would involve themselves with Old Order cooks and Edna for years. Edna loved the saga. ("It goes on and on," she wrote Harold Horwood in January 1985. "Big business — spies and intrigue coming to me at Sunfish and through me to the Old Order.")

Edna also made new friends, Rose and Kent Murray from Cambridge, and Elizabeth Baird from Toronto. Rose Murray and Elizabeth Baird were food writers and wonderful cooks. Murray had Edna's cookbooks and the article by Carroll Allen. Like so many others, Murray felt as if she already knew Edna. Seeing Edna at the market, she went up to her and said, "You're Edna Staebler." It was the beginning of a friendship that endures to this day; Edna usually spends New Year's Eve at the Murrays and stays overnight. "A very big spirit," Murray says of Edna. "I would like to be like her."[213]

Other new friends were Kit and Vern McDermott from Brantford, whom Edna met when Kit interviewed her the year before. "For some reason I was drawn to Edna." Soon the McDermotts were coming to Sunfish once or twice a week, feeling as though being with Edna was "like going on a brief holiday, away from everything. You feel encouraged and exhilarated."[214] It's another friendship that has lasted.

It was a wonderful summer.

In September of 1984 Gerald Noonan and Dr. John Weir, President of Wilfrid Laurier University, came out to Sunfish with exciting news. Would Edna accept an honorary doctor of letters degree? Edna was "thrilled and overwhelmed," she wrote Francoise. A few days later Gerry called and said the university wanted Edna to give the convocation address.

And now came the perfect day. The sun shone on October 28, 1984, for convocation at the Kitchener Memorial Auditorium. How could the day not be perfect? A friend in Goderich wrote Edna and said that "464 Canadian Jesuits and 3,400 Jesuits around the world" would be praying for Edna, who was wearing a new blue dress to match the scarf Francoise had given her, on her "special day."[215] Dr. Weir detailed Edna's writing career and praised her "unusual ability to absorb and articulate the texture of life in special communities."

Dr. Weir added that "Edna Staebler had almost single-handedly raised life in Waterloo County to near-mythical status," and quoted a Neil's Harbour fisherman: "Men was sayin' the other day seems just loike you be one of us."[216]

Edna had worked hard on her speech, even banning visitors for the last few days before convocation; she had finished it only that morning, she wrote Francoise.

Three thousand people, including her sisters and their families and Janet and Pierre Berton, waited to hear her speak candidly and naturally about her life. She had only ten minutes and had timed herself carefully.

Her speech was a brief recounting of her life after graduating from the University of Toronto: applying for the job as manager of the new Simpson's store, not doing so well counting change at the *Record*, and writing figures in bank books at the trust company, being fired from her teaching job because she did back somersaults, getting married and enjoying life "having a reasonable amount of fun."

> And always, there was that desire to write.
>
> One summer I drove with friends from Halifax to Cape Breton. We quarrelled and they left me alone in a bleak fishing village. I was nervous at first and wanted to leave but the spell of the sea and the Newfoundland dialect kept me there for three weeks. I lived in a fisherman's home, went swordfishing and hitch-hiked over the mountains. I became so excited about the place and the people that one morning I knew THIS IS IT. I'm going to write a book about Neil's Harbour.

I came home and started to work. I wrote every day — sometimes taking hours to make a sentence come right. I learned to say no to people who wanted me to do other things. During the first two years of writing, my mother kept saying, "Why waste your time?" And though I'd filled thousands of pages with typing, my husband said, "You're not a writer till you've had something published." And a neighbour said, "Put up or shut up."

I took weeks to write a story about my day sword-fishing and *Maclean's* bought it! They asked me to write about the Old Order Mennonites and the piece won an award. From then on *Maclean's* sent me all over Canada. Assignments were always an adventure and I couldn't resist them.

You can read all about them in *Whatever Happened to Maggie* — if you like. I was fortunate in having Pierre Berton as my first editor; he taught me a great deal about writing. I often tell Creative Writing classes about the time he said, "Get everything in this paragraph into one sentence and don't lose any of it. (Do you remember that, Pierre?)

Between *Maclean's* trips I kept rewriting my Neil's Harbour book. After five years of work I had filled a large carton with numerous drafts. Finally, I showed it to various publishers; they all said it was beautifully written but, because no one would be interested in such a remote part of Canada, it wouldn't make any money.

I put the book away in my filing cabinet for twenty years. By that time half a million tourists were travelling around the Cabot Trail in Cape Breton, and Jack McClelland said, "Let's have another look at your Neil's Harbour book."

After another year of revisions he published it.

It's sold out now but eventually it will be reprinted in a series of Maritime classics.

That's enough about my efforts in becoming a writer. I haven't mentioned the cookbooks —— they can speak for themselves. They've changed my life and the lives of thousands of people who've written me from all over the world. I'm probably responsible for Canada's declining birthrate because women — and men — tell me they like reading my cook books in bed at night. Maybe that's why I've been given an honorary doctorate today.

In a few minutes you'll be given your degrees. Then your practical education will begin. I truly wish for all of you that you may wake up every morning for the rest of your lives with a feeling of confidence and eagerness to keep on learning. At Wilfrid Laurier you have been given the tools to cope with whatever comes. Plato said, "This alone is to be feared: the closed mind, the sleeping imagination."

I hope your dream comes true.[217]

Edna received a standing ovation for her speech (so natural, so Edna-like to anyone who has ever heard her speak, but was it the first time she had said in public that Keith said you weren't a writer until you were published? Most people writing about Edna would repeat this), and at the reception the president kissed her and said it was the first time in the fifty-year history of the university that a convocation speech had been given a standing ovation and Edna hadn't even known, she'd just heard the applause. Pierre, Barbie, and Mardi Kersell from next door at Sunfish cried, she heard later, and after the reception, Gerry hovered over her at the dinner at the president's house and there were gifts and flowers.

The phone was still ringing at midnight; Edna was too excited to sleep after her "day of glory" — "a flawless day — nothing was wrong. I've never had or ever will again have anything as exciting and gratifying."[218]

Did she think about her winter musings to Harold Horwood? Did she remember them when she wrote the part of her speech about the magic of discovering Neil's Harbour and writing the book about it?

In October 1984 and the months that followed, there was the ongoing excitement about receiving the honorary degree. There were more than one hundred cards and letters to acknowledge and the book group toasted her with champagne, the first time anything alcoholic had ever been served there. Ruby started addressing her letters to "Dr. Edna Staebler."

Chapter Eighteen
The Cookie War

Could life get any better? Was it possible? Edna was seventy-nine on her birthday the following January. Dottie and Marnie sang "Happy Birthday" over the phone and Eva had people over for a dinner of fish, vegetable salad, mashed potatoes, grapes, and a huge chocolate cake. Eleven people sat around the big kitchen table; Hannah gave her Hasti-Notes, Mary a vase, Eva soap, May eggs, and Anna and Henry a baby doll dressed in Mennonite clothes. Norm, Ruby, Kit, Gerry, Rose, and another friend, Elsie, phoned later.[219]

Edna recorded this splendid day in her diary, unaware that some future birthdays would be big community events with lots of hoopla and media coverage. Was there ever an elderly woman so celebrated, so popular?

The older Edna got, the better life seemed to become. Well-known writers visited, but so did people like George Dawes, that strange, pessimistic young man, a hippie-like character with a beard and ragged jeans who lived in his camper truck.

Born in Cape Breton, George was a *Schmecks* fan. He had become a frequent visitor and showed Edna his writing. He was a big Hemingway fan, but Edna found his writing negative and unpublishable. Sometimes George stayed overnight in the spare bedroom. Her family wasn't keen on him: what was he doing there? But Edna accepted him the way she had Fred; Pierre Berton said Edna was always taking someone under her wing, that it was part of her interesting life.[220] Europe — Edna made another trip there in 1985 — or Sunfish: everywhere was interesting, fascinating and fulfilling.

Life became even more interesting with Edna's involvement in the cookie war. What could have been annoying and scary for someone else was a source of pleasure for Edna.

In 1983 a lawyer for Nabisco called Edna to ask about her rigglevake recipe in *Food That Really Schmecks*. Francoise was visiting at the time and Edna didn't call back. The lawyer didn't get back to her either, and Edna thought no more about it until Don Sim, a lawyer for Proctor and Gamble, visited her in May 1984.[221]

Rigglevake is the Pennsylvania Dutch word for railway; no one knew why the cookies were called that. The cookies were rolled like pinwheel cookies with light and dark parts. The recipe had come from Livvy's little black cookbook, but Edna had never made the cookies.

Proctor and Gamble had patented their recipe for cookies that were soft on the inside and crisp on the outside in 1979 in the United States, and in 1984 in Canada. When Nabisco began baking similar cookies, Proctor and Gamble sued for infringement of the copyright.

Bryan Dare of Dare Foods, a Kitchener firm that made cookies, explained to Edna that a recipe that had been published could not be patented; therefore, Nabisco was trying to show that Edna's rigglevake cookies were crisp and chewy, while Proctor and Gamble would argue her recipe did not represent the cookies they were making. Cookies were a million-dollar business, Dare told Edna.

For the next few years lawyers from Nabisco and Proctor and Gamble often visited Edna, bearing gifts of plants and cookies, even Cuisinarts for her Old Order friends, taking her out for dinner, accompanying her to the market, and visiting Mennonites, who baked cookies for them. Edna and her Old Order friends thought it was "fun," she wrote Harold Horwood in January 1985. Edna tried to be nonchalant when Don Sim, the lawyer for Proctor and Gamble, offered to pay Eva and Hannah twenty dollars an hour to bake rigglevake cookies. "Both girls were thrilled with the prospect of making so much money and said they'd practice the cookies first."[222]

It didn't seem like big business as lawyers Don Sim and Gordon Zimmerman, who grew up in Waterloo County, converged on Hannah and Eva to eat cookies and sticky buns. Eva had never talked to a lawyer before, but Edna told her they were "fun."

Sim, who weighed about three hundred pounds, even asked Eva to bake schnitz and shoofly pies for him. The lawyers were impressed with the grace and simplicity of Edna's Old Order friends, and Eva and Hannah were delighted to be making money for something they did all the time anyway.

Enter Anne Barschall, a lawyer for Nabisco, who called Edna from New York. What should she do? Edna asked Sim. Let her come, Sim advised. Edna would enjoy the experience.

Poor Anne. She arrived at Sunfish, dressed conservatively in dark colours and flat shoes at the advice of her mother. It was Anne's first assignment away from New York and she seemed excited. The next day Edna took her to the Waterloo farmers' market and introduced her to Ada, Livvy's unmarried granddaughter, who sold produce from her buggy. Ada said she'd bake rigglevake cookies for Anne.

Anne had never met a Mennonite before and was "delighted," but at the cider mill where they bought apple molasses, she talked on while the men waited at the door for their dinner. Later, she was disappointed to learn that Mennonites would not be witnesses if the case went to court. She shipped her apple molasses to New York — Edna gave her jars — and the molasses arrived in a sticky mess. Lawyers at her firm were soon baking rigglevake cookies; Anne's turned out black and hard. She'd never baked before.

Edna didn't care who won "the war" and remained friendly with both sides, accompanying Anne to Ada's house to watch cookie-baking, and receiving visits from Sim and Zimmerman. Lawyers for the two parties wined and dined Edna at expensive restaurants like Rundle's in Stratford and the Waterlot in New Hamburg.

Michael Manson, representing Nabisco, a biochemist as well as a lawyer, arrived with an azalea plant. He and Anne hoped Edna would appear in court. She'd get a trip to Delaware out of it. A few months later Anne called from New York and invited Edna there in November; they'd pay her expenses and show her the town. Edna wasn't interested. She'd been to New York in 1954 before sailing for Europe, and it didn't compare with London or Paris. Anyway, Edna was afraid she'd feel obligated after accepting their generosity. And who would stay with her cats?

Anne called back and said her boss said she should stay with Willie and Cecily. Nothing doing. Edna wasn't leaving her beloved cats with any New York lawyer. It wasn't long before the story hit the papers. June Callwood was the first to call the affair a cookie war. No blood had been spilled, but "the other traditional elements of human warfare are manifest: the combat is expensive; it is fundamentally silly; it is about money, vanity and power; and the people who declared war aren't doing the fighting. Their lawyers are."[223]

The press loved the story, but Edna was annoyed that Callwood hadn't referred to her as a writer.

"Of course I am a Canadian woman who writes cookbooks," she wrote Harold Horwood. "You warned me about that — about being called a cookbook writer. So I guess I shouldn't object — but coming from June who started writing for *Maclean's* at the same time I did — it was hurtful."

Judy Creighton, a journalist who'd met Edna in the seventies and become a friend, wrote about the story for Canadian Press, which carried it across Canada. The *Record* wrote about it, referring to Edna as "a soft-spoken, unassuming cookbook author who lives in a rustic cottage."[224]

After being interviewed by Peter Gzowski for *Morningside*, Edna received calls from radio stations from Buffalo, New York, Toronto, Saskatoon, Memphis, and San Diego, and from *Harper's* and *Forbes Business Magazine*. Reporters from the *Wall Street Journal* spent half a day at Sunfish ("As Long as They Really Schmeck, Who Cares if They're Patented?") and a film crew from the *Fifth Estate* arrived,[225] showing the crossroads at Erbsville ("only nine houses"), as well as the Old Order with their horses and buggies.

This was "cookiedom's promised land."

The program put the financial input of Proctor and Gamble into perspective: they had invested eighteen million dollars to bring these new crisp and chewy cookies to Canadian cookie lovers and showed footage of a huge factory.

In contrast to big business, there was Edna in her picturesque cottage, cheerfully passing around a heaping tin of rigglevake cookies, which she agreed were pretty hard; Edna strolling down to the lake; and Edna at the busy market.

She played up to the camera, telling viewers about the New York lawyer who offered to stay with her cats so she could go to New York. "Imagine, a lawyer looking after my cats!" It was the same lawyer who "left cookies in the oven for half an hour!"

Edna sounds almost girlish on film as she says she loved having the lawyers for both sides visiting. The fuss seemed like foolishness to Edna and her friends, but she was receiving five hundred dollars a day as a consultant, and the lawyers really loved the Mennonites; meeting them was "a metaphysical experience" for one of the lawyers. She spoke about the lawyers arriving in a Lincoln Continental.

Watching the program a year later, Edna thought she looked "like this nice little old grandmother."

The lawyer's boss said, "No more Lincoln Continentals," Edna wrote a new friend, David Luthy, an American convert to the Amish.[226]

Edna loved it all, although she worried about what she'd said to whom and she was concerned about the Mennonites being subpoenaed (until lawyers told her this would never happen; bad for the image). She was friendly to everyone and everyone loved being with her. Michael Manson picked her up in a stretch limo; Zimmerman drove her to Eva's, then Hannah's "where we had Chelsea buns … Don brought Eva a cookie jar … We took Eva to the market with her maple syrup, then shopped … had lunch at the Brittany … mussels in wine sauce…"[227]

Four days later Edna left for three weeks in France. Anne was back in June and some Mennonite friends asked her if she read the Bible and was she not afraid of hell? Anne and Edna ate dinner at Rundles ("Salmon mousse").

Edna was almost sorry when the brouhaha ended in 1989. She finally decided to support Nabisco, offered the lawyers her diary to confirm dates (they couldn't read her writing and sent along a tape recorder), and agreed to go to New York to meet the lawyers. Accompanied by her niece, Barbie, while Ruby stayed with the cats, she got royal treatment all the way: flying first class, "a gorgeous suite at the Waldorf Towers," a limo to ferry them for shopping and dining and a tour of a cookie factory.

The dispute was settled out of court.

"I thoroughly enjoyed it. It was great fun," Edna told a *Record* reporter, but added, "It was a crazy thing to pay all those legal fees for such an insignificant thing as a cookie recipe."[228]

The ongoing cookie war was wonderful publicity for Edna as she wondered what to write next. By 1985, McClelland and Stewart was anxious for her to write another cookbook, and she had a lot of recipes left over from *More Food That Really Schmecks*: the plum and rhubarb sections had been pulled out at the last minute because of the error in spacing.

As always, there was that nagging feeling she should be writing something else.

"Looked over recipes left over from *More Schmecks*," she wrote in her diary, "but do I want to bother typing recipes and writing another *Schmecks* — a lot of work involved, but I don't seem to do anything I should do — about Fred, Phillip, Molly, cats…"[229]

She quizzed her friends. Belle Playford next door thought Edna was "silly" to take on another cookbook, but Gerry Noonan thought it was "okay." "I don't think I'd do it if I didn't have 350 or more recipes already tried and typed out," Edna mused. "So why not?"

But she was shocked to discover *More Schmecks* being sold at Coles for $4.99. It was "incredible and scary." Apparently a salesman had sold 6,600 copies of *More Schmecks* to Coles for $1.50 each because the book was overstocked in the warehouse.

Edna was indignant. "Why should I bother writing another cookbook if they are going to give them away?"

And what about her royalties? she complained to Jack McClelland. Being called a cookbook author was one thing, but the books were hers, she had written them, and Edna, never shy about self-promotion or standing up for her rights, wrote McClelland, saying she had contacted a lawyer and the finance committee of The Writers' Union of Canada. She wanted the royalties they owed her. She typed the letter, mailed it before ten, and came home to bake a sugar cream peach pie while Kath, who was visiting from Devon, made a salad.

To distract herself from the royalty business, she reread Ruby's letters ("really enjoying them but [publishing them] would take another year's work and then what? no publishers"), noted a swan in the lake, went on a bus trip with Norm and Ralph to the Toronto Zoo where she saw pandas and a ghost tiger, read *Bodily Harm* ("not a happy book — few are these days except cookbooks") and took the bus to Toronto to have lunch with Carroll Allen at Le Petit Gourmet.

The royalty matter with M&S was settled to Edna's satisfaction when the publisher compensated her for the lost royalties.

On February 25, 1986, Edna made muffins, lemon snow, a potato flour sponge cake, and a quiche also made with potato flour. The food was for Jack McClelland, who was allergic to wheat flour and was visiting the next day. They had "a great session." Jack told her that her books had sold a quarter of a million copies, and Edna agreed to write another cookbook, with the deadline set for March 31, 1987.

Chapter Nineteen
A Wonderful Inspiration of What You Can Do With a Life

Edna's many fans eagerly awaited a new *Schmecks* cookbook, especially after watching the *Fifth Estate*, but Edna first had to complete a story about the cookie war that *Saturday Night* had asked her to write. She'd meant to write the story anyway and wondered if the *New Yorker* might be interested, but she gladly accepted *Saturday Night*'s offer.

As usual, she spent a long time working on it, writing and rewriting, and cutting — the last version in September 1986 was thirty-five pages long. And it was summer; as always, visitors flocked to Sunfish.[230]

She planned to use the story in the new cookbook. "[The article] is fun reading," she wrote an editor at M&S to report on the progress of the new book. She added that Liz McClelland, Jack's wife, was bringing "two bus loads of ladies to St. Jacobs this week and I must talk to them about Mennonite food. Always something."[231]

In August she explained to Jan Walter of M&S that the *Saturday Night* story was slowing things down; plus, it was summer.

"I'm afraid the cookbook has been relegated to the background this summer — as I expected. I've had a visitor from Devon for a month, two from Brittany for two weeks and many friends who come for just a few hours," she wrote.

The *Saturday Night* article appeared in May 1987. Lively and entertaining, the article created great interest, and when Edna attended the conference of the Writers' Union that month in Kingston, she was amazed at how many people had read it, she wrote Harold Horwood. Film producers contacted her, too, and soon filmmaker Gail Singer optioned the story, but a film was never started (although Singer, like so many others Edna met, continued to visit Sunfish. "I really liked her," Edna says).

However, the Blyth Festival staged Kathleen McDonnell's *The Cookie War*, a version of the original story, with a subplot involving conflict between a quilt shop owner and a mayor who wanted to build a mall.

Michael Manson and other lawyers from his firm accompanied Edna, by limo, to the premiere performance on June 17, 1988.[232]

Edna was the obvious star. Manson recalls people in the audience whispering and pointing to her. She spoke at the reception and was presented with a bushel basket of Bruce County produce and a Styrofoam container of chicken, T-bone steak, and sausage. It was wonderful, Edna noted.

By June 1987, Edna still had not signed a contract for the new book. Adrienne Clarkson, then president of M&S, offered a small advance, and an editor had rewritten Edna's recipe directions "in the explicit stereotyped way they do them in magazines because the people who do them use a formula — probably because they are not writers ... directions for the simplest things would go on ad infinitum," she wrote Harold. They'd wasted a whole month rewriting the whole book, Edna said.

The small advance was an insult, Edna felt. "Pierre said if they didn't give me what I want I should put the book up for auction — and he told Adrienne I had three other publishers that wanted it. She seemed to be quite impressed, offered an advance of $30,000 — which I think should be more because of the sales *More Schmecks* had in the first six months — far more than that. And the book sold for $14.95."[233]

Adrienne Clarkson spent half a day with Edna at Sunfish and "said I could have and do whatever I like — put in the cookie war story — have the jacket I want — the print, everything."[234]

"Sweet as honey," Edna noted. "Even kissed me on arrival — though I'd never seen her before."

With everything settled, Edna worked hard on the manuscript, getting up "between 4:30 and 5 to meet all the deadlines — and I did meet them," she reported to Kath Reeves, and wrote George Dawes that she worked "like a beaver all winter. Reached my March 31 deadline for my book because I was working at it from 5 in the morning and at my typewriter the rest of the day."

Barbara Naylor, who has been Edna's friend for about thirty years, recalls Edna arriving in town, carrying the manuscript in a plastic bag in case the house burned down. Hard at work, Edna did not fuss with choosing clothes to wear at home and alternated a few outfits. She had to remain focused, she explained to Naylor.

Writing the new cookbook also involved trying recipes Edna had not made before. Naylor remembers Edna preparing a rhubarb dish that turned out to be very watery. Edna, not at all embarrassed, served it with biscuits to sop up the juice.

Like everyone, Naylor loved being with Edna; so did Naylor's daughter, a child at the time, who delighted in all the things in Edna's cottage — people were always giving Edna small items like china cats — as well as the lake and the grass and just being with Edna. Even today, Naylor's daughter, who lives in Yellowknife, never returns to Waterloo County without going out to see Edna.[235]

Schmecks Appeal was published on October 3, 1987. "The Great Cookie War" chapter sets the tone. The book is a little more cosmopolitan than the earlier books, with a few little zany touches.

Edna tells Mennonite stories and explains the Old Order to new readers, but the recipes include ones Edna gathered on her travels, as well as Oktoberfest and "Kinderkochfest German Goodies," cakes, soups, breads, easy suppers and lunches, drinks, and the rhubarb and plum recipes that had been left out of the previous books. There are celiac recipes for people who, like Jack McClelland, could not eat wheat, and Edna tells all about Jack's visit to Sunfish and the little box of potato flour she used to make the quiche and the big sponge cake. There are fun recipes from children at a Waterloo School: "The Super-Duper Sandwich" and "Scratch Me Back Cookies."

But, too, there's Edna eating omelettes in Paris the entire eight days she was there, except for a pork chop meal au jus and another she couldn't remember because she was so taken with her companion (Alph, but unnamed). Edna eats octopus in Nice, accompanies Francoise's old cook to the market in Brittany, dines on what sounds like a gruesome concoction of gravy and leftovers with Harold Horwood, drinks three daiquiris one cold winter's day when Kit and Vern couldn't make it up the icy lane. There's something here very tongue-in-cheek of the much younger writer who wrote about Molly in Paris.

But she still appreciates Eva and Hannah's open-hearted ways of feeding people.

"This is a book for people who like to stay home and eat at their own table with family and friends whom they like to please but don't have to impress," Edna writes in the introduction. (Octopus was fine but there was a lot of good local food around, and you needn't be fussy.) And for people who like to read her stories in bed, she's added more "antidotes — as people often call anecdotes."[236]

As with the second *Schmecks*, she invited readers to write to her.

M&S had had a sort of contest to find a name for the new book. The prize was lunch for two at Sunfish. It was Doug Gibson who came up with *Schmecks Appeal*, and he took his seventy-seven-year-old mother, who was visiting from Scotland, with him to lunch.

Gibson enjoys telling stories about Edna.[237]

"There were the three of us and the place smelled good. Then we heard 'shit' from the kitchen. The quiche fell and landed vertically in the oven. We got it out — it was hilarious — delightful. My mother and Edna got along so well."

Edna was eighty-one years old, but that didn't stop her from enjoying the publicity tour.

"Great day," she noted in her diary on October 3. After a launch and book-signing in Waterloo, and lunch with the sales rep and Gerry Noonan, it was off to the airport to fly to Ottawa, where Michael Manson met her and dined with her at the "posh restaurant" of the Four Seasons Hotel (real tulips in the suite). Then autographing in Ottawa — and "smoked salmon, lobster bisque and scampi" for dinner.

It was on to Montreal (to the airport by private limo) and then to Toronto to visit M&S and autograph books at Simpson's and Eaton's. Home then for a few days, to take new books to Hannah and Eva and to entertain friends with muffins and tea, but by October 14 she was in Calgary, where she autographed at Eaton's and visited Bill and Merna Mitchell, who had a new golden Labrador puppy and served smoked Arctic char.

After Winnipeg, it was on to Vancouver for more promo and a visit to a new friend, Gordon Wagner, who had contacted her from Comox Bay, B.C., after reading the *Saturday Night* story.

He was seventy-three and had written a book. He came east while Edna was finishing work on the index to research his genealogy and visited at Sunfish where they talked about writing. He also worked in Hannah's garden. "A going concern… everyone loves him," Edna wrote Kath in August. He'd prepared his secret salmon salad, the recipe for which Edna used in *Schmecks Appeal*.

She also saw her old friends, the Salters. And watched salmon at a hatchery, ate oysters, had English tea, dined in a French restaurant, drove around with her friends, and appeared on television and radio.

A Twin Otter plane flew her to the Vancouver airport for the flight to Toronto. Then it was "home to Sunfish and cats" by limo.

"Very tired but glad I did the whole promotion tour. Everyone was scared that I wouldn't like it — at almost 82. They think I'm remarkable."[238]

On January 1, 1988, she wrote in her diary that "1987 was a very good year for me — 4 magazine pieces and a book published — the most I've accomplished in one year. I'm so grateful."

She did have a lot to be grateful for and she knew it. At an age when many older women were lonely and not paid much attention, she was a best-selling author whose fans wrote her delightful letters. Media people lined up to interview her, and at home she had her wide circle of friends who were always glad to see her, to visit for muffins or invite her out for a meal. She loved where she lived. She was healthy, enjoyed vigour and intelligence and curiosity about life.

She also had money, and money to spare. As she looked back over her life, she thought about all the wonderful things that had happened to her: all those lucky breaks and coincidences, even accidents — you could say the cookbooks started as an accident — that had enabled her to write and publish her work.

Besides private charity to friends, she had given money to start the *New Quarterly*, and now she decided to endow a literary award for creative non-fiction, the genre she wrote — a factual story told with fiction techniques — for a first or second book by a new Canadian writer. In 1950 the Women's Press Club Award had boosted her confidence, and she thought "it would be wonderful to do that for someone else."

She discussed it with Harold and Gerry Noonan; Noonan thought that Wilfrid Laurier University could administer the award. It took a little time to set up, but by 1991 Edna had donated twenty-five thousand dollars as a first installment to be invested for the yearly prize of three thousand dollars.

She was now a member of the Chancellor's Club, Edna wrote Dorothy Shoemaker, which entitled her to free parking, a lapel pin, a discount at the bookstore, invitations to athletic events, and a copy of a book on Laurier, which Shoemaker had already sent as a birthday gift; Edna exchanged Dottie's gift for an anthology of Mennonite short stories.

Pierre Berton, Farley Mowat, Harold Horwood, and Gerry Noonan were early judges. In 1991, *Ginger* by Susan Mayse won the award.

The award has become a big part of Edna's life, and she eagerly awaits the arrival of the books. "Are the books in yet?" she asks. By late March they begin to pile up on the back of Edna's sofa in the sunroom overlooking the lake. She's not shy about showing the books to visitors.

"Look at this — have you heard of this book? And this one?"

The judges, most of them academics, meet over the summer at Sunfish to draw up a short list of ten. They sit in the sunroom and have tea and muffins while they look at the sparkling lake and discuss books.

"No judge ever wants to quit," says Kathryn Wardropper, who has administered the award for Laurier since 1996. "Edna is a straight shooter; honest. You always know where you stand with her. She loves writers and being with writers."[239]

Like everyone else, Wardropper has become a close friend and often drives out to Sunfish to prepare dinner for Edna or just to have a visit. She is one of the people who got together in fall 2002 to make sure that there was always someone to fill Edna's birdfeeders and that she had food. She wakes up every morning and thinks about Edna, she says, and reminds herself to ask, the way Edna does, what surprises the world has in store.

Many of the award's winners have become Edna's personal friends, too. Two large canvases by Linda Johns, who won in 1994 for *Sharing a Robin's Life*, the story of Johns's relationship with a robin she rescued, hang in Edna's living room. Johns had visited Edna a few times and Edna encouraged her to exhibit at Laurier. Edna fell in love with Johns's lyrical but strong paintings of nature and animals, and not only bought two paintings for herself, but also purchased a larger one and donated it to Laurier. She also made sure her friends knew about the exhibit and Johns sold several other works of art in Waterloo (my husband bought one).

Johns went on to publish other books, including *For the Birds* and *Wild and Woolly*, and she and Edna often correspond and speak by telephone. Johns creates whimsical birthday books for Edna and named a rabbit after her, which died in March 2003 of a stroke at the great rabbit age of five years and eight months.

The award meant a lot to Johns, who lived alone in rural Nova Scotia where she worked as an artist and had a part-time library job; her annual income was about ten thousand dollars. She was (and remains) devoted to the birds she rescued, other wild creatures she has helped, and domesticated birds (two roosters, Bubble and Squeek, are now dead, but there's a hen, Chickpea, today). Her writing has been about kindness between creatures of different species, including human.

"I got the news of it on a very grim day. It was my birthday, which I didn't celebrate because of low self-esteem and the truck broke down in town. At home, I held the roosters on my lap and had a bit of a cry. Then I got this phone call from my art agent, Jeff Parker, who told me I had received the Edna Staebler Award for Creative Non-Fiction."

Edna helped Johns realize that she was a writer; she'd never even thought about writing until Nimbus in Halifax persuaded her to write a book about the robin (and she wouldn't have met Edna if she hadn't picked up that robin, Johns says); it took two months to even start writing. Edna's encouragement and faith made her feel she could be a writer. "I started looking at my life." Two more books about creatures followed, as well as self-published books of poetry, which she also illustrated.

"I think Edna influences everyone. Here's someone who's lived to be ninety-seven and who radiates joy. It makes you think there are calmer waters ahead."[240]

George Blackburn, who received the award in 1996 for *The Guns of Normandy: A Soldier's View*, which was published when he was seventy-nine, also became a close friend who keeps in touch with Edna, as does Charlotte Gray (*The Life and Times of Isabel MacKenzie King*, 1998), who hosted a dinner for award winners in the Ottawa area. Wayson Choy (*Paper Shadows: A Chinatown Childhood*, 2000) has been to Sunfish several times, and Taras Grescoe (*Sacré Blues: An Unsentimental Journey Through Quebec*, 2001) wrote Edna to say how much the award meant to him.

Edna was at Laurier on a freezing cold February night in 2003[241] when the sidewalks were covered with ice. It was a night when most elderly women, especially those who live down a treacherous lane deep in the country, would not dream of venturing outside. But Louis Silcox drove Edna right to her door, over the snow-piled lawn; he had to shovel to get back on the road.

(Kevin Thomason, Edna's next-door neighbour, drove her to town, but spent the evening at a meeting with other Sunfish residents, trying to convince the municipal council not to destroy the area wildlife by building on nearby Erbsville Road. Kevin, in his early thirties, and Edna often attend social events together. He might be the youngest person, and she the eldest — both first to arrive, the last to depart, he says.)[242]

But no way was Edna going miss Tom Allen receiving the 2002 award for *Rolling Home*, a book about going across Canada by train.

Edna, who rarely writes speeches beforehand, was at her informal best.

"I'm getting too old to make speeches, but here I am. Wait… I had a wonderful sentence to start — it's gone. Do you mind if I think for a minute? Oh dear. Too bad. It's wonderful to see so many people. First of all… I make up speeches in my head." She thanked all the proper people, and then she remembered the opening sentence: "I'm ninety-seven and I couldn't resist going out to meet a very nice young man."

After his reading, Allen ("What beautiful laughing eyes he has," Edna commented later) said that Edna is "a wonderful inspiration of what you can do with a life."

Chapter Twenty
The Good Things Just Kept Happening

Edna's good fortune continued. On October 17, 1988, Doug Gibson of M&S phoned Edna to see if she had any new books in mind.

Edna was still thinking about publishing a book about Fred, as well as Ruby's and Dr. Robins's letters; but also there was her journal, which she'd been rereading. She thought it was better and much more positive than L.M. Montgomery's journal ("such a sniveller," she said of Montgomery, who she felt didn't really like people and who'd had a far less exciting life than Edna), and Judith Miller, a friend who taught at Renison College, was interested in seeing the journal published.[243]

And maybe a book about Philip? She had all his letters and papers in her garage. And there was "Molly," her unfinished novella from long ago. And her book of quotations, the things Edna had copied from books and magazines over the years — "her bible," she called it; maybe someone would be interested in publishing it.

But the project she suggested to Gibson was something else she'd been thinking about: little cookbooks on specific categories, baking with yeast, pies, suppers, for instance. So often people asked about a specific recipe, say a pie recipe, and wouldn't it be a good idea to have favourite pies in one book?

Gibson liked the idea, and furthermore, was going to see about reprinting *Cape Breton Harbour* in a trade paperback edition, as well as reissuing *Sauerkraut and Enterprise*. Edna the star: everyone wanted her books.

Cape Breton Harbour, Edna's favourite book, was reprinted in 1990, but by McGraw-Hill, not by M&S. She donated the royalties to the school at Neil's Harbour. McGraw-Hill also reprinted *Maggie* in trade paperback, retitling it *People I've Known and Places I've Been*. (Two years later the two books were remaindered.)

It was "a time of revival for Staebler's powerful creative writing," noted the Kitchener *Record*.[244]

The problem with the series idea, however, was that McGraw-Hill Ryerson had published the first *Schmecks* book, and M&S the second and third. So popular were Edna's books that the two publishers worked together, with M&S doing the production and covers, and McGraw-Hill the inside.

There were several meetings between Edna and the two publishers.

Edna was never a slouch when it came to promoting her books and getting a good contract, and Gibson chuckles as he recalls Edna's outrageous demands about things like royalties.[245]

She was feisty with her publishers, and Gibson, who is from Scotland, feels he and Edna "have a special relationship. She can beat me up — I grew up in the country with feisty older women. I was the bad guy in one meeting. She was twisting us around her eighty-five-year-old finger while remaining smilingly immovable."

Six books came out in 1990, and six more in 1991. Each book had new recipes and folksy pen-and-ink illustrations, as well as an introduction by Edna. The titles were: *Baking with Yeast; Cakes and Frostings; Cookies and Squares; Lunches and Suppers; Meats, Fish and Fowl; More Baking; Muffins and Quick Breads; Pies and Tarts; Soups and Salads; Sweets, Sours & Drinks; Vegetables; and Desserts* — all *with Schmecks Appeal.*

Edna wasn't entirely happy with the books; she didn't like the covers, although "someone came up here and took cartons of stuff" to photograph, and the price, at ten dollars counting tax, seemed too high. Edna was always conscious of what people were willing to pay, and she was right about this, because the books were soon remaindered. Someone bought up the rest and placed them with Canadian Tire, she says; she saw copies at the Dutch Boy Supermarket.

Still, they are charming books. Judith Miller says reading one is almost like reading a novel — there's Edna canoeing across Sunfish

Lake to pick up corn in the vegetable book, for instance. Miller feels Edna's cookbooks have created a new genre, a different way of writing for and about women.[246]

In 1991 Edna and Janet Berton went on a ten-day cruise for food writers on the SS *Viking Sun*. Edna had heard about the "fancy trip" from the an M&S sales rep from Vancouver. "Edna, if I can get you on one of those trips, don't turn it down."[247]

Edna didn't turn down the chance when it came and asked if she could bring someone else because she didn't want to share a room with a stranger. What about Janet Berton? she wondered. Like Edna, Janet wasn't part of the "Toronto food mafia," and she wasn't a "foodie," but she'd written two cookbooks and wrote a food column for the *Region of York* magazine. Regular passengers paid twenty-three thousand dollars, according to the brochure, but the food writers only had to come up with the airfare. The idea was that chefs and restaurateurs in each port would show off their cuisine to the food writers, who would then — it was hoped — tell the world about the delicious food they had eaten.

Edna had her arm in a sling; Willie had bitten her badly — he was having strange seizures and she'd touched his head in the dark — but the injury didn't hold her back. She and Janet sailed on November 27 and shared "a fabulous suite with champagne, a box of chocolates, nuts and our own balcony."

They had a great time as the ship sailed to Puerto Vallarta, Acapulco, Costa Rica, through the Panama Canal, and back to Fort Lauderdale. They dined with the captain and the president of the Royal Viking cruise line; there were free massages and manicures, and the boutique had something new in it each morning. And wherever they landed, buses transported the food writers to another restaurant to be feted.

"An absolutely wonderful time," recalls Janet Berton. "The best chefs would speak to us. We ate better food than the rest of the boat. We got to tour the ship — we went through the meat floor, the dessert floor [where they prepared food] and so on. The most interesting thing was a box with a padlock on the first floor — it was filled with caviar!

"Edna was wonderful company. She's always up and wonderful company. She was eighty-six and a younger man asked her for a drink."[248]

"Janet and I were the only ones who'd published cookbooks, except for one person who'd published a little softcover book — nothing special," Edna recalls. "Neither one of us wrote about the trip and we were never invited again."

But the trip had a sad ending. Edna had boarded Willie with the vet, and he died while she was away.

Foodie or not, other foodies honoured Edna that year with the Silver Ladle Award, presented to Edna by the Toronto Culinary Guild at its annual meeting at the O'Keefe Centre in Toronto. The award honoured an individual who had made a substantial contribution to the food industry; Kate Aitken and Jehane Benoit were previous winners.

Food writers continue to respect and honour Edna, but the affection extends far beyond the cookbooks. Her good friend Rose Murray, herself the author of successful cookbooks, says:

> Edna was one of the first to write a cookbook … The cookbooks were an accident, but people were interested in the Mennonites themselves — people like to read about how the Mennonites cooked and why they did things the way they did. The things she makes in the books are approachable things. And it's down-to-earth chatter; you feel as if you're in the kitchen. Her biggest contribution was bringing the cookbooks forward and making them accessible for anyone… and for people who like folklore too.
>
> Edna's approach to life imbues her cookbooks. Indeed, she doesn't waste anything. I can see the love of simple things and good food… her wanting to share. Part of the reason for her longevity is her positive attitude.

Edna's attitude made all the difference. Murray recalls a young foreign exchange student, Sophie, who always wants to see Edna when she returns to Canada.

> Edna appeals to all ages. She makes people feel wanted, listens to people. She's one of the most insightful people I've ever met. At our New Year's parties, she never wants to go to bed until everyone has gone home. She'll analyze the party and people in a nice way.
>
> She's always on for an adventure. I remember her calling me and telling me the time she had taken her clothes to the laundromat. We had a lot of laughs. She takes everything in stride, sees the best in people. She's a very big spirit.[249]

Judy Creighton, a journalist for Canadian Press, who has written many articles about Edna and her cookbooks, and who first wrote about Edna and the *Tonight Show*, says *Schmecks* are wonderful and important reads. "I feel Edna is chatting to me."[250]

Creighton also admires Edna as "a first class journalist in the true sense of the word — she wrote about the Mennonites and the disadvantaged. Under the veneer of sweet Edna she could tackle these things. It was remarkable for those years, the fifties, when I was starting out and most women were just doing the women's pages."

Creighton met Edna after *More Food That Really Schmecks* came out. They chatted in a boardroom and liked each other immediately. Creighton was soon regularly visiting Sunfish. She and Edna have become very close over the years.

"I look to her as an example. When Paul [Creighton's husband] died, she'd call me often. We phone two or three times a week. Last Sunday she was sitting watching the rabbits on the patio."

In the summer of 2002, Crieghton, Rose Murray, and other friends had a work party to pull out weeds in front of Edna's cottage.

"She was watching us with so much tenderness… We're kindred souls."

All these kudos. Everyone you speak to says the same thing: Edna is wonderful, they want to be with her, they want to be like her. Sometimes you have to pause and remember the introspective and unhappy woman trying to cope with a bad marriage as she struggled to write *Cape Breton Harbour*. Her divorce at fifty-six and her tormented thoughts that her life was over have become almost a legend among her friends, but they probably do not know the extent of her confusion then.

And sometimes Edna is feistier than people recognize; her publishers see this.

And she did wonder just what people were tearing out of her garden during that work party, she admitted later with a chuckle.

As praise and success followed more praise and success, Edna did not forget those troubled times. Or the letters. Thinking about publishing the journals, she wondered how Keith would react to her revelations. And what about all the letters, many of them unsent, to the men she'd known in the forties? But she recognized that the letters and journal had helped her to write and to think things through and overcome her troubles and emerge as the person she had become.

The past, that time in the fifties when Edna was away on assignments for *Maclean's* and on her trips to Europe, must have been on her mind when in the early nineties she began working again on Ruby's letters from the fifties.

This time she had a publisher. She met Sandra Woolfrey, editor of Wilfrid Laurier Press, on a tour of the press. At least a year later, they saw each other again at a dinner. Edna came over to Woolfrey's table and said, "I really want to get to know you. Give me a call sometime."

Woolfrey was soon out at Sunfish, where Edna handed her two manuscripts — Dr. Robins's letters and Ruby's letters.[251]

A lot of hopeful writers sent Woolfrey manuscripts, and she wasn't too enthusiastic when she dipped into Ruby's letters that night. To her surprise, she enjoyed the letters so much that she didn't want them to end, and saved the last few to read with her morning coffee.

She was determined to publish them. "But my next task was to see if anyone else cared."

The manuscript met with mixed reactions among readers, but the press decided to go ahead with publication. It was wonderful news for Edna, who spent the next two years working on the letters she'd read so often over the years and which always cheered her up.

Ruby had to give permission for the book to be published. Edna waited until she was finished with editing before telling Ruby the good news. Ruby was hesitant, Edna wrote in the introduction. Could she be sued, would she embarrass her grown-up children? But names and locations had been changed. Ruby remained Ruby, but she lived in Barrie, and Edna was Kay who lived in London, not Waterloo County, and Norm became Jan.

"With some hesitation" Ruby agreed to publication.

Haven't Any News: Ruby's Letters from the Fifties, "edited by Ruby's sister Edna Staebler, Afterword by Marlene Kadar," was launched on a sunny day in May 1995 at the very packed Joseph Schneider Haus. It was just before Mother's Day, and people lined up to buy copies of the book with a picture of a smiling, attractive Ruby taken in the fifties, framed by a cheerful red. Edna and Ruby both autographed, Ruby signing, as she had her letters, "Love, Ruby."

"I always loved Ruby's letters," Edna says, "and thought for years they should be published. By the nineties they'd become social history. Pierre Berton tells me he dips into the book once in a while when he needs cheering up."

The letters are filled with everyday detail about a family, seen from the wife and mother's perspective, as they go about their daily lives. They are happy, hopeful letters, even when Ruby grumbles that the children won't go to bed or that they don't have very much money. Ruby thinks of ways to make money (a mushroom farm in the cellar), wishes she'd lose weight, and keeps working on a big rug. Like Edna, she's observant as she sits by her window and watches children walking or the antics of the squirrel in the tree. There's ironing to do, meals to be prepared, the house to clean, clothes to be sewn and mended. There are pickles to make. But there's also bridge, listening to CBC Radio while she works on her rug, and buying a new dress. There are the kids, whom she loves.

"Kay" the writer sister often sends things — a nightie, a handsome Harris Tweed coat. Ruby's happy when she finds a part-time job.

Ruby's Letters portrayed a life quite different from that of liberated women in the nineties — women with both a family and career — but no one could say that Ruby's life was unhappy. Reading them, I'm reminded of Edna, happily braiding her rug and sewing curtains in the thirties, before everything went wrong with her marriage.

Kadar's afterword put the book into context, saying *Ruby's Letters* was a "significant reclamation of Canadian women's ordinary voices" and discussing subtext and "epistolary narrative." She felt the letters were as absorbing as a novel.

Reviewers were ecstatic.

Jocelyn Laurence (Margaret Laurence's daughter), writing for the *Globe and Mail*, felt *Ruby's Letters* should be compulsory reading for courses in women's history. She found the afterword stuffy "compared to Ruby's bouncing ways. Ruby's wit leavens her complaints, and her obvious delight in all aspects of her world ('You'll be surprised at the houses built behind us. Have you see the moon?') provides a grace note throughout the collection." Laurence said she considered her review a form of a fan letter.[252]

So did Edna's friend Kit McDermott, in the *Brantford Expositor*: "Ruby, please consider this review among your fan mail. Because it is! The letters will give enduring pleasure to so many readers."[253]

London Free Press reviewer Nancy Schiefer also mentioned Ruby's obvious enjoyment of her world. "The charm of Ruby's letters lies in their open, ingenuous, full-hearted enjoyment of the daily round, of the everyday tasks, observations and surprises and random delights which season Ruby's days and give her jaunty messages such sparkle and verve." Schiefer ended by wishing a second collection of letters would be published.[254]

"Fun to read is the dominant aspect of this newest offering in the form of life-writing ... this collection is such a refreshing surprise," Eva Weidman wrote in *Vitality*.[255]

"There is never a dull moment in these letters, whatever Ruby is writing about," wrote Judith Miller for the *Waterloo Chronicle*. "She writes with urgency and vitality, spilling words onto the pages."[256]

"Ruby writes about her experiences as a housewife and mother — and later her work as a part-time store clerk — in letters that are engaging, warm, and funny and sometimes poignant. ... This excellent book is recommended for Canadiana and women's studies collections."

Unfortunately, despite the excellent reviews and fan mail she received, Ruby was less than happy with the book. She felt embarrassed that her spelling mistakes ("sangritches" for sandwiches) hadn't been corrected, for one thing. Even after the book was published with her approval, she wasn't keen on people reading her letters.[257]

"I'm not so sure I want them read and I certainly didn't want a book written," she told Judy Creighton in a Canadian Press interview.[258] Still, she admitted she did enjoy writing letters, which had become "a lost art."

"I'd rather write letters. I get excited when I talk on the phone and I say things I shouldn't have said and I'm sorry for."

Edna loved the book, but was disappointed with Laurier's distribution. It could have been a best-seller, she says, with more promotion.

She is probably correct. While Edna was the professional writer, Ruby shared her curiosity and delight in the world, and her capacity for happiness in whatever circumstances she found herself. It's interesting to speculate whether Edna would have written similar letters if her marriage hadn't fallen apart and she hadn't pursued her need to write. Ruby had the need, too, but she fulfilled it by writing letters to her mother and sisters.

Ruby's Letters was Edna's last book, and while she hadn't actually written it, she'd conceived the idea long before the cookbooks came to be. If it had not been for her vision and initiative, the letters might have mouldered away in a drawer to be eventually tossed out, or rested in the archives (Edna donated her papers to the University of Guelph), instead of becoming a book that cheered readers across Canada.

Ruby's Letters was a fitting ending to Edna's publishing career. If she hadn't put on her fancy hat and "new look" outfit and marched her swordfishing story to *Maclean's* she might not have written the story about the Old Order. Writing about the Mennonites led to the cookbooks, which brought fame and money. And if she hadn't published the first *Schmecks* book, perhaps her favourite book, *Cape Breton Harbour*, would not have been published; the *Maggie* book would not have appeared.

And if she hadn't had that unhappy marriage, perhaps, as she says, she would not have written at all. Without the bad times, she might not have figured out how to live with joy and the positive attitude that attracted so many people to her and created the spirit that infused her writing and made it so compelling.

It was like Linda Johns's story about the robin: if she hadn't picked it up, the rest wouldn't have followed. It was like Edna's faith when she went to Europe without plans: something or somebody would turn up.

Things had unfolded the right way.

While Edna still hoped to see her correspondence with Dr. Robins published, especially after her friend, Harry Froklage, then employed by the Kitchener Public Library, had the letters typed,[259] and she continued to think about the books she might have written — the one about Fred, for instance — her future writing would consist of letters and journal entries.

She was eighty-nine years old. But it was not over. Edna remained very much in the public eye, and more good things were coming.

Chapter Twenty-One
Order of Canada

On Monday, May 6, 1996, Edna wrote out a few last-minute instructions for Judith Miller, who was staying with Mally, and packed her New Zealand flight bag "with just enough clothes… my long dress, my lilac suit, pyjamas, etc."[260] She also put in a slender Edna O'Brien paperback for reading, and two books to give away: *Cape Breton Harbour* and *Maggie*.

The next morning at 7:20 a limousine picked up Edna and her niece, Barbie. They passed Lois Playford ("in her long blue nightgown and dressing gown… she looked so darling standing there alone in the cold."[261])

It was a momentous day. Edna and Barbie were flying to Ottawa, where Edna would receive the Order of Canada.

Edna was nominated by the Canadian Federation of University Women, Kitchener-Waterloo, and letters of support came from Wilfrid Laurier University; Pierre Berton; W.O. Mitchell; David Luthy of the Heritage Historical Library, "Preserving Old Amish and Old Order Mennonite History"; the University of Guelph Library Collection Department, which held Edna's papers; Fred Williams of Ingonish, who was born in Neil's Harbour; and the Joseph Schneider Haus, where there was a research fellowship in Edna's name and to which Edna had given money with a gentleman's agreement to keep *Sauerkraut and Enterprise* in print.

Everyone had glowing things to say about Edna. As always, it is Edna's personality that comes through in these testimonials.

David Luthy said:

> Mark Twain once wrote that the difference between a tourist and a traveller is that a tourist merely observes people and objects whereas a traveller encounters

> people and situations. Edna Staebler has been a traveller of the first class although often not having first-class accommodations. She has encountered and written about a great variety of Canadian cultural groups — from Cape Breton fishermen in the east to Hutterites on the western Prairies to Mennonites in her own locale of Waterloo County, Ontario.
>
> Generally there is little particularly noteworthy about journalists or reporters writing about other cultures. Most do it merely as an editor's assignment. Similar to a traveling salesperson, they are "here today and gone tomorrow," forming no lasting bonds.
>
> Edna Staebler, however, is an exception, feeling a kindred spirit with the people she encounters and writes about. Her friendship is long-lasting. For decades the has remained in contact with Cape Breton Island families, donating books she gathers for their high school library. Among her Old Order Mennonite neighbours, she is a frequent guest in their homes.
>
> It is a pity that Edna will probably go down in Canadian history as the "author of cookbooks." People will erroneously think she was a great gourmet cook, never realizing that it was friendship, not food, that she was best at serving. It just happened that the people she chose most to write about, the Mennonites, are good cooks. May Edna, who is a much better writer than a cook, receive the honour of becoming a Member of the Order of Canada.[262]

Fred Williams, Clara May's grandson, wrote about Edna's involvement with Neil's Harbour people over the years, especially his own family, and her generosity:

> Besides Edna shipping books from the library sale to Neil's Harbour … When *Cape Breton Harbour* and *People I Have Known*, which contained Aunt Maggie's

> story, were reissued … in 1990, Edna signed her royalties over to Cabot High School to purchase library materials. The school was given an immediate advance of $1,000.00, followed by a similar disbursement at a later date. That one donation was more than the yearly library budget.
>
> The two books were remaindered sometime in 1992 or 1993. Edna bought all the stock … and shipped them to Cabot High School. There were hundreds and hundreds of books! The students there still sell them to raise funds for the school.
>
> What is left to say? My long personal and professional association with Edna Staebler has developed in me the deepest respect for one I consider a true humanitarian. Apart from her feelings about the people and village of Neil's Harbour, here is a writer who has espoused the cause of a small high school (never more than 300 students from Grade 7 to 12), not some grand or popular issue which might advance her career and notoriety. This is one of those stories which will never catch media attention. But it is a story with substance: a story of one person's interest in a distant fishing village, its people, culture, economic well-being and unique outlook on life. Neil's Harbour was not a stage in Edna's life, it is part of her life, as she is part of it.[263]

The ceremony was videotaped, showing Edna looking elegant in a v-necked dark gown with a light design in the lower part of the skirt, and black pearls, her grey hair in a sort of Dutch pageboy. She watched intently as the recipients bowed their heads and received their medals.

"All through the investiture I felt so incredulous about me being one of this company of great, useful Canadians, who have done so much for their communities, their country. And I was one of them!"[264]

Forty-five Canadians ("nine men and thirty-six women," Edna counted) were honoured for philanthropy, heritage, the arts. Tiny Kokom L. Nottaway of Rapid Lake, Quebec, rose from her wheelchair to receive her medal for her contribution to the Algonquin tradition; David Smith, a successful restaurateur and caterer, was a fundraiser for the Heart Institute; Gordon Brown, President of the Allied Jewish Committee; newspaper people; a mining visionary; professors and teachers and volunteers and researchers.[265]

And then it was Edna's turn. She was the only one in the literary arts category, she said later.

Edna had asked if Barbie could accompany her when she received her award in case she stumbled. Edna was still tottery from a virus that had affected her balance and caused dizziness; sometimes she used a cane now (a big change, she wrote Alph. Most of her old friends needed canes or walkers, or were dead. "I was always so proud of being able to walk briskly and erectly, my Mennonite friend Eva said, 'Edna, you don't walk like an old woman'").

But she didn't use a cane at Government House. Barbie was on one arm and the handsome aide-de-camp (Edna noted the gold trim on his red outfit) on the other as she moved to the front of the room.

"Her accounts of life in small communities have become a valuable resource for historians. She is a continuing presence in our kitchens and at our dining tables, a mentor to young writers."

After it was all over — the hand-shaking and congratulations — Jean Pigott told Edna she had her cookbooks, and Donna Scott, who founded *Flare* magazine, said she knew Edna's work. Scott's husband was from Cape Breton and knew about *Cape Breton Harbour*.

Edna made note of everything at the dinner: "a centerpiece of pale, open roses, iris, and sprays of little orchids. The faded striped tent walls, ceiling, portraits —— all so elegant. The whole of Rideau Hall was like that —— & the flowers —— I wished Norm could be there to see them."[266]

Edna kept her sense of perspective, though.

"Of course we, the taxpayers, pay for all this grandeur —— but on seeing it one could not feel anything but pride." The next day Edna and Barbie attended a luncheon put on by the Media Club at the National Press Club. They were picked up by a van "with 3 little old ladies who could hardly get out of the van when we got to the N.P. Club."

Gladys Arnold was there. Edna had met her years ago when Arnold spoke at the Canadian Club in the forties, and Arnold had been helpful and encouraging. How far away those days must have seemed — before she was published, when she was writing *Cape Breton Harbour* on Simeon Street. Still married, struggling to make sense of things and discovering how to live and think. Now she and Gladys Arnold were both elderly.

Edna talked about *Ruby's Letters*, another visit to the past, but unfortunately the bookstore had not delivered any copies.

"There was a long table with mostly old ladies down both sides," noted the new recipient of the Order of Canada, age ninety.

Back home at Sunfish, Mally hid under the loveseat — "no friendly cat greeting." Edna napped then ate the Danish she had saved from Ottawa.

In Wilmot Township, Edna's friends and fans celebrated her investiture with a party for three hundred on Sunday, May 26, at Castle Kilbride, the restored stately home built in the late 1800s by a Scottish entrepreneur.

Edna was driven in a 1938 Rolls Royce, "greeted by fanfare by the New Hamburg Band, listened to speeches — and gave one — thank you — then watched Highland dancers and the dedication of an oak tree," she reported to Alph.

In her speech, Rose Murray said that Edna was the rock star of the cookbook world.[267]

Chapter Twenty-Two
There Is No Ending

I don't know how to end this book. There is so much to write about, and how can you include everything in Edna's long life? As she says, you'd need a series to do so. I have forgotten the gondola ride (the gondolier propositioned Edna; she told him to get lost) and I have just found out that Edna bought eleven straw hats at the market in Florence ("conical, in pretty colours. I thought I could give them as gifts but no one wanted one. I wore the blue one swimming for years until a squirrel ate it. And by the way I still have my mother's hats in the loft").

And the cats? I have mostly forgotten the cats, although Edna's voice was wistful when she asked if I was writing about Willie, Cecily, and Mally. (Cecily succumbed to fleas. Mally was not the friendliest cat until she developed a painful limp and then she became Miss Society, and Edna would want you to know that Mally is an indoor cat, "never having experienced the feel of grass beneath her feet.")

All these details: there are several books here. Edna could write volumes about Europe, as she could have written books about Fred, Philip, and Dr. Robins.

The awards? I thought a good ending would be the Order of Canada, but there have been so many other awards.

Another book could be written about Edna's awards, but speeches and functions and who said what: very boring. Unless Edna, who remembers and enjoys everything, were to write it.

Awards:

The same year she was awarded the Order of Canada, Edna received the first Cuisine Canada Lifetime Achievement Award at the Northern Bounty II Conference, held in November.

Michael Manson, lawyer for Smart and Biggar, who lived in Vancouver by then, was Edna's "date" for the evening.[268] The cookie war was eight years in the past, but Manson and Edna had developed a lasting friendship, an unusual outcome to what started as a professional relationship. Manson visited Edna whenever he was in the Toronto area, sometimes bringing along his wife and young son. "Great, amazing," is how Manson describes Edna. The only thing that mattered to her in the whole cookie war business, he says, was her friendship with the Old Order, and the trust they placed in her. Manson recently wrote Edna, "The years from '85 to now have provided me with the pleasure and honour of getting to know you and sharing a wonderful friendship with a truly exceptional person."

In her acceptance speech, "Edna ad-libbed and started to tell anecdotal stories about her life."

"300 people … laughed and clapped and stood in ovation," she wrote Alph. "I was the oldest person in the room and said I thought one must be old to achieve lifetime award."

The award became known as "The Edna."

Two days later she attended the award ceremony for George Blackburn, who was receiving Edna's award that year.

"Such a relief to have been able to do all that in 4 days."[269]

And then there were the local awards: two Waterloo Regional Arts Awards for contribution to the literary arts as well as a lifetime achievement award; Kitchener-Waterloo Woman of the Year; Waterloo-Wellington Hotel-Motel Association Hospitality Award; Regional Municipality of Waterloo Volunteer Award. And she was inducted into the Kitchener-Waterloo Hall of Fame.

And provincial: the Province of Ontario Senior Achievement Award.[270]

There have been gala birthday parties for her eighty-fifth, ninetieth, and ninety-fifth birthdays. The City of Kitchener even proclaimed an Edna Staebler Day in 1991.

All these awards: Edna appreciated the honours, but she enjoyed the events, too, noting everything and writing it down, either later the same day (sometimes Kevin sees her bedroom light shining through the trees[271]) or early the next morning if she wakes up to watch the sun come up over the lake.

You may not have noticed the flowers on the table, but Edna has. Lovely tulips, yes? Edna's eyes do not glaze over at speeches, although in recent years she uses a hearing aid that sometimes gives trouble. "Wasn't it a wonderful evening?" she will ask. Wasn't the speaker handsome? And the food delicious?

It's no wonder that a film about her, produced by Stephanie Walker in 1995, just before *Ruby's Letters* came out, was called *An Attentive Life*. The lake shimmers and Edna's cottage is cozy as she talks about her life to professor and writer Judith Miller; writer, artist, and professor Nancy Lou Patterson; and Sandra Woolfrey, a poet as well as editor for the university press. Once again Edna says that she is more than a cookbook author: the cookbooks happened almost by accident, *Cape Breton Harbour* remains her favourite book, and if she has regrets, they are about the books she did not write.

And what about her philanthropy? In 1996 Edna endowed the writer-in-library program at the Kitchener Public Library, where she had discovered magic as a child and served on the board, seeing through the construction of a new building. She gave the library one hundred thousand dollars.

And let me get myself in here. As mentioned in the foreword, I was the first writer-in-library under Edna's endowment. After publishing six literary books, I had stumbled onto mysteries with the story of Millicent Milroy, an eccentric woman who claimed to have been married to Edward VIII; she had this inscribed on the family tombstone at a cemetery in Cambridge. Mysteries? I never intended to write mysteries, rarely read them, and what was I doing, writing even more? They were fun, easy, but like Edna's cookbooks (not that you could compare them; the mysteries never made anything like the money *Schmecks* earned) they were almost an accident: I should have spent more time with Millicent's story and written the literary novel about her that I really wanted to write.

I was musing about my writing future (more mysteries or what?) when Harry Froklage called me and asked me if I wanted to be the writer at the library. Yes, yes; I needed the money and I enjoyed getting together with other writers, new and established, to talk about writing.

I didn't know all that much about Edna then. But I did know there was much more to her than the cookbooks. I recalled driving to Kitchener after the Writers' Union annual meeting one year with Harold Horwood and two other writers. Someone mentioned Edna Staebler, "the cookbook author," and I piped up, "But she also wrote *Cape Breton Harbour*," and Harold said *Cape Breton Harbour* was the best travel book ever written in Canada.

"Come and visit me at Sunfish," Edna said sometime in the late eighties at some literary do at Kitchener Public Library. (What was it? Edna would remember, probably.) "I have two cats."

I wish I had gone, but I didn't have my own car then, and I was allergic to cats and kept away from the wretched creatures that obstructed my breathing and made my eyes swell (I got over the allergy when I took in a stray cat; another story).

Maybe the next year we drove Edna to Kingston for another meeting: Edna squashed into the back of our Nissan, and when we stopped at McDonald's Rick wanted to photograph her under the yellow arches. She laughed, and later, at another roadside place, she praised the texture of — the sausages?

That was really all I knew when I went for lunch with Edna and the library people (but I did own one of her cookbooks). It was at Twenty King Street, let me be Edna-exact. I do not remember what we ate (pasta?) or if we had wine, or what. What I do recall is the librarians asking me about my requirements for the submission of manuscripts. How many pages, typed of course?

I said the writing didn't have to be typed. What if someone was really poor and could only write by hand? A baglady could be writing poetry.

Edna phoned me later and said, "Oh, by the way, I was glad you said that about the manuscripts."

We are both grinning, Edna and I, in the photo taken by Joyce Spring at the library reception for her column in *Today's Seniors*.

I have the clipping, photocopied from the Kitchener Public Library file, in front of me. I have just noticed, on top, in handwriting, that it says, "Staebler, Edna." And — in brackets — "(Mrs. Keith Staebler)."

Or perhaps I should end the book with the Margaret Laurence Memorial Lecture — an event held annually at the Writers' Union general meeting to honour the famous writer, who died in 1987 — and who was Edna's good friend.

Spring 1997. Edna was giving the lecture and Penny Dickens, then executive director of TWUC, asked me I'd like to accompany Edna by limo to Kingston.

Here was a dream — no train, no lugging a bag, but four hours with Edna in what I imagined would be a stretch limo (really a big white car, alas).

What I remember:

A sunny and warm day. The driver got lost going out to Sunfish. Edna wore a red blazer, which I have seen since — more than once.

The conversation. It wasn't long before we were talking away about writers and books. Margaret Laurence.

And Edna's life. I didn't know Keith had died in 1993, that a year before his death he had given an interview to the *Record* in which he talked, among other things, about his love for Helen. They were like Romeo and Juliet, he said, and he was fortunate to have experienced real love between a man and a woman. He had composed a song for Helen, "Lament for my Wife," which he played every day; it made him feel better.[272]

(Later I learned about the big turnout at his funeral. Hundreds came to honour the man who had helped them with things like finding jobs or overcoming addiction. Keith never drank again after the divorce. He even largely gave up coffee and tobacco, limiting himself to one cup and one cigarette each evening after dinner.)

As the miles whizzed by, Edna told me about her marriage and her early writing; about Keith's breakdown and the fact that his mother kept him at her house for two weeks, as if he did not have a wife to look after him. And about the rift that broadened between Edna and Keith, who no longer desired her.

Surprising revelations. She was bitter, especially about her mother-in-law, before we moved on to other subjects.

She was ninety-one years old in 1997.

As we neared Kingston, Edna's head nodded.

"Have a nap," I suggested, and she closed her eyes for a moment, but soon opened them again.

"I don't want to miss anything."

At Kingston, they gave Edna a suite in a university residence. She was supposed to stay at a hotel, but the room was booked; they'd move her the next day, they promised, but Edna said the suite was fine, she loved being with the others on campus. She'd stay where she was, thank you.

Introduced by Pierre Berton, she gave a stupendous speech, beginning with her childhood: "In 1906 I was born in a house two blocks from the public library in Berlin, Ontario (now Kitchener). My parents didn't read fairy stories to me in bed because we had gas lights downstairs, but not up, and my two younger sisters and I always went to bed in the dark."

She continued with her life as a university student, a young married woman, and the beginning of her writing career when she was first published by *Maclean's*, her marital problems, the divorce, writing assignments, the cookbooks, *Cape Breton Harbour*, and ending with *Ruby's Letters*. She mentioned her present life: "Because I've lived so long I could talk for hours about my life as a writer. I'm constantly grateful. I love living at Sunfish with my cat and the friends and strangers who call on me there. I keep writing in my journal every morning in bed; I don't know why, but I seem to be compelled to record."

Regrets:

> My great regret is that I haven't written some of the books that are still in my head. Pierre is still waiting to read about Fred, Philip and George, and a young woman who had many adventures in Canada and abroad. Professors at both Waterloo universities keep urging me to write memoirs. At the University of Guelph, with my literary papers, there is a carton of loose leaves from 80 years of my journal, and copies of letters I wrote to lovers and friends.[273]

She concluded by reading from *Cape Breton Harbour*, "my favorite of my 21 books." (Doug Gibson says Edna interrupted her speech to say, as if they were talking in her cottage, "I must say, Doug — I'm sorry Doug — the book was very badly handled." Now there is a different image. I do not remember, but Gibson, naturally, does. "She beat me up," he laughs.[274])

A book of tributes could be written, too.

Reporters have kept coming to her door — whether for news stories or just because journalists wanted to write about that unique person Edna Staebler, this woman of great age who had a full and independent life at Sunfish Lake ("A Recipe for Happiness" in the *Hamilton Spectator*).

The Sunfish setting was important. "I wish you could see the lake" was a constant refrain in her letters.

No town apartment for Edna; four years ago she was almost convinced she should go into town for the winter: what would happen if she were alone and fell? She even put down a deposit, but what would Mally look at from that high-up window? You couldn't even put a birdfeeder on the balcony. And wouldn't her many friends miss Sunfish? Edna stayed right where she was, reading, writing in her journal, sending letters, knitting mice while she watched television at night until Kevin brought the mail.

And, of course, too, entertaining friends old and new, all of whom have wonderful things to say about Edna.

"You come away with a smile," says author Betty Jane Wylie who was very moved by Edna's lecture at the annual Union meeting. "She's given younger writers courage."[275] (And now I remember Marian Engel writing to Edna: "You're the one with the sunshine.")

"She was always that way," says her cousin, Dr. Marcia Smith. "She gets a lot of reward from seeing and sharing."[276]

"I'm always amazed at her — her positive outlook on life. She's invigorating, a wonderful person; inspiring," says Bryan Dare. "She turned the [cookie] war into a positive — turned it into a joy, grabbed it and turned it into great fun."[277]

"Nothing phases her," says Kevin Thomason. "We have similar interests. I'll say, 'Get your coat on. We're going out to the swamp,' (to listen to frogs) and Edna says, 'That sounds exciting.'" They've looked at the northern lights, too, and watched a space station. "She's almost always cheerful. If not, one has the other laughing. In my work I'm shipped all over the planet. To have an hour to myself — forty-five minutes — carries a price but then at Edna's when I bring the mail at night, you get laughing, have a whole new perspective."[278]

"Edna has taught me that there are many ways to live a life," says Peggy Walshe, CEO of the Kitchener Public Library, "to defy and challenge norms and define success in a very personal way."[279]

You could write pages like this. I have included others, but writing everyone's accolades would take a whole book.

No one I interviewed has said one bad word about Edna.

(And cut my head off, but tributes can also be boring. And sometimes I wish someone would say — well, what? Edna swore at them, Edna got drunk?)

And yet.

She has been sharp and keen with publishers, not shy about promoting her books and sticking up for her rights. There is grit there, determination. People do forget she is a strong, accomplished writer who is proud of her work and stands up for the writing profession.

John Allemang, who writes for the *Globe and Mail*, has been Edna's friend for years; he and his wife and small son even stayed with the cats while Edna went a-travelling. Allemang lauds Edna's "early courage and bravery — she went her own way," and adds, "She's my kind of person — a very complete person. I'm struck by her craft. She's open to a lot of experiences. She was willing to listen to people, to their voices. Early on, it was important for me to see someone write about people and Food That way."

But Allemang hates the "Edna worship stuff." She is not always happy, he says, and he has even heard her being "a bit catty" about big-name Toronto writers.[280]

Harold Horwood told Edna that Margaret Laurence said "[Edna] sure as hell ain't no lady."[281]

Another honour? End it with this?

April 8, 2003: The Mayors' Dinner, held annually to honour a prominent citizen and to raise money for The Working Centre, is for Edna this year. It's spring, but it's cold and icy. I couldn't start my car, which was buried under a foot of ice. Some people from Toronto and beyond haven't been able to come, but George Blackburn, a recipient of Edna's award, is here from Ottawa; he's eighty-six now and drove to Toronto and took the train from there.

It had been touch and go with Edna, who worried that the swelling in her face, caused by the infection, wouldn't go down, but she looks splendid in a turquoise dress.

Over seven hundred people are here, including Edna's many friends (Kathryn; Kevin, who drove Edna, pulling his jeep right up to her door; Lawrence McNaught; Rose Murray; Ted Boyd — the list is endless), her niece Barbie and her grown children, Patty, a physician, and Ken, an engineer: names I have read in diaries and letters. And in the cookbook. There is a story about Patty and Kenny crying when a neighbour served up their dead pet rabbit for dinner. Never before have so many people attended the Mayors' Dinner, Edna tells me later.

The Bertons are here, all the way from Kleinburg. Pierre's foot is in a cast; you can tell he is in pain as he struggles to his feet. Luckily The Working Centre sent a limo for them, but Edna tells me later that Pam Berton had been prepared to drive through the snow.

The Working Centre has provided a wheelchair for Edna; later I notice Pierre sitting in it. He is fourteen years younger than Edna. I think about how long it has been since Edna met him. Fifty-five years of friendship. They're at the table next to mine and Edna's face is animated as she leans forward and speaks to her old friends.

Edna's three books, donated to the silent auction, go for eight thousand dollars.

Dr. Michael Higgins, graceful and witty, the president of St. Jerome's College at the University of Waterloo, is emcee. Mayors Carl Zehr (Kitchener) and Lynne Woolstencroft (Waterloo) speak, then Joe and Stephanie Mancini from The Working Centre, and then Harry Froklage and Kathryn Wardropper.

Harry is personal, talking about the many friends who visit Edna, her generosity and spirit, and his visit one Christmas when Edna happily displayed Kevin's present: Christmas lights on the lake worked by remote control. He mentions Edna's decision to remain at Sunfish instead of moving to an apartment in town for the winter; Dr. Robins; Edna's award. All the people who come to Sunfish, bringing food.

Then Kathryn: Before outlining Edna's achievements, endowments, the Gerald Noonan Bursary in Canadian Literature, and the George Blackburn Scholarship in Canadian History, Kathryn says she was supposed to speak about publishers in Brantford recently; once the people heard she knew Edna they talked about her for two hours.

Pierre Berton's voice is strong when he calls Edna "a national star," and firm in his praise. Edna had two special qualities in her writing: a sense of place and an ear for dialogue. She wrote about "ordinary people who meant something … She broke all the rules, made herself part of every story, and that brought the story to life." It is "the personality that comes alive; it shines through. The story 'Maggie Leaving Home' was important … Edna was really writing social history."

Pierre Berton concludes by saying, "Edna is really forty-two and always will be."

Edna sounds exactly the way she does in her own living room.

"I'm not going to talk long, I'm not going to make a speech. I'm ninety-seven, I'm just going to say thank you," and she chatters on about how much the Women's National Press Club Award meant to her in 1950. "I thought, Maybe I am a writer." She confides that she hasn't driven for a year and that she wore the dress she has on tonight when she was eighty-five.

"I haven't been to any store but Zehr's, Kevin brings my mail … I am surprised and grateful for tonight."[282]

A week later, Edna asks me if I heard the joke Michael Higgins told.

Sunday afternoon, ice gone now, and she was supposed to speak tonight at St. Andrew's Presbyterian Church where she went as a girl and imagined the sheriff riding in while she listened to the cat sounds Mr. Kerr's body made.

Dorothy Cressman, who has known Edna for years through the book group, and whose husband had been in Edna's class in Grade 12, was going to introduce her. "She doesn't change,"

Cressman says. "She's still the friendly, down-to-earth person she was then."[283] The story of the book group would make another book.

Edna told the minister she hadn't attended St. Andrew's since she was thirty-five, except for funerals and weddings, but he was so nice when he visited that she couldn't say no.

I was going to go, but Edna has a bad cold and she doesn't feel like talking in public.

May I visit on Wednesday?

Lawrence is coming on Monday, and Ardy, her massage therapist, on Tuesday, but Wednesday's fine.

"Oh — there's a fair strip of water at the edge of the lake. There were mergansers yesterday. And mallards today, and a whole row of Canada geese on the lake. Eleven of them. I love to see that. They're turning around. If you don't watch every minute, you miss something."

I picture Edna in her chair by the big window, with her binoculars, books, a stack of new mail, on the ledge.

"It's amazing how much you notice," I say.

Would *I* notice the birds if I lived at Sunfish? Because of Edna's influence? Or would solitude and nature send me hitch-hiking to K-Mart after a few days of no one coming?

Would so many people come to see me?

I think of Betty Jane Wylie, who also lives in the country. Betty Jane worries about being alone and says she doesn't inspire the devotion Edna's friends show.

Who does?

Edna says: "It's so wonderful. I'm so lucky to be here."

Is this the end?

No.

Edna wants to reread "Molly." I'll have the whole thing photocopied in Guelph soon. Edna even has an ending now. Molly returns to Ontario, alone. No titled husband, but she doesn't hitch up with George from the feed store, either. She gives talks (with slides?) to church groups in Inglenook, but she doesn't tell everything. She keeps her secrets.

Maybe someone will want to publish "Molly." Yes? Pierre read it long ago, but none of the people she knows now, except for me, have read it, or even know about it. She hasn't mentioned it in interviews, and in the Laurier film she even said she decided she didn't want to write about Europe. None of the women in the film has read it.

What would the *Schmecks* fans say to Molly cavorting around Paris?

I think of Edna returning from Europe in 1954, happy about Alph, but running to committee meetings, getting her house in order, back in Kitchener life. The fifties: green refrigerators, gelatin salads, casseroles, Norm's bridge club, girdles (Edna missed a tour in Europe because her panty girdle hadn't dried; another story I haven't told).

And in Kitchener, the Centennial celebrations, Edna giving an interview, a talk. I don't want her wearing a proper hat or baking cinnamon buns. I want to see her as the writer, at her typewriter. And as the woman quivering with the secret happiness of Alph and the Alps of Switzerland, the sunshine in the mountains and the flowers. She is looking back, but ahead, too, as she begins her novella.

She has survived the introspection — no more long letters questioning the meaning of life and no more unsent letters about fantasies. Her writing gets published now, *Maclean's* sends her all over to write about people, but here she is beginning something new and different: the novel she has always wanted to write.

She doesn't know what is in store for her: all the good things, the new life she will have.

Here she is, the writer, then and now.

I hope I have shown how she became the person she is, the woman everyone wants to be with, to see, as well as the successful writer.

She had lucky breaks with her writing, things fell into place, but it has been her spirit that made her writing so different. She is a talented writer with an understanding for people, a great curiosity, a non-judgemental attitude, an ear for dialogue. Her voice is unique. It is a large voice, whether describing Bevvy Martin's kitchen or the moonlight on the sea in Neil's Harbour.

Her way of looking at life, her thinking, affected her writing, and her writing drew an audience. Few would know her if she were just a nice, elderly lady. Would younger friends get together to arrange a schedule for filling the bird feeder and delivering soup for that person?

And sometimes it is easy to doubt that belief that so many things are wonderful. You know they are not. There are no wonderful things in war, or in poverty. Edna found little wonder in New Road, but it has to be said that, except for her long and unhappy marriage, she has had a good and easy life. No war, no poverty.

No displacement, no new beginnings in foreign lands, which has been the way for people torn from the countries of their birth. She has never suffered from discrimination. She knows where she comes from, where she belongs, and while European journeys brought adventure and a sense of sophistication, Edna's place in the universe was in Waterloo County and she knew it.

She wasn't prepared for the letdown marriage brought (all those embroidered things, after all) but the experience provided an edge, suffering, a platform on which to board a train she didn't know was coming.

Without the unhappy marriage and the divorce, instead a happy and long marriage: well, a widow, sad but content, cultured, someone with season's ticket to the opera. Maybe the happy wife wouldn't have discovered the way of looking at the world Edna found.

But is finding happiness always the way? I quote Frankl at the very beginning of this book. I am convinced his is an ideal, maybe even a possibility. But not always, and not possible for everyone.

Edna's life has been a writer's life.

It's easy to forget that the pleasant hostess who says, "Oh, look — there's a cardinal" is also a tremendous writer and proud of it, not "just" the author of the *Schmecks* cookbooks, but a literary writer whose non-cookbook writing has deserved more notice.

But if she had been, instead, "just" a literary writer — say she had published a few long-ago volumes of poetry — it's possible today only academics or book collectors would know about her.

Probably without the first successful cookbook, *Cape Breton Harbour* would not have been published. Without *Schmecks*, Edna would not have had the money to endow this and that, and would not have met so many younger writers.

But it's difficult not to have the feeling that even if she had not become the successful and famous author of the *Schmecks* books, she would still be this big spirit. Only you would not have heard of her; this biography would not have been written. She would have been an Unknown, like the people she wrote about for *Maclean's* (unknown no longer, then).

So how can this life story end?

Edna is still looking ahead, and who knows what will happen now?

Maybe "Molly" will be published.

Maybe Edna will be the author of a first novel at the age of ninety-seven.

Afterword

Edna suffered a stroke in May 2003.

"I wish you could see the moonlight on the lake," she told Kathryn Wardropper on the phone. And then her speech went.

Kathryn rushed out to Sunfish and called an ambulance. After a few weeks in hospital, Edna had recovered enough to enter Beechwood Manor in Waterloo, where she is reading books submitted for her creative non-fiction award. Photos of Mally and the blooming forget-me-nots and dandelions at Sunfish sit on a shelf. The room is filled with flowers sent by friends; the stack of get-well cards must be ten inches high. Her niece Barbie has driven her back to Sunfish for a visit, as have Kathryn and Lawrence. Mally was overjoyed to see her.

Edna longs for Sunfish and hopes to return home.

Until then: "One day at a time," she told me when I visited last week. It was early afternoon. Edna was resting after lunch. I was her sixth visiter that day.

She is still eager to reread "Molly."

June 2003

Notes

The author's interviews with Edna took place weekly from summer 2001 until the end of March 2003. Edna's archive, including letters, journals, clippings, various writings, etc., is held at the University of Guelph (UG). Most of the materials referred to below can be found there.

Please note that an asterisk following a name indicates the name has been changed.

1 Edna Staebler, *Cape Breton Harbour* (Toronto: McGraw-Hill Ryerson, 1990), p. 92.
2 Edna Staebler, *Food That Really Schmecks* (Toronto: Ryerson Press, 1968), p. 21.
3 Edna Staebler, entry in journal, January 1953.
4 Edna Staebler, letter to Keith Staebler, 1956.
5 Canadian Press, "Staebler says no to Leno," *The Record* [Kitchener-Waterloo], October 4, 2002; *Record* staff, "Leno is toast," *The Record*, October 7, 2002.
6 John English and Kenneth McLaughlin, *Kitchener: An Illustrated History* (Toronto: Robin Brass Studio, 1996), p. 166.
7 Edna Staebler, letter to Earl Bailey, February 21, 1945.
8 "*Familien Nachrichten, Gebören*," (Family News, Births), *Berliner Journal*, January 17, 1906.
9 Barbara and Peter Wurtele, interview with the author, 2002. The Waterloo Historical Society records, held at the Kitchener Public Library, also provided information on Edna's family history.
10 Hilde Froese Tiessen and Paul Gerard Tiessen, eds., *Ephraim Weber's Letters Home, 1902–1955* (Waterloo: MLR Editions, 1966), p. 27.
11 Edna Staebler, *Sauerkraut and Enterprise* (Kitchener: Friends of

Joseph Schneider Haus, reprinted in 1973), p. 73.
12 *The Daily Telegraph*, January 1905.
13 Edna Staebler, quoted in *Maclean's*, April 1, 1950.
14 Edna Staebler, letter to Louise Cress, June 20, 1921.
15 Ibid.
16 School report cards, 1919-1926, UG.
17 Rules of Queens Hall, 1926, UG.
18 University marks and courses, 1926-1929, UG.
19 *The Record*, March 29, 1993.
20 Edna Staebler, letters to Keith Staebler, largely undated in this period.
21 Edna Staebler, letter to Keith Staebler, undated.
22 Mac MacLean, letter to Edna Staebler, May 8, 1930.
23 "Staebler-Cress," *The Record*, October 1933.
24 The gift register is at UG.
25 Marcus Adeney, "Kitchener — city of a song," *Saturday Night*, June 17, 1933.
26 Tiessen, *Weber's Letters*, p. 83.
27 Edna Staebler, letter to Tom Glover, November 25. (Year unstated, but probably 1946.)
28 Edna Staebler, essay, UG; later published in *Canadian Home Journal*, date unknown.
29 Edna's "commonplace book."
30 "Local folk to see brilliant play," *The Record*, May 1937.
31 Rules of Little Theatre, 1930s, UG.
32 Edna Staebler, *The White Waistcoat*, play manuscript, late 1930s.
33 "2 exacting dramas given by Little Theatre group," *The Record*, January 30, 1937; "'The White Waistcoat' wins first place in contest," October 8, 1937; "Prize winning plays given," January 27, 1938.
34 Edna Staebler, *The Departure*, play manuscript, late 1930s.
35 "Many Kitchenerites 'dare' Lindbergh to speak here," *The Record*, November 1, 1938.
36 Ibid.
37 Thelma Craig, "London group wins honors at Kitchener," *Globe and Mail*, April 1, 1940.
38 Edna Staebler, letter to Earl Bailey, March 30, 1944.
39 Edna Staebler, entry in journal, 1948.

40 Edna Staebler, letter to Geoff Henson, 1944.
41 Edna Staebler, letter to Geoff Henson, February 20 (year unstated).
42 Fred Kruger, "Decriminalization," unpublished memoir.
43 Harold Horwood, letter to the author, 2003.
44 Edna Staebler, letter to Newspaper Institute of America, 1944.
45 Edna Staebler, writing assignment for Newspaper Institute of America, 1944.
46 Edna Staebler, letter to Earl Bailey, March 1944.
47 Ibid.
48 Ibid.
49 Edna Staebler, letter to Keith Staebler, August 5, 1945.
50 Edna Staebler, letter to Tom Glover, November 5, 1945.
51 Dr. John Robins, letter to Edna Staebler, February 3, 1946.
52 Ibid.
53 Edna Staebler, unsent letter to Tom Glover, "Saturday."
54 Letters from Fay* and Howard* are in Edna's archives at the University of Guelph.
55 John Robins, letter to Edna Staebler, January 8, 1947.
56 Ibid.
57 Edna Staebler outlined her emotions re Fay* and Howard* in unsent letters to Tom Glover, 1946 and 1947.
58 Keith Staebler, suicide note, undated.
59 Edna Staebler, letter to Tom Glover, 1946.
60 Ibid.
61 Dr. Robins, letter to Edna Staebler, 1946.
62 The archive of Philip Knowling has been lent to the author by Edna Staebler.
63 Edna Staebler, letter to Keith Staebler, "Thursday."
64 Ibid.
65 Edna Staebler, letter to Keith Staebler, "Saturday evening."
66 Edna Staebler, letter to Keith Staebler, "Wednesday."
67 Edna Staebler, letter to Keith Staebler, 1947.
68 Edna Staebler, letter to Keith Staebler, "Saturday evening," 1947.
69 Edna Staebler, letter to Dr. Robins, May 1948.
70 Edna Staebler, letter to Helen Kergin, June 1948.
71 Ibid.

72 Edna Staebler, letter to John Anderson*, 1948.
73 Edna Staebler, letter to John Anderson*, undated.
74 John Anderson*, telegram to Edna Staebler.
75 Edna Staebler, letter to Helen Kergin, July 1948.
76 Edna Staebler, letter to Dr. Robins, August 21, 1948.
77 Ibid.
78 Edna Staebler, "Moonlight," late 1940s.
79 Edna Staebler, "Prelude," late 1940s.
80 Edna Staebler, *Cape Breton Harbour* (Toronto: McGraw-Hill Ryerson, 1990), p. 146.
81 Edna Staebler, letter to Philip Knowling, 1948.
82 Edna Staebler, letter to Dr. Robins, October 2, 1948.
83 Edna Staebler, letter to Dr. Robins, January 1949.
84 Dr. Robins, letter to Edna Staebler, January 1949.
85 *Cape Breton Harbour*, p. 84.
86 Edna Staebler, *Whatever Happened to Maggie and Other People I've Known* (Toronto: McClelland and Stewart, 1983), p. 16.
87 *Maggie*, p. 39.
88 Edna Staebler, letter to Helen Kergin, 1950.
89 Weber, p. 173.
90 Edna Staebler, as quoted in "In the Editor's Confidence," *Maclean's*, 1950.
91 Edna Staebler, letter to Dr. Robins, October 10, 1949.
92 Edna Staebler, letter to Dr. Robins, December 5, 1949.
93 Edna Staebler, letter to Dr. Robins, March 1950.
94 Edna Staebler, letter to Dr. Robins, March 12, 1950.
95 Edna Staebler, letter to Helen Kergin, 1950.
96 A list of flowers and gifts is at University of Guelph archives.
97 Canadian Press article, unspecified newspaper, 1950.
98 *Record* staff, "Kitchener author's sotry ranked best of the year," 1950, otherwise undated clipping.
99 Edna Staebler, letter to Dr. Robins, 1950.
100 Edna Staebler, letter to Dr. Robins, September 1950.
101 Photos can be found in *The Record*, 1950, UG; photo collection Endla Loney.
102 Edna Staebler, letter to Dr. Robins, 1959.

103 Edna Staebler, letter to Dr. Robins, February 22, 1951.
104 Edna Staebler, letter to Dr. Robins, March 23, 1951.
105 Edna Staebler, letter to Keith Staebler, July 17, 1951.
106 *Maggie*, p. 167.
107 *Maggie*, p. 81.
108 *Maggie*, p. 84.
109 Edna Staebler, letter to Bill Mitchell, October 28, year unclear but probably 1950.
110 Edna Staebler, letter to Keith Staebler, 1951.
111 Ibid.
112 *Maggie*, p. 89–90.
113 *Maggie*, p. 100.
114 Particulars regarding John Gray and Macmillan: Edna Staebler, letter to Keith Staebler, 1951.
115 Edna Staebler, letter to Dr. Robins, 1951.
116 Edna Staebler, entry in journal, December 1953.
117 Except where otherwise indicated, the information and quotes in the following pages are from entries in Edna Staebler's journal, 1954.
118 Edna Staebler, letter to Keith Staebler, also to Louise Cress and family; the European letters are often addressed "Dear Gang" and were passed from one family member to another. Edna asked the recipients to keep the letters for her.
119 Edna Staebler, letter to Keith Staebler, 1954.
120 Canadian Press, "Kitchener marking its 100th anniversary," *The Record*, June 22, 1954.
121 Edna Staebler, "Molly," unpublished novella, 1954, UG.
122 Ibid.
123 Edna Staebler, "The Blue-Headed Cat," unpublished short story, 1954, UG.
124 Edna Staebler, letter to Keith Staebler, September 1955.
125 Edna Staebler, "Would you change the lives of these people?" *Maclean's*, May12, 1956, p. 30.
126 Ibid.
127 Ibid.
128 *Dartmouth Free Press*, letter to the editor, 1955.
129 Anonymous letter to Edna Staebler, 1955.

130 Edna Staebler, letter to Helen Kergin, 1957.
131 Edna Staebler, letter to Helen Kergin, January 1958.
132 Edna Staebler, letter to Norm Hodgson, December 6, 1960.
133 Edna Staebler, letter to Clara May, January 1961.
134 Edna Staebler, letter to Laci, 1960.
135 Edna Staebler, letter to Alphonse, 1961.
136 Edna Staebler, letter to Philip Knowling, 1961.
137 Edna Staebler, loose writing, 1961.
138 Ibid.
139 Information on Keith's life with Helen: Greg Kittel (Keith Staebler's step-grandson), interview with the author, 2003; also, Jack and Mardi Kersell, interview with the author, 2002.
140 Edna discussed her car and possible travels in letters to Philip Knowling and Kath Reeves, 1963.
141 Waterloo Trust Company booklet.
142 Information re Canada Council grant is from a letter to "Evelyn," undated.
143 Edna Staebler, letter to Sheila Burnford, 1966.
144 Edna Staebler, letter to Ruby Dimma, 1964.
145 Edna Staebler, letter to Alphonse, 1965.
146 There are many fan letters from this period in Edna's archives at the University of Guelph.
147 Edna Staebler wrote to Sheila Burnford about the township book during this period.
148 Edna Staebler, letter to Sheila Burnford, March 1967.
149 "*Food That Really Schmecks* launched at lunch," *The Record*, June 27, 1968.
150 *Food That Really Schmecks*, p. 15.
151 Various review clippings for *FTRS* are at UG.
152 Jo Carson, "Book follows 18 years' research in kitchen," *Globe and Mail*, May 9, 1968.
153 *Country Guide*, November 1968.
154 *FTRS*, p. 1.
155 *FTRS*, p. 5.
156 *FTRS*, p. 3.
157 *FTRS*, p. 28.
158 *FTRS*, p. 136.

159 *FTRS*, p. 171.
160 Edna Staebler, letter to Alphonse, 1968.
161 Ibid.
162 Edna Staebler, letter to Joan MacKenzie, November 20, 1969.
163 Edna Staebler, letter to Joan MacKenzie, November 29, 1969.
164 Edna Staebler, *Cape Breton Harbour* (Toronto: McClelland and Stewart, 1972), p. 23.
165 *CBH*, p. 114.
166 *CBH*, p. 57.
167 *CBH*, p. 171.
168 Various fan letters for this period are in Edna's archives at UG.
169 Anne Montages, "A warm assurance against urban strictures," *Globe and Mail*, June 3, 1972.
170 Jean Johnston, "Staebler novel paints earthy people," *The Record*, May 6, 1972.
171 Harold Horwood, letter to the author, 2003.
172 Carroll Allen, "Edna Staebler tells what it's like to be suddenly famous for writing a best-selling cookbook when you don't regard yourself as a cook," *Homemaker's*, Mar./April 1973.
173 Ibid.
174 Ibid.
175 Letters from the publishers mentioned in this period are at UG.
176 Edna Staebler, letter to *Ladies' Home Journal*, 1960.
177 Edna Staebler, letter to Jack McClelland, 1975.
178 Edna Staebler, letter to Jack McClelland, September 10, 1975.
179 Ibid.
180 Edna Staebler, letter to Jack McClelland, February 6, 1977.
181 Edna Staebler, entry in diary (not journal), which she lent to the author. Quotes following in Chapter 14 are from this diary except where otherwise indicated.
182 Edna Staebler, letter to Jack McClelland, February 1977.
183 Edna Staebler, *More Food That Really Schmecks* (Toronto: McClelland and Stewart, 1979), p. 1.
184 *MFTRS*, p. 124.
185 *MFTRS*, p. 123.
186 *MFTRS*, p. 109.

187 *MFTRS*, p. 110.
188 Canadian Press, "More Mennonite recipes on the way," *Toronto Star*, March 21, 1979.
189 Edna Staebler, entry in diary, June 5, 1979.
190 Edna's day-to-day activities are taken from her diary, 1979.
191 Edna Staebler, letter to Alphonse, 1979.
192 Fan letters from this period in Edna's archives at UG.
193 Wende Gregory-Frei, interview with the author, 2002.
194 Jim Morris, interview with the author, 2002.
195 Pierre Berton, interview with the author, 2003.
196 Janet Berton, interview with the author, 2003.
197 Brenda Hoerle, "Next cookbook 'simmering'," *Galt Reporter*, November 8, 1984.
198 Cathy Williams, *Highlights*, 1984.
199 Laurence McNaught, interview with the author, 2002.
200 Harold Horwood, letter to the author, 2003.
201 Edna's ideas for books are taken from 1980 diary entries.
202 Edna Staebler, entry in diary, 1980.
203 Harold Horwood, letter to the author, 2003.
204 Accounts of Edna's activities are from her diary, 1981.
205 Edna Staebler, correspondence re Fred Kruger, 1981.
206 *Maggie*, Foreword by Pierre Berton, p. 7.
207 Nancy Shiefer, "On average Canadians," *London Free Press*, May 4, 1983.
208 Ibid.
209 Harold Horwood, letter to Edna Staebler, January 25, 1984.
210 Edna Staebler, letter to Harold Horwood, 1984.
211 Edna Staebler, letter to Alphonse, December 1984.
212 Ibid.
213 Rose Murray, interview with the author, 2002.
214 Kit McDermott, interview with the author, 2002.
215 Edna Staebler, letter to Harold Horwood, November 28, 1984.
216 Dr. John Weir, convocation speech, October 28, 1984. (Edna has a transcript of the speech in her records.)
217 Edna Staebler, convocation speech, October 28, 1984.
218 Edna Staebler, diary entry, 1984. Also contains a record of cards received, etc.

219 Edna Staebler, diary entry, 1985.
220 Pierre Berton, interview with the author, 2003.
221 An outline of the Cookie War is in *Schmecks Appeal.* The original article appeared as "Cooking the evidence," *Saturday Night*, May 1987, p. 28.
222 Edna Staebler, letter to Harold Horwood, January 14, 1985.
223 June Callwood, "Companies wait to see how legal cookie crumbles," *Globe and Mail*, December 11, 1985.
224 Canadian Press, "Edna Staebler wooed by both sides in lawsuit," Judy Creighton, *The Record*, December 13, 1985.
225 *The Fifth Estate* videa is available at UG.
226 Edna Staebler, letter to David Luthy.
227 Edna Staebler, diary entry, 1985.
228 Margaret Terol, "Posh life is over for Staebler," *The Record*, September 14, 1989.
229 Quotes that follow in Chapter 18 are from Edna's diary, 1986.
230 Edna Staebler, entry in diary, 1986.
231 Edna Staebler, letter to McClelland and Stewrat, June 23, 1986.
232 Michael Manson, interview with the author, 2003; Edna wrote about the premiere in her 1988 diary.
233 Edna Staebler, letter to Harold Horwood, June 2, 1987.
234 Ibid.
235 Barbara Naylor, interview with the author, 2003.
236 Edna Staebler, *Schmecks Appeal* (Toronto: McClelland and Stewart, 1989), p. 9.
237 Doug Gibson, interview with the author, 2003.
238 Edna Staebler, entry in diary, 1987.
239 Kathryn Wardropper, interview with the author, 2003.
240 Linda Johns, interview with the author, 2003.
241 The author was present at the Edna Staebler Creative Non-Fiction Award ceremony, 2002.
242 Kevin Thomason, interview with the author, 2003.
243 Edna Staebler, journal, May 1988; fuller excerpts published in Kathryn Carter, ed., *The Small Details of Life: 20 Diaries by Canadian Women* (University of Toronto Press, 2002), foreword by Judith Miller for the excerpt from Edna's journal.

244 *The Record*, 1991.

245 Doug Gibson, interview with the author, 2003.

246 Judith Miller, interview with the author, 2002.

247 Janet Berton, interview with the author, 2003.

248 Ibid.

249 Rose Murray, interview with the author, 2002.

250 Judy Creighton, interview with the author, 2002.

251 Sandra Woolfrey, interview with the author, 2003.

252 Jocelyn Laurence, "Sparkling bulletins from '50s homefront," *Globe and Mail*, August 3, 1995.

253 Kit McDermott, "Collection of letters an 'ordinary voice' on a woman's life in Ontario, 1950s," *Brantford Expositor*, May 13, 1995.

254 Nancy Schiefer, "Staebler's sister reviews her life in the '50s," *London Free Press*, 1995.

255 Eva Weidman, "Haven't Any News," *Vitality*, October 25, 1996.

256 Judith Miller, "Four winning books of creative non-fiction," *Waterloo Chronicle*, September 25, 1995.

257 Ruby Dimma, interview with the author, 2002.

258 Judy Creighton, "Housewife letters have plenty to say about life in the '50s," *The Toronto Sun*, June 26, 1995.

259 Harry Froklage, interview with the author, 2003.

260 Edna Staebler, entry in journal, May 6, 1996.

261 Ibid.

262 Letters of support re the Order of Canada were lent to the author by Edna Staebler.

263 Ibid.

264 Edna Staebler, letter to Alphonse, 1996.

265 The author watched the video of the investiture at UG.

266 Edna Staebler, letter to Alphonse, 1996.

267 Rose Murray, speech at Castle Kilbride, May 26, 1996. (Edna has a transcript of the speech in her records.)

268 Michael Manson, interview with the author, 2003.

269 Edna Staebler, entry in diary, 1996.

270 Details about awards are at UG and Kitchener Public Library.

271 Kevin Thomason, interview with the author, 2003.

272 Info re Keith Staebler: *The Record*, March 29, 1993; September 21,

1987; December 26, 1992.

273 Edna Staebler, Margaret Laurence Memorial address, spring 1997. (Edna has a copy of her speech in her records.)

274 Doug Gibson, interview with the author, 2003.

275 Betty Jane Wylie, interview with the author, 2003.

276 Dr. Marcia Smith, interview with the author, 2003.

277 Bryan Dare, interview with the author, 2003.

278 Kevin Thomason, interview with the author, 2003.

279 Peggy Walshe, interview with the author, 2003.

280 John Allemang, interview with the author, 2003.

281 Harold Horwood, letter to Edna Staebler, April 1988.

282 Edna Staebler, speech at the Mayor's Dinner, April 8, 2003. (Author was present.)

283 Dorothy Cressman, interview with the author, 2002.

Selected Bibliography

Books by Edna Staebler:

Sauerkraut and Enterprise. University Women's Club of Kitchener-Waterloo, 1960; McClelland and Stewart, 1966.

Food That Really Schmecks. Toronto: Ryerson Press, 1968.

Cape Breton Harbour. Toronto: McClelland and Stewart, 1972; McGraw-Hill Ryerson, 1990.

Whatever Happened to Maggie and Other People I've Known. Toronto: McCelland and Stewart, 1983; reprinted by McGraw-Hill Ryerson as *Maggie*, 1990.

More Food That Really Schmecks. Toronto: McClelland and Stewart, 1979.

Schmecks Appeal. Toronto: McClelland and Stewart, 1988.

The Schmecks Appeal Cookbooks (a series of 12 cookbooks), 1990–1991.

Haven't Any News: Ruby's Letters. by Ruby Cress and edited by Edna Staebler. Waterloo: Wilfrid Laurier Press, 1995.

Historical Pamphlets by Edna Staebler:

"The Electrohome Story," Paris, ON: Walker Press, 1956.

"The Waterloo Trust and Savings Company: A Brief History." Kitchener, Waterloo Trust and Savings Company, 1963.

Others:

Berton, Pierre. *My Times*. Toronto: McClelland and Stewart, 1995.

Berton, Pierre and Janet Berton. *Pierre and Janet Berton's Canadian Food Guide*. Toronto: McClelland and Stewart, 1974; originally published as *The Centennial Food Guide*, 1966 (revised for the 1974 edition).

Carter, Kathryn, ed. *The Small Details of Life: 20 Diaries by Women of Canada*. Toronto: University of Toronto Press, 2002.

Chadwick, W.R. *The Battle for Berlin, Ontario: An Historical Drama*. Waterloo: Wilfrid Laurier University Press, 1992.

English, John, and Kenneth McLaughlin. *Kitchener, An Illustrated History*. Waterloo: Wilfrid Laurier Press, 1983, 1996, under license by Robin Brass Press.

Epp, Frank H. *Mennonites in Canada, 1786-1920: The History of a Separate People*. Toronto: Macmillan, 1974.

Mills, Rych. *Images of Canada: Kitchener (Berlin) 1880-1960*. Charleston, S.C.: Arcadia Publishing, 2002.

Nolan, Tom. *Ross Macdonald: A Biography*. New York: Scribner, 1999.

Sutherland, Fraser. *The Monthly Epic: A History of Canadian Magazines*. Markham: Fitzhenry and Whiteside, 1989.

Tiessen, Hilde Froese and Paul Gerard Tiessen. *Weber's Letters Home, 1902-1955: Letters from Ephraim Weber to Leslie Staebler of Waterloo County*. Waterloo: MLR Editions, 1996.

Trager, James. *The Women's Chronology*. New York: Henry Holt and Company, 1994.

Uttley, W.V. *A History of Kitchener*. Waterloo: Wilfrid Laurier Press, 1975.

White, Randall. *Too Good to Be True*. Toronto: Dundurn Press, 1993.

Betty Crocker's Picture Cook Book, Text Edition. New York: McGraw Hill, 1950.

Related Reading:

Burke, Susan M. and Matthew H. Hill. *From Pennsylvania to Waterloo, Pennsylvania-German Folk Culture in Transition*. Kitchener: Joseph Schneider Haus, 1991.

Dunham, Mabel. *The Trail of the Conestoga*. Toronto: McClelland and Stewart, 1942.

Hayes, Geoffrey. *Waterloo County: An Illustrated History*. Waterloo: Waterloo Historical Society, 1997.

Russell, Ruth, ed. *Women of Waterloo County*. Waterloo: Natural Heritage, 2000.

Silcox, Nancy. *Roads of the Heart*. Once Upon Your Memory Publishing, 2002.

Walker, Stephanie Kirkwood. *A Waterloo County Album: Glimpses of the Way We Were*. Toronto: Dundurn, 2002.

Acknowledgements

Many people have helped me with this book, and I am very grateful to all of them for sharing information, insight, and advice.

I would like to acknowledge, first of all, Edna Staebler, who welcomed me to her home often over a period of two years, sharing stories about her life. The biography was her idea, and I thank her for her trust in me and for her belief in my writing ability. She has been generous, open, and wise. I am eternally grateful to her for her permission to see everything in her large archive at the University of Guelph. Her vision of the world has affected me. It was a gift I had not expected.

Kathryn Wardropper, administrator of the Edna Staebler Award for Creative Non-Fiction and manager of the Wilfrid Laurier Bookstore, deserves a big thank you. Kathryn suggested Dundurn to me in the first place and provided invaluable advice and encouragement. I especially thank her for reading the manuscript and offering excellent comments. She was always ready to listen and very generous with her time.

A very special thank you goes to the staff of the archives at the University of Guelph, specifically Ellen Morrison and Lorne Bruce, as well Darlene, Amy, and Linda. Their courtesy, friendliness, and helpfulness made my trips to the archives a pleasure. This book could not have been written without their help.

Susan Hoffman and staff of the Grace Schmidt Room at the Kitchener Public Library and other library staff were also very helpful and I am grateful. Thanks, too, to staff at Woodside National Park who arranged a special screening of films about old Berlin.

The folks at Dundurn have been wonderful. Tony Hawke, Beth Bruder, editor Jennifer Bergeron, and designer Jennifer Scott were all great.

Joyce Spring, a friend of many years, kindly read the manuscript and made insightful comments. I also thank Joyce for the times she either accompanied me or drove me to Sunfish Lake in all kinds of weather. My colleague with the Industrial Artifacts Project in Kitchener, Betty Reinders, also offered to read the manuscript and I thank her for her input.

Also, thanks for interviews and other help to: John Allemang, Carroll Allen, Pierre and Janet Berton, Susan Burke of the Joseph Schneider Haus, Bert Coates, Judy Creighton, Ruby Cress, Dorothy Cressman, Leonard Croth, Bryan Dare, Harry Froklage, Doug Gibson, Wende Gregory-Frei, Harold Horwood, Rosalee Howlett, Kim Jernigan (editor of *The New Quarterly*), Jack and Mardi Kersell, Greg Kittel, Endla Loney, David Luthy, Kit McDermott, Laurence McNaught, Michael Manson, Nancy Martin, Professor Judith Miller, Rych Mills, Jim Morris, Rose Murray, Barbara Naylor, Frank O'Brien, Nancy Lou Patterson, Ted and Janni Schafer, Hannah Schlenker, John Shannon and staff (who allowed me to tour Edna's birthplace), Tricia Siemens, Nancy Silcox, Dr. Marcia Smith, Peter Etril and Marilyn Snyder, Eric Staebler, Isabella Stefanescu, Kevin Thomason, Professor Paul Tiessen, Stephanie Walker, Peggy Walshe (CEO of the Kitchener Public Library), Fred Williams, Sandra Woolfrey, Barbara and Peter Wurtele, and Betty Jane Wylie.

Also, thanks to the group of Edna supporters who invited me to their meeting. I have mentioned most of them, but Steve Notar and Louis Silcox were also there. And thanks to the Waterloo Regional Arts Council for general encouragement, and to Pirak Studios Limited for their photography.

I hope I have not left anyone out and I apologize if I have. I spoke to so many people. Others also briefly discussed Edna with me. From a furniture store to a doctor's waiting room: everywhere I went in Kitchener I met someone who has Edna stories.

Last of all, the biggest thanks must go to my husband, Richard O'Brien, for encouragement, patience, and support. His computer expertise made it possible for me to write in my beloved old WordStar, which he "translated" into acceptable transmissions to the publisher. He also scanned photos, dealt with computer glitches that drove me nuts, sent things along to Dundurn, looked up newspaper references, and walked all three dogs when I was still writing late at night.

Many, many thanks to everyone.

Veronica Ross
July 2003
Kitchener

Index